D1807186

INTERPRETATION OF LAW IN THE AGE OF ENLIGHTENMENT

Law and Philosophy Library

VOLUME 95

Series Editors:

FRANCISCO J. LAPORTA, *Department of Law,*
Autonomous University of Madrid, Spain

FREDERICK SCHAUER, *School of Law, University of Virginia, U.S.A.*

TORBEN SPAAK, *Uppsala University, Sweden*

Former Series Editors:

AULIS AARNIO, MICHAEL D. BAYLES†, CONRAD D. JOHNSON†,
ALAN MABE, ALEKSANDER PECZENIK†

Editorial Advisory Board:

AULIS AARNIO, *Secretary General of the Tampere Club, Finland*
HUMBERTO ÁVILA, *Federal University of South Brazil, Brazil*
ZENON BANKOWSKI, *Centre for Law and Society, University of Edinburgh,*
United Kingdom
PAOLO COMANDUCCI, *University of Genoa, Italy*
HUGH CORDER, *University of Cape Town, South Africa*
DAVID DYZENHAUS, *University of Toronto, Canada*
ERNESTO GARZÓN VALDÉS, *Institut für Politikwissenschaft, Johannes*
Gutenberg Universitat, Mainz, Germany
RICCARDO GUASTINI, *University of Genoa, Italy*
JOHN KLEINIG, *Department of Law, Police Science and Criminal Justice*
Administration, John Jay College of Criminal Justice, City University of New York,
U.S.A.
PATRICIA MINDUS, *Università Degli Studi di Torino, Italy*
YASUTOMO MORIGIWA, *Nagoya University, Japan*
GIOVANNI BATTISTA RATTI, *"Juan de la Cierva" Fellow in Law, Faculty of*
Law, University of Girona, Spain
WOJCIECH SADURSKI, *European University Institute, Department of Law,*
Florence, Italy
HORACIO SPECTOR, *Universidad Torcuato Di Tella, Argentina*
ROBERT S. SUMMERS, *School of Law, Cornell University, U.S.A.*
MICHEL TROPER, *Membre de l'Institut Universitaire de France, France*
CARL WELLMAN, *Department of Philosophy, Washington University, U.S.A.*

For further volumes:
http://www.springer.com/series/6210

INTERPRETATION OF LAW IN THE AGE OF ENLIGHTENMENT

From the Rule of the King to the Rule of Law

Edited by

MORIGIWA Yasutomo

Graduate School of Law, Nagoya University, Nagoya, Japan

Michael STOLLEIS

Max Planck Institute for European Legal History, Frankfurt/Main, Germany

Jean-Louis HALPÉRIN

École Normale Supérieure, UMR 7074 "Centre de Théorie et Analyse du droit", Paris, France

 Springer

Editors
MORIGIWA Yasutomo
Graduate School of Law
Nagoya University
Furo-cho 1
464-8601 Nagoya Aichi
Japan
morigiwa@nagoya-u.jp

Jean-Louis HALPÉRIN
École Normale Supérieure,
    UMR 7074 "Centre de Théorie
    et Analyse du droit"
boulevard Jourdan 48
75014 Paris
France
jean-louis.halperin@ens.fr

Michael STOLLEIS
Faculty of Law
University of Frankfurt
Frankfurt
Germany
and
Max Planck Institute for European
    Legal History
Hausener Weg 120
D-60489 Frankfurt/Main
Germany
stolleis@rg.mpg.de

ISSN 1572-4395
ISBN 978-94-007-1505-9   e-ISBN 978-94-007-1506-6
DOI 10.1007/978-94-007-1506-6
Springer Dordrecht Heidelberg London New York

Library of Congress Control Number: 2011929885

© Springer Science+Business Media B.V. 2011
No part of this work may be reproduced, stored in a retrieval system, or transmitted in any form or by
any means, electronic, mechanical, photocopying, microfilming, recording or otherwise, without written
permission from the Publisher, with the exception of any material supplied specifically for the purpose
of being entered and executed on a computer system, for exclusive use by the purchaser of the work.

Printed on acid-free paper

Springer is part of Springer Science+Business Media (www.springer.com)

Foreword

Our project: the "Hermeneutic Study and Education of Textual Configuration" (HERSETEC), commenced in June 2007, after official notice was delivered by the Society for the Promotion of Science. The Society organized peer reviews with advice from distinguished scholars both within and beyond the borders of Japan, and authorized us to launch. As this project was to focus upon the pedagogical dimensions of the doctorate course, we called upon doctorate students for their willing participation in our project, in order to enrich both their knowledge and their experience in their respective research fields.

Our scientific assumptions about textual configuration can be explained as follows: in general, texts constitute a kind of imaginary constellation of homologues: both those of pre-textuality – a prerequisite for textual existence – and other related texts, which realize inter-textuality through cross-references among them; meta-texts, which assign annotations or interpretations to texts; and para-texts, which are titles that indicate genres of texts or categories to which the texts belong, as well as their forms and constitutions. A particular text exists as a closely-knit gathering of textual constituents, and their overall configuration is characterized as "text" in the broad sense. Based on the theoretical ideas explained above, which have already been cultivated and elaborated on in the sphere of literature, we have examined what is called the "hermeneutical point of view," which is, as I see it, one of the most important devices of modern science for the understanding of the written text.

As the fruits of labor in the educational sphere are, regrettably, less visible when compared to the research results, I would explain the activities of our project over the past four years by presenting the trajectory of various international meetings that we have organized and hosted.

First, we inaugurated the series with a conference entitled "Philological and Grammatical Studies of English Historical Texts," which was held in Nagoya, in September 2007. The late Professor AMANO Masachiyo was its organizer and the proceedings were published in 2008 from Peter Lang. The second international colloquium that we organized was named *Balzac, Flaubert. La genèse de l'oeuvre et la question de l'interprétation* and was held in December 2007. The third was held in February 2008, titled "Identity in Text Interpretation and Everyday Life". In July 2008, we hosted the fourth international conference on the subject of "The Global Stature of Japanese Religious Texts: Aspects of textuality and syntactic methodology". The fifth international conference was organized by MATSUZAWA Kazuhiro in collaboration with Gisèle SÉGINGER: *La mise en texte des savoirs*, in March 2009, at the *Université de Paris-Est*, of which proceedings were published in November 2010 from *Presses Universitaires de Strasbourg*. Almost simultaneously, we held the sixth international meeting with the theme *Herméneutique du texte d'histoire: orientation, interpretation et questions nouvelles* on the 7th and 8th of March in 2009, in Tokyo. The seventh, titled "The Sixth Workshop on Altaic Formal Linguistics" was held in September 2009 in Nagoya. The proceedings of this colloquium were published by the MIT Press in 2011. Once again, almost contemporaneously, the eighth international meeting was hosted in association with the Charles University of the Czech Republic, in Prague: "Historical Trajectory of the Written Text in Japanese: Interpretation, Re-contextualization and Configuration". The ninth meeting was based on the theme "Japanese Academic Knowledge Aiming for Language" in September 2010. Finally, it was the tenth international meeting that our colleague MORIGIWA Yasutomo organized in association with Professors Drs. Michael STOLLEIS and Jean-Louis HALPÉRIN, titled "Interpretation by Another Name: The Uses of Legal Texts in the Age of Enlightenment", from which this book has ensued.

I would stress the fact that the conference was our first to discuss the problem of law and juridical texts. I do not doubt that our scientific attempt ended successfully, thanks to the collaboration of all the contributors gathered at this meeting. To conclude, I would like to express my sincere gratitude to my colleague MORIGIWA Yasutomo, and Professors Drs. Michael STOLLEIS and Jean-Louis HALPÉRIN for their scientific patronage and advice.

Academician of the Japan Academy   SATO Shoichi
Professor at Nagoya University
Project leader of HERSETEC

Preface

Legal interpretation was a matter of great controversy in 19th century Germany. The conflicts that took place between the historical school and what was deemed the school of *Begriffsjurisprudenz* is well known. This debate increasingly broadened divisions between the Germanisten and the Romanisten, and Savigny, Puchta, Jhering are just some of the names that come to mind as the major actors at play. The issue of legal interpretation has continued to be discussed in the 20th century; a great part of the works of Zitelmann, Ehrlich, Gény, Kelsen, Holmes, Cardozo, Llewellyn, Hart and, more recently, of Ronald Dworkin, Joseph Raz, and Neil MacCormick have been devoted to pressing interpretive questions. These questions include those concerning the issues of "judge-made law," silences in the law, the idea of "one right answer", the Janus-faced character of legal interpretation, and the nature of legal reasoning itself. In addition, the "linguistic turn," influenced by the views of L. Wittgenstein, J. L. Austin, and H.-G. Gadamer, among others, accentuated this focus on the role of interpretation in the creation of legal norms.

Compared to what we know of the 19th and 20th centuries, our understanding of what occurred in 18th century Europe on this issue is much less evident. However, just as the knowledge of 19th century controversies aids our understanding of those of the 20th century, a sound understanding of how legal interpretation was regarded in the eighteenth ought to help us better understand these later developments.

Further, legal interpretation in the Age of Enlightenment is a topic of great interest from the point of view of legal theory. How did the ideology of the era, with its emphasis on the power of reason, affect the practice of legal interpretation in the courts? As in the case of Kant, the 18th century was the period during which the concept of public reason was developed. Is it possible that the judiciary had been operating upon such a concept, perhaps without being aware of it? If there were enlightened judges, would they not have espoused the idea that through reason, a code could be derived with two main functions: first, unification of the then various and conflicting sources of law which necessitated interpretation; and second, to be so clear and systematic that no interpretation would be needed? Further, because none existed, that the judges can and should interpret the law according to natural law principles so that a functional surrogate of such a code could be derived in practice?

While Friedrich the Great aspired to bring about such a Code, and although there were attempts to systematize positive law under natural law principles in the universities, such tendencies seem not to have been the case with the judges of the courts in his official realm. As the work by Heinz MOHNHAUPT and Jan SCHRÖDER in this volume demonstrates, history tends to contradict our expectations. Finding reasonable solutions through legal interpretation, and reading reason into the law was mainly a pre-18th century practice. In contrast, what developed in the 18th century was the replacement of reason by authority. More and more, as Hobbes said, authority, not reason, made the law. The power of absolutist kings controlled the judiciary, and directed them to follow the wishes of the sovereign; the concept of authority was thus firmly rooted in this century, and the scope for judicial interpretation became increasingly narrower.

Furthermore, in contrast to the spread of Enlightenment philosophy from France to Germany, and the high level of communication among the literary and scientific circles of England, Scotland and Continental Europe, there was relatively little exchange of ideas and practice between the courts divided by the Rhine. Entirely different ways of addressing the needs of a new, modern state were developed in each area respectively.

These preliminary findings prompted a more thorough investigation of the subject, with the aim of finding out in more detail how the German and French judges interpreted law in their respective courts. This in turn provided a foundation for a better understanding of the development of legal interpretation during the Age of Enlightenment.

The first idea of this collective work, initiated by MORIGIWA Yasutomo, was to question the German and the French systems during the Age of Enlightenment. The working hypothesis was that the well known contrasts between French legalism ("legicentrism", prevalent Napoleonic codification, and disallowance of judicial review of statutes), and the German theory of interpretation (Savigny's system, later adapted to the Kelsenian context of constitutional review) could find their roots in 18th century differences between each country's philosophical, political and legal contexts. The working hypothesis was exactly that: nothing more than temporary scaffolding, thus in need of further refinement and elaboration as the enquiry progressed. The most well-known writings discussing legal interpretation during the 18th century – such as Montesqieu's famous expression of the judge as the "mouth of the law" – seemed, *prima facie*, foreign to any interpretivist understanding of the law. It was as if they spoke of interpretation "by another name" if at all. This was consonant with the changing practice of the judges in France and Germany, but admitting no room for interpretation is by far an exaggeration. Thus, it was necessary to further investigate the works of less notorious writers and those engaged in judicial practice.

Thanks to the financial support of the Hermeneutic Study and Education of Textual Configuration (HERSETEC, a Global Centre of Excellence Program organized by the Nagoya University Graduate School of Letters), a symposium was organized and held in Paris, September–October 2010. In preparation, Michael STOLLEIS (former Director of the *Max-Planck-Institut für europäische Rechtsgeschichte*) in concert with MORIGIWA, provided scientific perspective on the issue at hand, and the *Centre de Théorie et Analyse du Droit* (UMR 7074 represented by Jean-Louis HALPÉRIN, *École normale supérieure*, Paris) kindly provided the venue for the conference, utilizing both campuses of the *École normale supérieure*. In addition, as co-organizer, HALPÉRIN provided a wealth of ideas for the conference.

At the conference, the discussion was particularly rigorous, not only on the papers presented, but also concerning the subject matter as a whole, especially on the links between older and more recent debates. It became apparent, first, that the Age of Enlightenment should be understood as a period beginning in the middle of the 17th century (with Hobbes' *Leviathan*) and concluding after the French Revolution with the German debates on the works of Savigny. Differences between French and German doctrine were also more precisely contextualized, and were shown to be linked with the developments of the modern State on both sides of the Rhine.

The changes that intervened during the Age of Enlightenment came to be considered as beacons for our contemporaneous understanding of the nature of legal interpretation. These changes can be aptly described by the sub-title: "from the Rule of the King to the Rule of Law", which depicts the transition from judges devoted to the service of the Prince to judges subjected to a significantly more abstract sovereignty. Through the historical investigation of legal interpretation in Germany and France during this era, the legacy of legal cultures created by the Age of Enlightenment began to appear as clues that could fuel renewed debates about legal interpretation today.

The chapters in this volume were organized with the idea above in mind. The volume begins with a work by STOLLEIS, which goes well beyond the introductory function it serves. The second and third parts are comprised of works in legal history written by representative legal historians of France and Germany, and concentrate on the issue of legal interpretation. Heinz MOHNHAUPT and Brad WENDEL kindly joined us post-conference, which allowed us to change this volume from a record of proceedings to a well-balanced and informative collection of essays.

Part IV is a collection of chapters by philosophers of law. MORIGIWA provides an introduction discussing the way in which a theory of general interpretation can illuminate legal interpretation, given the heritage of philosophy stemming from the "linguistic turn." Michel TROPER then illustrates the modern French judge's broad interpretive scope, despite the official ideology that the French judge merely applies and never interprets law. This may give the appearance that the French judge has liberal scope in interpretation that may be little more than arbitrary. Contrary to this perspective, WENDEL discusses the interpretation of law by American lawyers, and demonstrates that they ought to be responsible for the quality of the reasons given to explain and justify their legal interpretations. This may be understood as an anti-thesis to TROPER, as it claims that there is (in the case of lawyers) a normative reason to rule out discretion in interpretation, *a fortiori* for the case of the judge. In this sense, modern day theories of legal interpretation may be seen to return to the system of reading reason into law. This is the position MORIGIWA takes, in arguing that the interpretation of law is a never-ending spiraling process of reason-giving.

The volume closes with a synthesis of the findings, presented by HALPÉRIN. We hope that this will give the reader a panoramic view of the state of legal interpretation in the Age of Enlightenment. The book should offer as well a taste of the contemporary theoretical situation on the issue of legal interpretation. With this prospect in mind, we hope that the collection of these texts, made possible with the kind support given us by *Springer Verlag*, will provoke further research and debate surrounding the question of interpretation on the use and creation of law.

Last but not least, the editors would like to thank everyone who made this volume possible. We were fortunate enough to receive papers from the leading writers in the field. The audience at the Paris symposium, their questions and critique from the floor were most helpful. Professor SATO Shoichi of the Japan Academy and leader of the HERSETEC project gave invaluable moral as well as financial support. The *Max-Planck-Institut für europäische Rechtsgeschichte* and the *École normale supérieure* were generous in allowing us the use of their premises for our meetings and the symposium. Our special thanks go to Thomas ROBERTS for his speedy and excellent translation of the work by Heinz MOHNHAUPT, NODA Yukari for her always timely secretarial work, Leah HAMILTON for her tireless polishing, formatting and all types of editorial work, and Neil and Diana at Springer for their warm support; without their help, this book would not have seen the light of day.

Nagoya, Japan   MORIGIWA Yasutomo
Frankfurt, Germany   Michael STOLLEIS
Paris, France   Jean-Louis HALPÉRIN
February 2011

Contents

Contributors

Serge DAUCHY Centre d'Histoire Judiciaire, CNRS, Lille, France, serge.dauchy@univ-lille2.fr

Hans-Peter HAFERKAMP Institut für Neuere Privatrechtsgeschichte, Deutsche und Rheinische Rechtsgeschichte, Universität zu Köln, 50923 Köln, Deutschland, Hans-Peter.Haferkamp@uni-koeln.de

Jean-Louis HALPÉRIN École Normale Supérieure, UMR 7074 "Centre de Théorie et Analyse du droit", Paris, France, jean-louis.halperin@ens.fr; jean-louis.halperin@wanadoo.fr

Heinz MOHNHAUPT Max-Planck-Institut für europäische Rechtsgeschichte (Max-Planck-Institute for European Legal History), Frankfurt am Main, Germany, mohnhaupt@rg.mpg.de

MORIGIWA Yasutomo Graduate School of Law, Nagoya University, Nagoya 464-8601, Japan, morigiwa@nagoya-u.jp

Jan SCHRÖDER Faculty of Law, University of Tübingen, Geschwister-Scholl-Platz, D-72076, Tübingen, jan.schroeder@jura.uni-tuebingen.de; ejschroeder@web.de

Michael STOLLEIS Faculty of Law, University of Frankfurt, Frankfurt, Germany; Former Director, Max Planck Institute for European Legal History, D-60489 Frankfurt/Main, Germany, stolleis@rg.mpg.de

Michel TROPER Centre de Théorie et Analyse du Droit, Université de Paris Ouest – Nanterre, Paris, France, troper@u-paris10.fr

W. Bradley WENDEL Law School, Cornell University, Ithaca, New York, US, bradley-wendel@lawschool.cornell.edu

About the Authors

Prof. Serge DAUCHY has studied history and law at the Universities of Ghent and Paris. He is the research director at the Centre National de la Recherche Scientifique, director of the Centre d'Histoire Judiciaire (UMR 8025 CNRS – Lille) and a professor at the Facultés universitaires Saint-Louis in Brussels. He is currently working on the history of civil procedure, case law and on the circulation of legal literature in early modern Europe.

Prof. Dr. Hans-Peter HAFERKAMP PhD in 1994, habilitation in 2002. From 2003, director of the Institute of the History of Modern Private Law at the University of Cologne. Fields of study: history of private law in the modern age, history of jurisprudence, contemporary legal history.

Major publications: *Die heutige Rechtsmissbrauchslehre – Ergebnis nationalsozialistischen Rechtsdenkens?,* Berlin 1995; *Georg Friedrich Puchta und die Begriffsjurisprudenz',* Frankfurt on the Main, 2004.

Jean-Louis HALPÉRIN École Normale Supérieure (Paris), UMR 7074 CNRS "Centre de Théorie et Analyse du droit". Professor of legal history, successively at the Universities of Lyon (1988–1998) and Burgundy (1998–2003), then at the Ecole Normale Superieure (Paris) from 2003, author of various books about French codification.

Major publications: (*L'Impossible Code civil*, Paris, PUF, 1992), European legal history (*Histoire des droits en Europe*, Paris, Flammarion, 2004) and comparative law (*Profil des mondialisations du droit*, Paris, Dalloz, 2009).

Heinz MOHNHAUPT Jurist and legal historian, is an emeritus fellow of the Max-Planck Institute for European Legal History in Frankfurt am Main. His research is currently focused on the theory and practice of using legal sources, the history of constitutions and of legal terms, and comparative history in natural and human sciences.

Major publications: "Potestas legislatoria . . .," in: *Ius Commune* 4 (1972), 188–239; "Untersuchungen zum Verhältnis Privileg und Kodifikation," in: *Ius Commune* 5 (1975), 71–121; *Verfassung* (together with D. Grimm), 2. ed., 2002; *Prudentia legislatoria*, 2003.

MORIGIWA Yasutomo is Professor of Law at the Graduate School of Law, Nagoya University. LL.B., LL.M., University of Tokyo. Teaches philosophy of law, legal ethics and anti-corruption in English and Japanese. Acting President, International Association for Philosophy of Law and Social Philosophy (IVR). After beginning his career at the University of Tokyo as Research Associate, worked on theories of law and language at Oxford with Profs. Hart, Dworkin, and Raz. Now active in work on interpretation and in promoting the practical import of legal philosophy; e.g., uses his findings on legal validation to explain to the practicing jurist the binding nature of legal ethics. He has also edited a textbook on legal ethics *Ethica Juris Peritorum* (Nagoya University Press, 2005), with translations in Chinese and Mongolian. Examples of works available in European languages: "Die philosophischen Grundlagen der Richterethik," *Schleswig-Holsteinische Anzeigen*, Teil A Nr. 4, 110–115 (2009), "The Semantic Sting in Jurisprudence," *Archiv fuer Rechts- und Sozialphilosophie*, Beiheft 40, 16–24 (1991), "Authority, Rationality, and Law," *Southern California Law Review* 62, 897–912 (1989).

Jan SCHRÖDER was born in 1943 in Berlin. Professor of law, Eberhard-Karls-Universität Tübingen. Chair for German legal history and civil law since 1989, retired October 2009. Member of the Academy of Science and Literature Mainz 2001. Honorary doctor of the University of Stockholm, faculty of law, 2003.

Major publications: (1) *Wissenschaftstheorie und Lehre der "praktischen Jurisprudenz" auf deutschen Universitäten an der Wende zum 19. Jahrhundert*, 1979; (2) *Recht als Wissenschaft. Geschichte der juristischen Methode vom Humanismus bis zur historischen Schule (1500–1850)*, 2001; (3) (Co-author with Gerd Kleinheyer): *Deutsche und europäische Juristen aus neun Jahrhunderten*, 5th edition, 2008 (translations of former editions: Japanese 1983, Chinese 2004); (4) *Rechtswissenschaft in der Neuzeit: Geschichte, Theorie, Methode* (selected essays), 2010.

Michael STOLLEIS was born in 1941. He was a Professor for Public Law and History of Law at the University of Frankfurt from 1975 to 2006. From 1992 to 2009 he also directed the Max Planck Institute for European Legal History. He has been awarded both the Leibniz Prize of the Deutsche Forschungsmeinschaft (1991) and the Prize of the International Balzan Foundation (2000). He is a member of several Scientific Academies and obtained honorary degrees from the Universities of Lund, Toulouse, Padova and Helsinki.

Major works: *History of Public Law in Germany (1600–1945)*, 3 vol., 1988, 1992, 1999, second and third volume appeared in english (vol. II 1800–1914, New York (Berghahn Books) 2001; vol. III. 1914–1945, Oxford University Press 2004). Collected articles appeared under the title *The Law under the Swastika. Studies on Legal History in Nazi Germany*, Chicago 1998. See also: *The Eye of the Law. Two Essays on Legal History*, Birbeck Law Press, London 2009.

Michel TROPER is professor emeritus at the Université de Paris X-Nanterre, a member of the Institut Universitaire de France. He created and was the first President of the SFPJ (Société Française de philosophie politique et juridique). He is also honorary president of the French association of constitutional law. TROPER has taught and lectured in several universities around the world.

Major publications: *La séparation des pouvoirs et l'histoire constitutionnelle française*, Paris, LGDJ (new edit. 2010); *La philosophie du droit*, Paris, PUF (Que Sais-je?), 3rd edit. 2011; Le droit et la nécessité, Paris, PUF, 2011; HAMON F. & TROPER M., *Droit constitutionnel*, Paris, LGDJ, 31st. edit., 2009; TROPER M. & CHAGNOLLAUD D. (ed.), *Traité international de droit constitutionnel*, Paris, Dalloz, 3 vol. (forthcoming).

W. Bradley WENDEL Professor of Law, Cornell Law School. B.A. Rice University; J.D. Duke University; LL.M., J.S.D. Columbia University.

Major publications: *Lawyers and Fidelity to Law* (Princeton University Press 2010); *Professional Responsibility: Examples and Explanations* (Wolters Kluwer, 3rd ed. 2010); and co-editor of *The Law and Ethics of Lawyering* (with Hazard, et al., Foundation Press, 5th ed. 2010).

Part I
Introduction

Chapter 1
Judicial Interpretation in Transition from the *Ancien Régime* to Constitutionalism

Michael STOLLEIS

There are few statements more universally accepted than Thomas Hobbes's famous gloss: that "All Laws need Interpretation".[1] This idea has remained an ongoing jurisprudential theme since antiquity, as even before legislation in the modern sense existed, judges were required to determine "the right" interpretation of any given law.[2] The deficiencies of laws and legal texts are acknowledged and well known: those both obvious and latent, and those actual or claimed. Not only this, but the law also contains a well-known blindness towards the future, and like all texts, can be interpreted differently depending on the context. Therefore, if society is to function harmoniously, an authority is required: an authority which ends the battle of interpretation.

This battle has been a constant jurisprudential problem. All texts are ambiguous, be they divine commandments or human norms; simple directions or instruction manuals. When the word "interpretation" is entered into Google, sixty-nine million hits are returned, revealing that in any sense of the word, interpretation is a fundamental problem within human communication.

---

[1] T. Hobbes, Leviathan, Oxford 1909, 212.

[2] So the often quoted sentence from the speech from Feb. 23rd 1803 concerning the tabling of the code civil of Portalis, *Il y avait des juges avant qu'il y eût lois...* (*Mohnhaupt, Potestas legislatoria und Gesetzesbegriff im Ancien Régime, in: id., Historische Vergleichung im Bereich von Staat und Recht*, Frankfurt 2000, 223).

M. STOLLEIS (✉)
Faculty of Law, University of Frankfurt, Frankfurt, Germany; Former Director, Max Planck Institute for European Legal History, D-60489 Frankfurt/Main, Germany
e-mail: stolleis@rg.mpg.de

MORIGIWA, Y. et al. (eds.), *Interpretation of Law in the Age of Enlightenment*, Law and Philosophy Library 95,
DOI 10.1007/978-94-007-1506-6_1, © Springer Science+Business Media B.V. 2011

I The Concept of Sovereignty

To determine a starting point within the *polemic* surrounding juridical interpretation, we shall begin with Thomas Hobbes. Insofar as Hobbes appoints the secular sovereign as the final authority – whoever he may be: whether one man, as in a monarchy; or an assembly of men, as in a democracy or aristocracy – Hobbes simultaneously appoints him as the legislator of civil law.[3] This sovereign is not only able to make, abolish or change laws; he is also able to interpret them. This was previously noted by Bodin, in his acknowledgment that the sovereign both *donne & casser la loy* and can *changer & corriger* the law also.[4] To support this, here Bodin refers to the works of Bartolus, Baldus and Accursius, and in a direct way to the Roman law Digest and institutions.

In addition to this, throughout the High Middle Ages canon law permitted the pope to *omne ius tollere et de iure supra ius dispensare*. Thus, whoever held the right to legislate was also able to interpret the law authentically and legitimately: *Unde ius prodiit, interpretatio quoque procedat* (*Liber extra* 5.39.31, *Dekretale Inter alia*).

Thomas Hobbes can be situated within this debate on absolutism, which ran from the era of Justinian to the medieval juristic popes; and from Bodin to the absolutism of Hobbes's own time. Hobbes recognized the sovereign's inability to make every interpretive and juridical decision alone. Thus, Hobbes legitimated the judicial right of interpretation as a product of delegation between social actors. Judges are appointed by a sovereign, and make decisions in the sovereign's name.[5] These decisions do not acquire validity by virtue of being the private sentences of judges, but because they are made within the authority of the sovereign. In this way, judicial decisions become not only the *sovereign's* sentence, but also binding and enforceable law. Even interpretations of common or local laws are only legitimate if they implicitly or explicitly suit the will of the sovereign. In other words: the sovereign's power over the law subdues the interpretation of it. In Hobbes's model there is no independent justice, no separation of state functions and no autonomous interpretation by the judge.

---

[3]T. Hobbes, Leviathan, Oxford 1909, 204: The Soveraign is Legislator.

[4]Bodin, *Six livres*, Chap. I, 8. *Principi leges a se latas sua voluntate ac sine subditorum consensu abrogare, vel ex parte legibus derogare vel subrogare vel abrogare licere.* In the French version: *Le Prince souverain peut déroger aux lois, ou icelles casser ou annuler cessant la justice d'icelles.*

[5]M. Stolleis, Im Namen des Gesetzes, Berlin 2004.

Although we are familiar with the distinctions between "legislation", "administration" and "jurisdiction", under Roman law only the singular term "jurisdiction" existed. This term contained the connotations of both *imperium* and *potestas* (power). (Ulpian D. 2.1.3).[6]

Initially, jurisdiction was defined as an authoritarian power (*maiestas*); a power that determined, established, changed, and declared in one pronouncement both the law, and what was right. On this point, Bartolus expounds: *facere statuta est iurisdictio in genere sumpta*, and Baldus follows to state that *statuta condere est iurisdictionis: Quia qui statuit, ius dicit. . .*: he who has determined, has determined the law; he who has jurisdiction, is sovereign. In Spain and France, "he who determined" was the king. In Germany, the emperor and the estates of the empire had to collectively agree upon the establishment of new laws. In these circumstances, the jurists' debate over claims to "jurisdiction" in the Roman sense (D 2.1.3.) revolved around this contentious problem of power.

From the time of medieval jurisdiction to the time of Hobbes, Bodin's aim was to examine and clarify the earlier debates. Even Bodin himself was initially unsure of his direction. Nonetheless, first, within the "Methodus" from 1566, he declared the appointment of leading clerks to be the most significant attribute of sovereignty, and after that, the enactment or the repeal of laws. In *Les six Livres de la République* from 1576, the power to make legislation is mentioned above all as the *première marque de souveraineté, c'est donner loy à tous en général, et à chacun en particulier* (Lib. I, chap. X). Since then, the concept of sovereignty has defined – and allowed – the concentration of law-making power to rest in the hands of the sovereign.

II The Judge as an Agent of the Prince

Thomas Hobbes – with whom we started – did not change anything in relation to this concept of sovereignty. In a complex interplay between power politics and political and legal theory, the various spheres of the sovereign's power were consolidated under the central title of "sovereignty". As a consequence, the "states" (*Stände*) lost their position: they were overthrown by the power of the sovereign, and eluded by the powers that could bypass them completely. An example of this is the situation in which a prince could make new taxes without the assent of the states. The states were convened less and less often, or even not at all; they were being abandoned.

---

[6]M. Stolleis, *Geschichte des öffentlichen Rechts in Deutschland*, Bd. I, München 1988, 156 ff.

The language of commands makes this hierarchical power structure clear: *nous disons, déclarons, ordonnons*, or *volumus et iubemus* or *ordenamos y mandamos*.[7] In this world of absolutism the judge became nothing more than the organ of the will of the sovereign. In this world, every interpretation made by the judge automatically embodied an act of finding justice on behalf of the monarch. While in practice it was the judge who was acting and who adjudicated upon each case (*ius dicit*), in theory it remained the monarch. Even so, during this period, no monarch could directly influence or control the verdicts of his judiciary. Instead, he led the judges' work, and interfered from time to time where deficiencies were reported. Judges were controlled in the same way as other higher or lower officials, fiscals, military men or diplomats, court officials or scullions. During this period, the guiding principle was the "machine", driven by a central controller or energy point.[8]

However, within the judicial institution itself, the monarch's theoretical involvement did not in fact extend to individual cases or typical lawsuits, and therefore cannot be interpreted in any real sense. Nonetheless, the theoretical situation was exactly the way Hobbes had described it. Any given judge was authorized to consolidate the legal order on behalf of the sovereign (or the proper authority).

In fulfilling this role, judges focused upon the wording of Roman law – or indeed other sources of law – and also concerned themselves with the doctrine of precedent. In some circumstances, judges even consulted academic texts for their opinions. However ultimately, these tasks were little more than preparation. This was because the final decision – made after all interpretation – was one in the name of the king (*au nom du roi*), or in the name of the empire. As the last legitimating point, the sovereign remained at the top of the hierarchy; at the apex of the pyramid.

Consequently, the judiciary's function of interpreting the law became a part of the executive branch. The judiciary was not independent, but instead was an instrument of the sovereign's will. Montesquieu's famous description of the judiciary as the *bouche de la loi* (*De l'Esprit des Lois*, XI, 6) aptly describes this relationship. This description is often misunderstood, as well as the connotations that it implies for the separation of powers.[9] It does not imply that judicial interpretation is not useful, but only that the law – in the

---

[7]Following Mohnhaupt (fn. 2) 225 ff.

[8]B. Stollberg-Rilinger, *Der Staat als Maschine. Zur politischen Metaphorik des absoluten Fürstenstaats*, Berlin 1986.

[9]U. Seif, *Der missverstandene Montesquieu: Gewaltenbalance, nicht Gewaltentrennung*, in: *Zeitschrift für Neuere Rechtsgeschichte* 22 (2000) 149 ff.

mechanical sense – contains solutions for everything, and the judge plays the part of the mouth to speak it aloud.[10]

Montesquieu's statement is not an endorsement of the modern-day commitment to the "rule of law" (*état de droit*), nor of the idea that the judiciary is forbidden to deviate from it. Montesquieu is merely describing the legal relationship between the monarch and the judiciary, and in this respect the metaphor is apt. It merely denotes the hierarchy of law as stemming from the sovereign. All legal historians agree that a modern idea of law did not exist during this period, as modern law was a product of the constitutional movement of the 19th century. Modern law can be seen as a product of an evolving parliamentarianism, and its distinction between the executive (which can only enact decrees), and the legislature, which can enact the law.[11] In 1748, during Montesquieu's time, modern legal ideas had not yet developed in either France or Germany (which remained relatively underdeveloped and politically disparate).[12]

III On the Way to Independence

During the Enlightenment period, from the middle of the 18th century onwards, criticism towards absolutism grew. In France this criticism was directed towards the church much earlier and much more strongly, while in Germany it was more moderate and subtle. In 1750 this criticism intensified and became more widespread. By this stage, the attention of the educated classes was focused upon questions of state order, reform and the limits of sovereignty.[13] In a theoretical sense this movement was strong, but in practice it was weak. In Germany, for example, at the level of the realm (the particular territories of autonomous cities) men reacted very slowly, or they

---

[10]R. Ogorek, *De l'Esprit des légendes oder wie gewissermaßen aus dem Nichts eine Interpretationslehre wurde* (1983), in: id., *Aufklärung über Justiz*, Bd. 1, Frankfurt 2008, 67 ff.; id., *Die erstaunliche Karriere des Subsumtionsmodells oder wozu braucht der Jurist Geschichte?*, aa0., 87 ff.

[11]Chr.-F. Menger – H. Wehrhahn, *Das Gesetz als Norm und Maßnahme*, in: *Veröffentlichungen der Vereinigung der Deutschen Staatsrechtslehrer* (VVDStRL) 15 (1957) 3 ff.; G. Roellecke – Chr. Starck, *Die Bindung des Richters an Gesetz und Verfassung*, in: VVDStRL 34 (1976) 7 ff.; K. Eichenberger – R. Novak – M. Kloepfer, *Gesetzgebung im Rechtsstaat*, in: VVDStRL 40 (1982) 7 ff.

[12]Th. Unverhau, *Lex. Eine Untersuchung zum Gesetzesverständnis deutscher Publizisten des 17. und 18. Jahrhunderts*, jur. Diss. Heidelberg 1971; Mohnhaupt (fn. 2) 248 ff.

[13]Chr. Link, *Herrschaftsordnung und Bürgerliche Freiheit. Grenzen der Staatsgewalt in der älteren deutschen Staatslehre*, Wien – Köln – Graz 1979.

did not react to demands for reform at all. Despite this sluggish response, in the theoretical sense state sovereignty had been newly founded.

Throughout this movement tensions developed between old ideas and new. One dissent existed between the idea of *ius publicum universal* – or, the natural law foundations of state power – and the practical implementation of the social contract theory. The acceptance of the idea that the sovereign was not appointed through God, but that his position was legitimated through a fictitious social contract, symbolizes one of the biggest secularization processes in the modern era.

The development of the social contract idea (whereby unrestrained individual power enjoyed in the "state of nature" is surrendered to the state in return for political order) illustrates some of the main ideas which were debated from the time of Hobbes to Rousseau. While Hobbes' primary argument was that the sovereign had to establish a monopoly over the use of force to ensure social order and prevent warfare, in the 18th century the underlying premise was an expectation that the state would provide for individual happiness.

The sovereign was now no longer expected to be a mere protector and guarantor of safety (this much was taken for granted); rather, the sovereign was expected to be a provider of welfare for his citizens. In line with the Aristotelian tradition, it was assumed that each citizen would find his or her own "good life" and attain happiness. As the expectation of "safety" changed into "happiness" or "welfare", the former emphasis upon the collective shifted to an emphasis upon the individual citizen. The individual citizen was now a fictive partner in a social contract with the state. As partners to this contract, citizens expected welfare from the state, as well as the protection of their freedom to grow and develop as individuals. The mantra of "freedom and property" became an active and powerful force from 1750 onwards, and came to play a tremendous role in determining what was expected from Parliament throughout the 19th century. Text books on natural law published during this period asserted freedom in a variety of areas: indeed, "freedom" was not seen as simply the ability to fulfill an individualized or personal conception of welfare or happiness. For example, economic freedom was also asserted in opposition to overarching state regulation. The new civic entrepreneurs complained of state regulations, and of corruption and a lack of administrative efficiency.

Even so, not less important in the eyes of contemporaries was the desire that religious freedom should gain its own sphere of free operation: first through the guarantee of the *forum internum*; afterwards through the permission of the house service; and even later through allowing the public exercise of religion. Moreover, this idea further extended to the realm of civil freedom. Most especially, however, demands centered upon the realm of personal freedom – with a focus on liberation from the agrarian lifestyle, liberation from tributes, freedom of emigration, and freedom of personal property. This was in addition to demands for freedom of speech, and calls for reducing censorship: essentially, a demand for freedom of communication.

Originally, the idea of *libertas naturalis* was perceived by the state as a dangerous concept, but even so, it was something that only the state could concede. By this stage, however, it was too late: the people desired the remnants of their natural liberty – their "lost paradise". This concept was embodied in the well-known writings of Rousseau, which described the "noble savage" as a happy individual, living in a state of natural freedom. These demands for freedom defined the intellectual scene of the second half of the 18th century: now, "justice" was put forward as one of the main arguments opposing absolutism.

Slowly, the question of whether the model of absolutist justice should continue to exist was raised more and more. Under absolutism, the codes of procedure mentioned a list of cases, in which the judge was required to immediately inform the bench or the monarch. These were cases such as treason, blasphemy, scandalous libel, cases of emigration, and serious crimes.[14] Besides this, cases that were doubtful in the eyes of the judges, or unclear in themselves, also had to be immediately reported.[15] In other words, during absolutism interpretation was left to the monarch. He could *ex plenitudine potestatis* (out of his comprehensive power) repeal a verdict or change it;[16] he could rearrange the proceeding, or refer it to some other court; and he could even explicitly determine the interpretation of a law.[17]

Further doubts about absolutism arose when a legally unsophisticated monarch undertook to interpret the law in a certain case in virtue of his authority, and blundered. The monarch in question was Friedrich II, who decided a civil process incorrectly. This case is famous, because it marked a turning point in Prussian and German legal history.[18] From that time on,

---

[14]W. Ogris, *Maria Theresia Iudex*, in: id., *Elemente europäischer Rechtskultur*, Wien 2003, 643 f.

[15]Ogris, loc. cit., 644.

[16]In 1730 Friedrich Wilhelm I. of Prussia decided against the mild judgment of the court martial against Hans Hermann von Katte. He was sentenced to death because of desertion.

[17]Comprising R. Ogorek, *Richterkönig oder Subsumtionsautomat? Zur Justiztheorie im 19. Jahrhundert*, 2. Aufl. Frankfurt 2008, 18 ff.

[18]R. Stammler, *Deutsches Rechtsleben*, vol. II, München 1932, 411, 496; E. Schmidt, *Rechtssprüche und Machtsprüche der preußischen Könige des 18. Jahrhunderts*, Leipzig

judgments from the sovereign (*ex plenitudine potestatis*)[19] were viewed as not only deviations from the norm, but when they were brought they were now perceived to be the opposite of legal decisions. As Werner Ogris says, in this respect there was a swing in opinion, and some even tried to forbid such *dicta*. However, these attempts at banning *dicta* did not eventuate, in either the case of the Prussian civil code from 1794, or in that of the general civil code from 1811.[20]

IV The Independent Judge as Limited Interpreter

Unsurprisingly, it was more than just a swing in opinions. Other factors at play were the French revolution and the replacement of the monarch by abstract law. Furthermore, the gradual fragmentation and specialization of the *plenitudo potestatis* also influenced the course of events. Finally, it was the enforcement of the judges' independence as a direct contrast to the monarchs' power. Rather than a swing in opinions, the historical and jurisprudential change was about important power shifts: shifts by which interpretation was viewed from a new perspective.

I shall not describe the entire shift from the absolutist state to the constitutional state here. The constitutional movement that spread throughout Europe took place under different political conditions and traditions, which varied between countries. In France, for example, the movement was the transition from absolutism to constitutional monarchy; from the *Régime du Terreur* to the constitution of 1791; the step by step transition to the *Directoire*; and finally, the empire of Napoleon and the return to the constitutional monarchy in the *Charte Constitutionnelle* in 1814. While these events were observed in other countries, they were not adopted.

In the case of Germany, the first constitutions appeared in 1814, and the southern German (Bavaria, Baden, Wuerttemberg) constitutions in 1818–1819. These constitutions embodied a significant legal shift, in that they proclaimed judicial independence from the sovereign. This independence

---

1943; id., *Die Justizpolitik Friedrichs d. Gr., in: Heidelberger Jahrbücher* 4 (1962) 95 f.; J. Regge, *Kabinettsjustiz in Brandenburg-Preußen*, Berlin 1977; M. Dießelhorst, *Die Prozesse des Müllers Arnold und das Eingreifen Friederichs des Großen*, Göttingen 1984; David M. Luebke, Frederik the Great and the Celebrated Case of the Millers Arnold (1770–1779): A Reappraisal, in: Central European History 32/4 (1999) 379–408.

[19] W. Ogris, *De sententiis ex plenitudine potestatis. Ein Beitrag zur Geschichte der Kabinettsjustiz vornehmlich des 18. Jahrhunderts*, in: *Festschrift H. Krause* 1975, 171 ff.

[20] W. Ogris, *Machtspruch*, in: *Handwörterbuch zur Deutschen Rechtsgeschichte* (1. ed.), vol. III, Berlin 1984, 126–128 (127).

was secured by the prohibition of the *dicta* which had prevailed in the 18th century. Even so, justice was still "owned" and influenced by the king, as long as he held the title of sovereignty. In other words: the model remained absolutist, but the possibility for the monarch to intervene directly in the justice system was abolished. Judicial errors could only be corrected via judicial processes, rather than by monarchical dismissal of judges. The new constitutions declared this point explicitly. For example, it was written in the Bavarian constitution of 1818 that jurisdiction was left to the king ("The king is the head of the state, united in himself all the rights of state authority and exercises given to him under the current constitutional provisions"). The Baden constitution of 1818 also declared that: "The courts are independent within the range of their responsibilities". Finally, the Württemberg constitution from 1819 stated that: "Jurisdiction is in the king's name and under his supervision by educated collegial courts in statutory bodies managed in in-order. The courts, civil and penal are within the limits of their profession independently".

At this stage of constitutional development, this compromise between the monarchy and the judiciary seemed to be a reasonable one. On the one hand, justice remained in the hands of the sovereign; on the other it was bound to the law, and was given practical and factual independence. Thus, the judges were free to interpret the law on their own account. They no longer had to fear the possibility that the monarch could claim this task as his own. This solution was accepted as reasonable, due to the arrangement of the German states, and their perceived need for a practical, centrally-controlled system of justice. Especially in the southern German states that had grown throughout the Napoleonic era, this perceived need for a centralized justice system was particularly strong. In these states, some clerical jurisdiction remained, as well as the patrimonial courts. In addition, strong regional and territorial differences meant that without the regulating hand of the state, the new system would have failed. Despite these developments, one important political fact must be emphasized: power still remained with the monarch, and was not to diminish under the new system. Most especially, the sovereign retained all classical rights as to law-making and sovereignty. A parliamentary influence on the provision of justice – for example through the election of judges – was unthinkable.

However, the literature of political science in this period placed emphasis on other things. For instance, Romeo Maurenbrecher, a conservative author, wrote about the "monarch's judicial power" and placed emphasis on individual agency, following the liberal tradition of the 18th century. On the contrary, Klüber, a liberal author, stated that: "all administration of justice is down to the state". The reference to the "state" did not mean the monarch, but the "state" as an abstract person that had become the "legal person" and no longer the *persona moralis*. The legal person was first described by Georg Arnold Heise in 1807, and later by Savigny as an "artificial subject admitted by means of a pure fiction". Most especially, due to the work of Wilhelm Eduard Albrecht, the "legal person" became – against the opinion of Maurenbrecher – the fundamental principle for the understanding of the state.[21]

Thus, the abstract state came to embody the political compromise between the sovereignty of the monarchy, and the sovereignty of the people. If the state was the holder of justice there would be no more *dicta*; the judges were now independent (within the limits of the law) and they interpreted "in the name of the state", but were no longer legitimated through the monarch.[22] They were bound to the law, but independent. Even the obligation to inform the monarch, his chambers, or the legislative commission in cases of questionable interpretation, was omitted. In any event, this obligation was not feasible in practice, as the process engendered significant delays. In addition, the judge, as a servant of the state, could now decide cases independently of the monarch – and thus he did. For the people of the liberal civil society (who were now able to fill the positions of the judiciary), the law became a beacon of hope and justice became the most important protective shield of freedom.[23]

Even so, until the middle of the century, "justice" was still viewed as a dissident idea. For example, in Hesse (Germany) "justice" acted as a major driving force in the riot of civil servants and the military against their ruler. However, the criminal justice system now followed the legal model advocated by Feuerbach, which required accurate statements of facts,[24] prohibited claw-back regimes, and guaranteed the position of the "legally determined judge".[25] Civil justice provided protection from arbitrary interventions in freedom and property, and it also replaced the absent system of administrative courts by allowing claims of compensation against the treasury, or *fiscus*. Thus, to quote Dieter Simon: "the supply of freedom

---

[21] E.A. (= Wilhelm Eduard Albrecht), review in: *Göttingische gelehrte Anzeigen* 1837, S. 1489, 1492 f., 1496 f. (Reprint 1962).

[22] So was the judgment in Prussia, Bavaria, and Württemberg and so on until the end of the monarchy "in the name of the king". For details see Stolleis (fn. 4).

[23] Ogorek (fn. 15) 37 f.

[24] Ogorek (fn. 15) 39 ff.

[25] U. Seif, *Recht und Justizhoheit. Historische Grundlagen des gesetzlichen Richters in Deutschland, England und Frankreich*, Berlin 2003. The guarantee of the judge according the law was qualified by the Federal Constitutional Court as a "solid element of the German constitutional development" Decisions vol. 82, 159 (194).

guaranteeing factors like they were gained up to and discussed in the pre-March Era was delimited: autonomous courts that were organizationally shielded against influence by the executive or the legislative (separation of powers, independence of justice), that were staffed by neutral, personal and independent judges, as well as the judges' obedience to the law and the guarantee of the legal judge were instruments established to guaranty civil freedom".[26]

Constitutional law textbooks only slowly followed this fundamental change in understanding justice. Until the middle of the 19th century the judiciary was viewed as branch of the executive. However, the overriding demand was clear – a completely independent justice system. This was emphasized in several constitutions of the pre-March era (the *Vormärz* period), but even in the constitution of the Paulskirche, which stated that: "jurisdiction is down to the state. Patrimonial courts aren't allowed" (§174); "the legal power is exercised by the courts independently …" (§175); and finally, "judicature and administration shall be distinct and independent from each other" (§181). This paved the way for the German judicature act in 1877,[27] after the delay of the imperial constitution in 1871 due to political conditions.[28] From 1871 onwards, justice became a separate "third power". This continued under the Weimar constitution (Art. 102), and is still embodied in Article 97 of the basic law today. Only insignificant semantic changes were made, such as: "The juridical power is practiced by independent courts that are loyal to the law", was changed to: "Judges shall be independent and subject only to the law" (Art. 97 Abs. 1GG).

V Interpretation and the Will of the Parliaments

Nonetheless, even uncomplicated formulae are full of difficulties. Every jurist knows that complete adherence to the law can cause a multitude of problems. For example, at this stage of the 19th century, the law was not completely codified. In many places, a "common law" was established (through textbooks of academic jurisprudence) but its existence meant that some obvious or hidden deficits in the law still remained. However, the debate was not about creating a perfect system. A query to the legislator (*référé législatif*) was no longer possible. In fact, the civil judge of the 19th

---

[26]D. Simon, *Die Unabhängigkeit des Richters*, Darmstadt 1975, 5.

[27]Which only contained the state powers for "the legal process" (Art. 4 Nr. 13).

[28]Constitutional law of the court from Jan. 27th 1877 (RGBl 77), § 1: "The legal power is down to independent courts that are obliged to the law".

century now used many, ever changing methods to reach a legal decision, such as grammatical methods, historical, logical, and systematic methods.[29] In addition – if the judge was required to interpret a text – he may even have resorted to hermeneutics, a discipline first described by Schleiermacher.[30]

During this period, the key events that defined the legal landscape of the 19th century took place. The first such occurrence was the disappearance of the jus-naturalistic argument, and its substitution for a modern "philosophical" one; second, the transformation of the Roman law from the *Usus modernus* into "modern roman law"; third, the dispute over the presumption of innocence and the common law; and finally, the qualification of science as a source of law and the attempt to construct coherent legal concepts. These were all, in a certain way, a reflection of the philosophical constructions of the 18th century, as described by Christian Wolff. During the 19th century the legal order was made more flexible in several ways, namely via arguments of "equity"; through the doctrine of "preconditions" (*Voraussetzung*); by the application of the *clausula rebus sic stantibus* according to the civil law and finally by the adaption of Husserl's concept of intentionality and the idea of teleological interpretation.

This complicated area was examined by Regina Ogorek, Hans-Peter Haferkamp and Jan Schröder, but I do not wish to explain it any further. While this debate is important, its constitutional frame is more so. I will now describe how the 1789 European "break" or "discontinuity" affected the role of judges in the interpretive sphere. First, the monarch and the monarchical administration lost their monopoly on legislative power. *La Loi est l'expression de la volonté générale* is written in Article 6 of the *Déclaration des droits de l'homme et du citoyen*, August 26 1789. The "*voluntas principis*" was substituted by the law itself – although it was a long process that spanned the length of the 19th century. The making of legislation was (in theory) transferred from the monarch to Parliament, freed from *dicta*, and also became more independent in several ways. Namely, the wording of the legislation itself became the subject of judicial interpretation, and new laws were created by Parliament alone. This prompted the question of how far judges could stretch their interpretive license without stepping outside the boundaries of the text.

---

[29]F.C. v. Savigny, *System des heutigen Römischen Rechts*, Bd. I, 1840, 215. See H. Mohnhaupt, *Richter und Rechtsprechung im Werk Savignys*, in: *Studien zur europäischen Rechtsgeschichte*, ed. by W. Wilhelm, Frankfurt 1972, 243 ff.

[30]W. Dilthey, *Die Entstehung der Hermeneutik* (1900), in: *Gesammelte Schriften* vol. V, Leipzig und Berlin 1924.

Although judge-made law is now viewed as a legitimate ally that can supplement – and act as a substitute for – the law, some authors criticize some aspects of judicial interpretation. For example, even today it is frowned upon if judge-made law appears to step outside the "right" or intended meaning of a text (*contra legem*).[31] In the 19th century the judiciary was vastly more independent in areas where there was no legislation, for instance in the flexible and open-textured realm of civil law. Here they made use of contemporary Roman law, the common law and of approaches based on "philosophy", "fundamental principles", "evidence" and a "natural approach" to the text (*natürliche Betrachtungsweise.*) But nevertheless, interpretation was too flexible. Traditions existed in teaching interpretive techniques; the presumption of innocence; the constraints and pressures of working within a judicial hierarchy; and the rapid development of juridical journals that critically discussed legislation.[32]

However, in contrast to the official stance, and the constitutions that declared independence, the judiciary was still constrained by the practical requirements of interpretation. For example, an obligation to follow precedent existed, and the deviation from which could influence the career of a judge. In addition, the judiciary had to consider the volume of relevant precedent; and finally, was constrained in whether or not they could grant an appeal. Furthermore, the state remained the employer (*Dienstherr*), paid the salary of the judiciary, and in addition, dictated the educational requirements for – and the chances of – becoming a judge.

Recent scholarship illustrates that the direct and indirect discipline of the judiciary throughout the 19th century was very effective in shaping judicial interpretation.[33] For example, after 1850, special salaries and personal politics slowly transformed the liberal judges of the pre-March era into conservative, monarchical, and nationalistic judges. In other words: contrary to the judicial independence that the constitutions proclaimed, in reality, the judiciary remained influenced and constrained by the monarchy.

These normative and factual restrictions on judicial independence – and thus upon freedom of interpretation – are known and are still valid today.[34] Even so, my discussion of them ends here. To close, I wish to describe the

---

[31] B. Rüthers, *Rechtstheorie*, München 1999, § 24. *Richterliche Gesetzesabweichungen*, especially RdNr. 947 f.

[32] M. Stolleis (ed.), *Juristische Zeitschriften. Die neuen Medien des 18. – 20. Jahrhunderts*, Frankfurt 1999.

[33] Th. Ormond, *Richterwürde und Regierungstreue. Dienstrecht, politische Betätigung und Disziplinierung der Richter in Preußen*, Baden und Hessen 1866–1918, Frankfurt 1994.

[34] For details see Simon (fn. 26).

long-ranging development of constitutional jurisdiction. A historical survey of the role of the judiciary in Europe from the mid-18th century to the present reveals that the French Revolution was the primary event at play. The constitutional movement of the 19th century paved the way for an autonomous and independent "third power". At the end of the 19th century – at least in Germany – the position of the judiciary was reinforced once more, when judges were given the power to check acts of administration and declare them unlawful. The administrative branch of the judiciary was established between 1863 and 1875. Other branches were later established, such as the finance courts in 1919, the labor courts in 1927, and the social jurisdiction in 1951.

At the same time, the judiciary also began to develop a system of judicial review, by which they assessed the constitutionality of the civil law. The first stage of this development involved a formal analysis, in which the judiciary examined the legality of the law's creation and structure. After the First World War, the judiciary also undertook a second stage of review: analyzing the substantive content of the law for compatibility with the constitution. Eventually, the judiciary came to possess its own constitutional jurisdiction, which allowed it to check the law in formal *and* substantive ways.[35] The old form of the bill for the sovereign – the *référé legislative* – had now become a bill for the federal constitutional court (Art. 100 GG) where "authentic" or "legitimate" interpretation took place. The federal constitutional court had become the final arbiter on matters of interpretation, although the sovereign could still pass legislation through Parliament.

As a consequence, a completely new model was born: one that was radically different from that of the 18th century. In this new model, an independent judge would interpret and decide upon the law, and was thus quasi-sovereign. If the judge had any reasonable doubts, he would present the law to the federal constitutional court. The federal constitutional court's right to be the final arbiter of the law necessarily implied that it was also quasi-sovereign. Parliament – actually the real sovereign – could also only be quasi-sovereign, due to its obligation to the constitution and to the federal constitutional court. This quasi-sovereignty produces a paradox within constitutional states with fully independent judiciaries. This model was once known as the "judges' state" (*Justizstaat*) and much discussion surrounded

---

[35]Chr. Gusy, *Richterliches Prüfungsrecht: eine verfassungsgeschichtliche Untersuchung*, Berlin 1985; N. E. Herrmann, *Entstehung, Legitimation und Zukunft der konkreten Normenkontrolle im modernen Verfassungsstaat*, Berlin 2001; M. Stolleis, Judicial Review, Administrative Review, and Constitutional Review in the Weimar Republic, in: *Ratio Iuris* 16 (2003) 266–280.

the enlargement of judicial powers of interpretation. Indeed the judiciary's reputation and actual influence on the federal republic was tremendous. By 1949 the judiciary was described as the "third pillar of democracy".[36]

However, these developments may have been influenced by other factors. In particular, the shift that I have described can also be viewed as the transformation from an 18th century agrarian society to an industrial one. Politically controlled legislation was a process that was too slow, and too defective for the rapid changes that were occurring. These changes, and the resultant abundance of individual cases, required a greater degree of control by the judiciary. The tasks of the judiciary itself were divided two ways: first, the judiciary split into specialized jurisdictions; and second, the *référé legislative* was utilized to refer cases to the constitutional court if there were any doubts as to interpretation. In the light of this division of labor, it is plausible that an institutional sovereign no longer exists, but that instead there is a functionally differentiated legal system that is able to resolve conflicts in a much more appropriate way.

In conclusion, the battle of interpretation has ended with the truism that judicial interpretation is only legitimate if it is undertaken through a permanent alignment of the interpretation of the law and the constitution. However, while the constitution is the highest legal norm, this norm itself has been formed through the "interpretation" of the judiciary, which itself is obliged to the constitution in turn.

---

[36]*Jahrbuch des öffentlichen Rechts*, New Series 1 (1951); new edition Tübingen 2010, 728.

Part II
The Case of France

.

Chapter 2
Legal Interpretation in France Under the Reign of Louis XVI: A Review of the *Gazette des tribunaux*

Jean-Louis HALPÉRIN

This chapter examines judicial interpretation of the law during the final years of France's *Ancien Regime*: in particular, the 15 years of Louis XVI's reign that preceded the French Revolution. I shall explore this interpretation through the lens of a periodical law report from the period, called the *Gazette des tribunaux*. To this end, first it will be necessary to present this publication's political and legal context. Second, I shall analyse the evolution of methods of publishing judgments, before proposing hypotheses about the evolution of legal interpretation itself.

France, as an absolutist kingdom, had afforded complete power to the monarchy since the 17th century. Furthermore, the *États généraux* (an assembly representing the Three Estates) had not been convened from 1614 to 1789. Thus, the only remaining force of opposition to the king was the higher courts, or the *Parlements*. Over the course of the 18th century, questions of the registration of royal ordinances and the interpretation of legislative texts had become central to the *Parlements'* struggle with the monarchy, and with this context in mind, the following propositions may be put forward. First, the problems associated with legal interpretation were recognised and discussed during this period. Legal dictionaries contained articles referring to the "interpretation" of the law – a discussion often grounded in the Roman law tradition. Second, the recognition of the judiciary's power to interpret legal texts was controversial. Indeed, the judiciary faced a constant pressure from philosophers, lawyers, and most especially, the royal power, who all sought to limit the judicial function to nothing more than a "mechanical" application of the law (to use a phrase from Beccaria's syllogistic scheme for a penal law). Third, the controversy over the role of

J.-L. HALPÉRIN (✉)
École Normale Supérieure, UMR 7074 "Centre de Théorie et Analyse du droit",
Paris, France
e-mail: jean-louis.halperin@ens.fr; jean-louis.halperin@wanadoo.fr

MORIGIWA, Y. et al. (eds.), *Interpretation of Law in the Age of Enlightenment*, Law and Philosophy Library 95, DOI 10.1007/978-94-007-1506-6_2, © Springer Science+Business Media B.V. 2011

the judiciary in legal interpretation was complicated by the practice of the courts not to publish their reasons. Fourth, the main goals of the law reports of this period were to construct the reasons behind judgements, and to identify standards of legal interpretation. Finally, the Age of Enlightenment in France provoked a critical examination – led by the French *philosophes* and their readers – of the discipline known as hermeneutics, and the possibility of a singular text bearing several differing meanings at the same time.

As Paul Hazard has shown, the work of the Enlightenment philosophers was preceded by the evolution of a critical Biblical exegesis. In France, this critical outlook was embodied in Richard Simon's *Histoire critique du Vieux Testament* (1678). This work questioned the literal and historical interpretations of a text, the weight of tradition, and the possibility of this tradition being discarded.[1] For all these reasons, and to better understand the French "cult of statute law" or "legicentrism" after the French Revolution,[2] this period of the end of the 18th century can be seen as a turning point in legal history.

The Context of the *Gazette des Tribunaux's* Publication (1775–1789)

Louis XVI's accession to the throne in 1774 corresponded with a great crisis within the French judiciary. At the end of his reign, Louis XV had decided – after years of struggle against the *Parlements* over the registration of royal legislation – to support the reforms of his Chancellor, René Maupeou. In response, the *Parlement de Paris* undertook a "justice strike", which was considered to be a "forfeiture" of their offices. This strike provoked the arrest of dissident judges and the disbanding of the *Parlement* in January 1771. Shortly afterwards, the patrimonial magistrates of all twelve *Parlements* (who could sell and transmit their offices hereditarily, thereby securing independence from the royal power) were replaced by new judges who were nominated and chosen by the king. For the next three years, this

---

[1]Paul Hazard, *La Crise de la conscience européenne 1680–1715*, Paris, Boivin et Cie, 1935, pp. 186–197.

[2]Through the word "legicentrism", some French legal historians want to describe the ideology (supposed to dominate from 1789 onwards) of strict submission of judges towards statute law, with the obligation to give reasons (law of the 16th and 24th August 1790), the institution of *référé législatif* (the judge must ask for a legislative interpretation in case of doubt about the meaning of the statute law, according the same 1790 law) and the creation of the *Tribunal de cassation* (Law of the 27th of November – 1st of December 1790) to control the respect of laws by the judges.

coup d'État was followed by a sweeping reform of the entire judiciary. This reform included the suppression of process fees paid to the judges, the breakup of the judicial constituency of the *Parlement de Paris* (through the creation of six Superior Courts), and the disappearance of many specialised courts. Finally, new rules were established regulating the power of high courts to remonstrate to the king (i.e. to address respectful observations to the king about the statute concerned).[3]

Maupeou was then confronted with a violent pamphleteering campaign from those who supported the revoked members of the *Parlements*. Nonetheless, he succeeded with the clear support of the king and the approval of several philosophers (including Voltaire). However, when Louis XV died, his grandson and successor – only 20 years old when he became King – preferred to undertake a policy of reconciliation with the traditional judicial elite. Consequently, Maupeou fell into disgrace in August 1774 and by November the *Parlements* had been reinstated with their prerogatives and their patrimonial officers. Thus, the reign of Louis XVI began with an apparent victory for the *Robinocracy*, or the "robe nobility". The "Robinocracy" (which included the judicial elite) was given the power to settle trials as a last resort, with the rather scarce exceptions of recourse before the *Conseil du roi* and the use of the *cassation* process. In addition, they could also give a "sovereign" interpretation of laws.

From the 17th century onwards, (namely, the period of the *Fronde* troubles between 1648 and 1653 during the reign of Louis XIV, and the absolutist policies of his personal reign from 1661 onwards), the central debate between the royal power and the High Courts revolved around the participation of the "Sovereign Courts" in the legislative process, through their use of registration and remonstrations (*remontrances*).[4] If an ordinance had not yet been registered, any remonstration was prohibited. This prohibition was closely connected with the question of legal interpretation of royal ordinances, and acted as a barrier against any blockage of royal legislation. However, it was removed by the Regent after the death of Louis XIV in 1715. Louis XIV had also forbidden any judicial interpretation of royal legislation under the pretext of doubt or difficulty, in the royal ordinance of 1667 on civil procedure (Article VII of Part I). This prohibition was based upon the

---

[3]Michel Antoine, "Sens et portée de la réforme Maupeou", *Revue Historique*, vol. 288/1, 1992, pp. 39–59; Julian Swann, *Politics and the Parlement of Paris under Louis XV 1754–1774*, Cambridge, Cambridge University Press, 1995, pp. 352–368.
[4]François Saint-Bonnet, "Louis XIV, les parlements et la souveraineté" *in* Gauthier Aubert, Olivier Chaline (eds.), *Les Parlements de Louis XIV. Opposition, coopération, autonomisation?*, Rennes, Presses Universitaires de Rennes, 2010, pp. 173–183.

principle of the monopoly of royal interpretation, and it was neither a new
policy (it had been repeated several times in the 16th century[5]), nor a solid
success.[6] This debate reared its head once more during the Maupeou crisis.
The *Maximes du droit public français* (1772), one of the texts critical of the
Chancellor's policy – written by the well-known Jansenist barristers Mey,
Maultrot and Aubry – proposed to distinguish between two kinds of interpretation: authoritative interpretation (*interprétation d'autorité*) reserved to
the king; and doctrinal interpretation (*interprétation de doctrine*), a necessary attribute of the judicial function.[7] Can we disregard the fact that the
very same expressions were used once again in 1801 by Portalis in the
famous *Discours préliminaire,* which sparked the development of the future
Napoleonic Code? Was this not a turning point for the question of legal
interpretation for 18th century France: one with great repercussions during
the French Revolution and the codification period?

Before I attempt to examine the development of new interpretive doctrines
at the end of the 18th century in more depth, we must take note of several
features of the French legal order during the *Ancien Régime*. As a country
that had been unified and centralised since the Middle Ages, the kingdom
of France had developed the idea that all justice and law emanated from
the royal power. From the 16th century onwards, the existence of "French
Law" (*droit français*) – as distinct from Roman law – was well established.
In this period, legal writing was published in French more frequently, and
these writings presented French law as original and independent. However,
the French legal order remained a pluralist one, incorporating many different
sources of law. For example, in northern and central France, French law drew
upon regional customs, which were officially written down during the 16th
century. In southern France, Roman law (as the "written law" or *droit écrit*)
was also considered a valid legal source. Other sources included canon law
(which was applied in cases of marriage and ecclesiastical affairs) and royal
ordinances. As a consequence, a tension existed between the cohesive legal
framework which stemmed from the king (formed by the development of
legislation and interpretive declarations) and the plurality of legal sources
based on authoritative texts and established legal opinion. Whereas statutory
law was rather underdeveloped in the field of private law, a broad scope

---

[5]Jacques Krynen, *L'État de justice. France XVIIIe–XXe siècle. L'idéologie de la
magistrature ancienne*, Paris, Gallimard, "Bibliothèque des Histoires", 2009, p. 157.
[6]Nicola Picardi, *Introduzione, Code Louis, Ordonnance civile*, Testi e documenti per la
storia del processo, Milano, Giuffrè, 1996, p. XXVIII.
[7]Paolo Alvazzi del Frate, *L'interpretazione autentica nel XVIII secolo. Divieto di interpretatio e "riferimento al legislatore" nell'illuminismo giuridico*, Torino, Giappichelli,
2000, pp. 63–64.

still existed for the use and the interpretation of Roman texts and of written customs. For this reason, French law was also a *Juristenrecht* (law created by jurists) and judges were free to interpret a plurality of laws (and to decide in the first instance which law was applicable to the case at hand).[8] Thus, the royal power was forced to concede to judges a very broad scope for interpreting a complex patchwork of legal sources.

This balanced conception of judicial interpretation is well expressed in the legal dictionaries which were published in France during the 17th and 18th centuries. One such dictionary is Claude de Ferrière's *Dictionnaire de droit et de pratique*, first published as the *Introduction à la pratique* in 1684, and later as a dictionary in 1734, 1740 and 1749. De Ferrière was a professor of both civil (i.e. Roman) and French law. Indeed, French law was taught at law faculties as an independent subject after its introduction by Louis XIV in 1679. De Ferrière wrote that the interpretation of royal ordinances was a power reserved to the king, according to the Roman maxim: *Ejus est legem interpretari, cujus est legem condere* (see C. 1, 14, 1; C. 1. 14, 9; C. 1, 14, 12 and C. 1, 17, 2, 21). However, the courts could make a "just interpretation" by extending or restricting ordinances and customs according to reason and equity.[9] The same principles are repeated in the *Nouvelle Introduction à la Pratique* (1745), written by Claude-Joseph de Ferrière (Claude's son, also a law professor at a Paris Faculty). The *Nouvelle Introduction* defines interpretation as the process of determining the intended meaning of any given law, so that an interpreter can extend or restrict its scope as required by reason and equity. This meant that if a valid interpretation could be gleaned from the law itself, judges (especially those in higher courts) could interpret and make the law. The *Nouvelle Introduction* also provides that the king's power to intervene was reserved for cases of interpretation that were contrary to the wording and intended meaning of the law.[10] In 1779, during the reign of Louis XVI, the new *Répertoire universel* also noted the same thing. The *Répertoire*, written by Guyot (and reputed to be open to the ideas of the Encyclopaedists), stated that in France, judicial interpretation of ordinances

---

[8]The cassation recourse before the *Conseil du Roi* was conceived to make the royal ordinances respected, although it was not impossible to quash a decision of a *Parlement* for violation of Roman or customary law.

[9]Claude de Ferrière, *Dictionnaire de droit et de pratique*, 3rd ed., vol. II, V° Interpretation, Paris, 1749, pp. 83–85 and V° Loy, p. 140. The author considers that almost every law needs an interpretation, and that this interpretation can be found in the reason (i.e. the decisive reason for the legislator) and the spirit of the law, without making distinctions in front of a silent law or interpreting clear and precise articles.

[10]Claude-Joseph de Ferrière, *Nouvelle Introduction à la Pratique*, Paris, vol. II, 1745, pp. 75–76.

had always been reserved to the king. However, the judges that represented the sovereign were granted the capacity to interpret the law (judging *vice sacra principis*), in direct contrast to inferior judges who were bound to the black letter of the text.[11]

One cannot speak of genuine theories of legal interpretation in these dictionaries for they merely repeat the traditional tenets of Roman law.[12] In particular, they repeat the distinction between the extension and restriction of legal texts: those both good, and odious respectively, and reiterate the notion of the "spirit of the law". It must also be noted that there is no discussion of judicial interpretation of the law in the works of Robert Joseph Pothier – one of the best-known professors of French Law from the 18th century (*professeurs de droit français*) – who taught jurisprudence in Orléans. Pothier wrote his famous treatises during this period, but his lack of commentary on interpretation is significant, and was absent even from his treatise about civil procedure. This treatise quotes article VII of Part I of the 1677 ordinance, but does not include a thorough discussion of it. Pothier was necessarily aware of the conflicts between the *Parlements* and the king, as during this period he was a judge in the *présidial*, an intermediate-level court in Orléans. Thus it could be inferred that he did not wish to intervene in this political debate, and had no personal ideas to propose about legal interpretation.

Throughout the 18th century, only two French authors developed theories of legal interpretation: Jean Domat and Henri François d'Aguesseau, linked by the respect of the latter for the former. Domat was a royal advocate (*avocat du roi*) in Clermont, pensioned by the king to set the Roman law "in order". Domat's monumental work, *Les Lois civiles dans leur ordre naturel* (1689) was re-edited several times during the 18th century. In its opening discussion, which was intended to be a treatise on laws (*Traité des Lois*), Domat devotes an entire chapter to the use and interpretation of the law. In line with Roman texts, he considered that it was the interpreter's role to find the spirit, intention, and rationale behind every law; the mischief the law wished to deal with; and its relationship with, and changes to other laws.[13] Domat also contributed to the discussion of the incompleteness of legal texts – noting that legal texts cannot foresee the potentially

---

[11] Joseph-Nicolas Guyot, *Répertoire universel et raisonné de jurisprudence civile, criminelle, canonique et bénéficiale*, Paris, Panckoucke, vol. 32, 1779, V° Interprétation, p. 371.

[12] Especially from D. 14, 1, 1, 20 (interpretation according the black letter of the law), D. 35, 1, 64 (favorable interpretation of the law), D. 50, 16, 219 (intention more important then the expressions of the Law) or C. 1, 14, 5 (importance of the spirit of the law).

[13] *Traité des lois*, Chapter XII, 7.

infinite circumstances of future cases.[14] Pursuant to this, he also pointed to the necessity of extending general rules to the maximum possible number of individual persons and cases.

This desire to rationalise legal interpretation (most likely inspired by Descartes' method of reasoning) was based on the conviction that French law was, like other legal orders, (to use the modern term) a complex mixture of natural laws (many of them discovered by the Roman jurists) and "arbitrary" laws (developed by customs and royal legislation).[15] Another section of the first part of *Les Lois civiles dans leur ordre naturel* was devoted to the use and interpretation of rules.[16] Domat repeated his distinctions between the interpretation of the true meaning behind the law (discovering what the law has said) and the interpretation of the scope of the law (considering what the law wishes to cover). In addition, he emphasized once more the difference between the interpretation of natural laws (those according to equity), and the interpretation of arbitrary laws (those according to the intention or whim of the lawmaker). He encouraged interpreters (or judges) to discover equity in every rule according to the "light of reason" (*la lumière de la raison*), and to only resort to the king in cases where a broad interpretive method would be inefficient or contrary to public utility.

The influence of Domat was clear, especially in the works of Henri-François d'Aguesseau (1668–1751), who served as the royal advocate at the *Châtelet* Court of Paris in 1690 and later at the *Parlement de Paris* in 1691, where he also became the Attorney-General (*Procureur Général*) in 1700. He also assumed the role of the Royal Chancellor from 1717 to 1750. D'Aguesseau's discourses, pleadings and treatises were gathered and published by his sons between 1759 and 1789, and in nineteen discourses concerning the judicial discipline (the *Mercuriales*, published from 1698 to 1715), d'Aguesseau reminded the judiciary of their duties to the law. His exhortations betray a sense of pessimism (which was likely influenced by Domat's Jansenism), in relation to younger legal practitioners, who often took a superficial view of the law and preferred to engage with wit rather than knowledge.

D'Aguesseau depicted a good magistrate as one who worshipped the law (*religieux adorateur de la loi*), and one who was learned in the science of

---

[14]Ibid., Chapter XII, 17. This idea, coming from D. 1, 3, 12 (all cases cannot be foreseen in the statutory law), is repeated by all the legal writers during the 18th century.

[15]Ibid. Chapter XI, 1–11 (especially the idea that many arbitrary laws are consequences of natural laws, which provokes the coexistence of two laws inside one arbitrary law).

[16]Jean Domat, *Les lois civiles dans leur ordre naturel*, vol. I, tit. I, sect. II, especially n. 1 and 12, éd. Héricourt, Paris, chez Nyon, 1777, pp. 4–10.

Roman law (as the Romans, through the superiority of their genius, discovered "the first principles and the last consequences of natural law"). A good magistrate would also try to understand the spirit of the laws and remedy their inevitable lacunae with his wisdom.[17] In his extended discussions on the complex interpretation of different legal sources, d'Aguesseau adopted the method proposed by Domat. This method combined Roman texts ("the reason of the law"), royal legislation ("the authority of law") and customs ("the interpretation of the law"). D'Aguesseau attempted to use this method in a clear (and apparently logical) manner, and to this end he relied upon the maxims of natural law.[18] The recourse to Descartes' geometrical reasoning was the means, according to d'Aguesseau, by which one could reach a "common reason": a reason that could inform the decisions of the judiciary.[19] One can ask whether this "systematic" (but not fundamentally new) approach to the interpretative functions of the judiciary had any real effect on judicial practice during the second half of the 18th century, and further, whether it conflicted with a more legalistic method as defended by French "philosophers".

It would be an overstatement to say that the French philosophers had developed a coherent theory of legal interpretation. First, the question of legal interpretation is not deeply examined in Montesquieu's *Esprit des Lois* (1748), a title which evokes Domat's reflections upon judicial functions. In this text, Montesquieu's famous words, which describe the judiciary as the "mouth which speaks the law" (*Esprit des Lois,* XI, 6, *De la constitution d'Angleterre*), are applied only to "republican" governments, whereas in monarchies the judge follows the law when it is precise, and looks for the spirit of the law when it is not (VI, III, likely inspired by Domat). Furthermore, the image of the magistrate "speaking the law" (*lex loquens*) as put forward by Cicero (*De legibus*, III, 1, 2) and mentioned in the Digest (1, 1, 8 which describes the praetor as the *viva vox* of civil law), was a "cliché" of judicial rhetoric: a cliché used by many French judges before Montesquieu, and repeated afterwards by d'Aguesseau.[20] In addition, even

---

[17]Jeanne-Marie Tuffery-Andrieu, *La discipline des juges, les Mercuriales de D'Aguesseau*, Paris, LGDJ, 2007, especially pp. 84, 99–100, 130–131.

[18]For example the 41st pleading (1697 about donations made by a father who was married twice) *in* D'Aguesseau, *Oeuvres*, vol. 4, 1764, pp. 25–41.

[19]Marie-France Renoux-Zagamé, "Lumières de la pensée juridique: le Chancelier d'Aguesseau", conference at the Court of Cassation, 28th of November 2006.

[20]Jeanne-Marie Tuffery-Andrieu, op. cit., p. 99. Furthermore, in his *Pensées* (that were not published during the 18th century), Montesquieu wrote that the *Parlement* was in the same time the slave of the letter of the law and the repository of the spirit of all laws (*Pensées*, n. 2266, ed. Louis Desgraves, Paris, Robert Laffont, 1991, p. 658).

the Great Encyclopaedia of d'Alembert and Diderot did not alter the definitions of "interpretation" in legal dictionaries.[21] Voltaire specified that every
law had to be clear, uniform and precise, because interpretation was almost
always a "corruption" of the text.[22] Therefore, it is hazardous to infer a complete theory of judicial syllogism (such as that inspired by Beccaria) from
the Encyclopaedia. Any judicial ideas about legal interpretation were most
likely indebted to the maxims of Domat and d'Aguesseau, which were presented in the oral conclusions articulated by king's advocates. Unfortunately
it is difficult to know the opinions of individual judges, as the decision of the
judiciary was a collective one. Furthermore, from the 14th century onwards,
French courts did not supply the reasons for their judgments.[23] Based upon
the desire to keep the authority of the courts intact – and supported by the
canonical and Romanist doctrine of the Middle Ages – this "judicial custom"
afforded a central role to private law reports. These law reports developed
after the Middle Ages and the *Ancien Régime,* of which the *Gazette des
tribunaux* is the final example.

A Clear Evolution in the Method of Publishing Judgments

From the time of the Middle Ages to that of the 16th and 17th centuries,
the works of several authors played a vital role in developing the literature
of private law reports (*recueils d'arrêts*). These works include the writings of Jean Le Coq, known as *Johannes Gallus* from 1340 to 1399, and
his *Questiones*, which gathered the judgments of the *Parlement de Paris.*
Other works that may be mentioned here include the *Decisiones Parlamenti
Dalphinali*, written by Gui Pape (who passed away in 1477); the *Aufrerius*
from 1458 to 1511, and the *Recueil des 74 arrêts du Parlement de Toulouse*,
both of which were written by Étienne Aufréri. Law reports were devoted to
a selection of decisions of one *Parlement*: for example in Toulouse, the decisions of Maynard were edited in 1603, d'Olive in 1638, Cambolas in 1659,
and Maynard once again in 1705. These books were completed by ambitious
compilations in alphabetical order; by Louet at the beginning of the 17th

---

[21] Paolo Alvazzi del Frate, op. cit., p. 116.

[22] Voltaire, *Dictionnaire philosophique*, V° Des lois civiles et ecclésiastiques, Paris, ed.
Garnier, 1967, p. 290.

[23] Serge Dauchy, Véronique Demars-Sion, "La non-motivation des décisions judiciaires
dans l'ancien droit: principe ou usage?", *Revue Historique de Droit français et étranger*,
82(2), 2004, pp. 223–239.

century,[24] Bouguier in 1622, Henrys in 1638, Bretonnier in 1718, and Guy
Rousseau de la Combe in 1736. Journals also began to develop during this
period, such as the *Journal des principales audiences,* which began under
Jean du Fresne in 1648. This journal produced seven volumes, and gathered
judgements of the *Parlement de Paris* from 1622 to 1722. Furthermore, the
Journal du Palais was founded by Gabriel Guéret in 1672 and continued
by Claude Blondeau in 1737, and produced two volumes containing judgements from 1660 to 1700. Finally, legal dictionaries were published. In 1711,
Brillon's *Dictionnaire des Arrêts* was published in 3 volumes; followed
by Denisart's *Collection des décisions nouvelles,* published in 6 volumes
between 1754 and 1756. Subsequently, Guyot's *Répertoire universel* was
published in 1775.[25]

These law reports were written by lawyers or judges (with the chief editor
usually present during the pleadings), and they were vehemently criticized
by many authors (including the authors of other reports). This criticism
towards the law reports was, for the most part, levelled against their numerous faults, (especially their old-fashioned style) and any errors of dates,
names or facts.[26] However, the real – and not seriously discussed – problem was with their methodology, which attempted to infer the reasons of
the judgment from the pleadings of the lawyers, and those of the winning
litigants in particular. The increased publication of these law reports was,
nonetheless, proof of their utility and of the growing reliance on precedent. Even if a rule of precedent did not explicitly exist, judgments were
quoted as authoritative by lawyers and king's advocates. During the reign
of Louis XVI, new dictionaries – for instance, Guyot's *Répertoire universel,* the *Encyclopédie méthodique,* and Prost de Royer's *Dictionnaire de
jurisprudence et des arrêts* – reported debates about what was now called

---

[24]Serge Dauchy, "Les recueils privés de 'jurisprudence' aux Temps Modernes", in Alain
Wijfells (ed.), *Case Law in Making,* Berlin, Duncker & Humblot, 1997, vol. I, pp. 237–
247 about Louet, a member of the *Parlement de Paris* at the end of the 16th century.
[25]Gerhard Walter in Helmut Coing, *Handbuch der Quellen und Literatur der neueren
europäischen Privatrechtsgechichte,* Munich, 1976, Band II, Teilband II, p. 1223;
Serge Dauchy, Véronique Demars-Sion (dir.), *Les recueils d'arrêts et dictionnaires de
jurisprudence, XVIe–XVIIIe siècles,* Paris, La Mémoire du Droit, 2005.
[26]Christian Chêne, "L'arrestographie, science fort douteuse", *Recueil des travaux et
mémoires publiés par la Société d'histoire du droit et des institutions des anciens pays
de droit écrit,* 1985, pp. 179–187; Nicolas Derasse, "La mise en valeur des recueils
d'arrêts et des dictionnaires de jurisprudence à travers leurs préfaces", *in* Serge Dauchy,
Véronique Demars-Sion, op. cit. (note 25), pp. 41–68.

jurisprudence des arrêts, and the focus shifted onto whether the reasons (*motifs*) of one judgment could be applied to another similar case.[27]

Similarly, the reign of Louis XV – with its successive disputes between the royal power, the *Parlements* and the Parisian barristers[28] – had seen a dramatic increase of published *memoires* (or *factum*). An ordinance in 1670 had banned oral pleadings for criminal trials, and these *memoires* were written by lawyers to publicise the cause of their clients in these types of cases. Courtroom literature gained an audience among the nobility and the middle classes, and the Enlightenment movement established a desire for debates on criminal justice, based primarily upon "public opinion".[29] A publisher from Lyon, François Gayot de Pitaval, was the first to understand this opportunity, and in 1734 he launched a collection of twenty volumes about famous trials – the *Causes célèbres et intéressantes*.[30] Then, after a period of lessened creativity in the middle of the 18th century (the same also holds true for the law reports), in 1772–1773 Nicolas Le Moyne des Essarts began constructing the great collection of *Causes célèbres, curieuses et intéressantes de toutes les Cours souveraines du royaume*, which reached 179 volumes by 1789. In the first volume, the publisher's aim was to present judgments with descriptions of facts to his readers, and the "reasons which could have influenced the judges' decisions".[31] Despite this promise, the periodical instead chose to focus upon the sensational facts of cases, rather than publishing legal arguments. This entailed that from the beginning of the reign of Louis XVI (1774), an ever increasing scope existed for a new periodical more strongly dedicated to the discussion of legal precedent.

---

[27]Joseph Nicolas Guyot, op. cit., vol. I, 1775, V° Arrêt; *Encyclopédie méthodique. Jurisprudence*, Paris, Panckoucke, vol. 5, 1785, V° Jurisprudence, p. 365; Antoine-François Prost de Royer, *Dictionnaire de jurisprudence et des arrêts*, Lyon, vol. VI, 1787, v° Arrêt, pp. 720–728 reporting a debate among Metz lawyers 20 years before.

[28]David Avrom Bell, *Lawyers and Citizens. The Making of a Political Elite in the Old Regime France*, Oxford, Oxford University Press, 1994, has shown that the Order of Parisian Barristers, created only at the end of the 17th century, has developed from the years 1720 onwards (and the so-called "*affaire des avocats*" about memoires defending Jansenist priests) a clear strategy of publicizing judicial affairs, pp. 150–183.

[29]Hans-Jürgen Lüsenbrik, *Kriminalität and Literatur im Frankreich des 18. Jahrhunderts*, Munchen-Wien, Oldenbourg, 1983, p. 105.

[30]Sarah Maza, *Private Lives and Public Affairs. The Causes célèbres of Prerevolutionary France*, Berkeley-Los Angeles,-London, The University of California Press, 1995, p. 25.

[31]*Causes célèbres, curieuses et intéressantes de toutes les Cours souveraines du royaume*, vol. I, 1773, p. 6.

Between 1775 and 1789, a Parisian barrister called Mars published 28 volumes of the *Gazette des tribunaux*,[32] which appeared quite novel in several ways. Namely, it had a more professional goal in mind, and bar the *Causes celebres*, it became the most long-lasting legal periodical in the course of the *Ancien Régime*. The later development of a smaller format of the periodical (in-octavo, the *Causes célèbres* being an in-12) and its publication in separate sheets of 16 pages, brought it into direct contrast with the heavy folios of the classical law reports (for example, Blondeau's *Journal du Palais*) and even the in-quarto size of the current dictionaries. Mars justified the new periodicals on the basis that an increased individual independence had led to an escalation of disputes, offences and penalties, as well as a greater reliance upon – or claim to – the law (justice), and its interpretation (*la réclamation des lois, leurs interprétations*). In addition, commentators, defence counsels, judges and journalists began to gather seemingly interesting or entertaining material, (such as in the *Causes celebres*), so as to appeal to interested persons outside the circle of the legal profession. Mars decided to insert "notices about the trials" (*la notice des causes*); memoires; pleadings; reviews of new books concerning the law,[33] the bar, and eloquence; and abstracts of new statutes in each issue. Thus, it can be seen that a new and increased desire had arisen: a desire to provide the most comprehensive information about innovation in the legal sphere. This desire was most likely influenced by the belief that the new reign would bring about important changes in both legal ideas and rules. Hence, in 1775, the third issue of the *Gazette des tribunaux* relayed the discourse pronounced at the opening of the session of the criminal chamber in the *Parlement de Paris*: a discourse which lauded Louis XVI as the restorer of morality and of law.

Each issue of the *Gazette des tribunaux* presented notices about cases first, and also contained papers about recent judgments (usually from a few weeks before the issue) of the *Parlement de Paris*, the *Parlements de province* (mostly from Nancy, Douai, Grenoble, Dijon, Toulouse), the Royal Council and the *Châtelet* Court in Paris. The majority of these judgments concerned civil affairs, but ecclesiastical litigation was also important, and some criminal trials were reported. The length of these notices varied from one or two pages – a simple abstract – to an article of four, six, or even ten pages in some cases. After a title indicating the legal subject concerned, the

---

[32]Mars was a former advocate before the Royal Council ("*avocat aux Conseils*") and seigniorial judge of the duke of Bouillon. The *Gazette des Tribunaux* was published in Paris, Le Jay, rue Saint-Jacques.

[33]One finds some of the well known titles of the new legal literature: Guyot's *Répertoire universel*, the journal of the *Causes célèbres*, Boncerf's *Inconvénients des droits féodaux*,

facts were briefly described. Many of these notices focused upon the legal
arguments developed in written *memoires* or in oral pleadings, and also acted
as a method of prompting readers of the *Gazette* to consult these *memoires*.
It can be presumed that Mars, or perhaps one of his probable collaborators,[34]
attended the proceedings in question in each notice.[35] Among the terms used
to present the texts of the proceedings, we find expressions such as: "before
reporting the judgment and making known the respective claims of the litigants, we will expose their conclusions",[36] "let us come to the opinion of
the public ministry",[37] and "the pleading of the Advocate General Séguier
has been presented in two sessions of more than two hours each".[38]

In comparison with previous law reports, initially the notices of the
Gazette des tribunaux were longer than those present in the works of Louet,
Brodeau or Rousseaud de la Combe (which were often alphabetized, simple
quotations of different judgments in a specialized article). However, they
were shorter than the organized "dissertations" of the *Journal du Palais*
(which was chronological, but focused on a selection of judgments decided
some decades earlier), and older *"recueils d'arrêts"*.[39] In 1779 the publisher
proposed a new plan: a method of presenting these notices as a kind of
"miniature", or summary. This gave readers all the parts of a larger picture (the judicial scene as a whole)[40] in a smaller format. Some of these
short notices reproduced the arguments of cases, as in the previous law
reports, without identifying the litigants and their lawyers: "it has been
said... It has been answered". However, in many cases, there was a con-
certed effort to make a living synthesis of arguments in relation to the
identities of the lawyers concerned. It can be seen that the number of quoted
barristers is rather limited, and in many cases involves well-known lawyers
such as Tronchet, Target, Treilhard, Camus in Paris, Merlin in Douai, and
Thouret in Rouen or Lanjuinais in Rennes. It is also important to note that

---

[34]*Gazette des tribunaux*, vol. 27, 1788, n. 13, p. 196 alluding to the help of a lawyer to
take notes of the conclusions of the Advocate General in the *Parlement de Dauphiné*.

[35]For an example of avowed presence in the audience of the Court, *Gazette des
tribunaux*, vol. 8, 1779, n. 37, p. 164.

[36]*Gazette des tribunaux*, vol. 1, 1775, n. 5, p. 65.

[37]Ibid., vol. 8, 1779, n. 27, p. 7.

[38]Ibid., vol. 13, n. 22, p. 339 (with the use of the formula *"attendu que"* which began to
be the common one until today in the decisions of French judicial courts).

[39]For example, Augeard, *Arrêts notables des différents tribunaux du royaume*, Paris,
vol. I, 1710 alternates very short and longer notices, in many cases with the name of the
Advocate General and the indication that the decision was "conform" to the conclusions
of the Public Ministry.

[40]Ibid., vol. 7, 1779, n. 8, p. 127.

these lawyers would later become members and leaders of the Constituent Assembly in 1789.

From volume two (1776) onwards, on several occasions the *Gazette des tribunaux* chose to present the conclusions expressed by king's advocates or Advocate Generals, in either a few lines or in a few pages (but not in every issue). The most quoted members of the Public Ministry were a number of well-known royal servants (*gens du roi*) in the Paris Courts. These were individuals such as Guillaume-François-Louis Joly de Fleury, (and, then his nephew) who undertook the role of the General Prosecutor from 1774 to 1787, and the Advocate General Antoine-Louis Séguier (from 1755 to 1790). Also prominent were the Advocate General Henri-Cardin-Jean-Baptiste d'Aguesseau from 1772 to 1789 (grandson of the Chancellor) and Louis-Michel Lepeltier de Saint-Fargeau, the Advocate General at the *Châtelet* Court in 1777.[41] Hérault de Séchelles, who assumed the role of Advocate General at the *Châtelet* (and then at the *Parlement* in 1780), was also commonly quoted.[42] Some of the conclusions of these Advocates appear to be directly quoted by the *Gazette des tribunaux*, whereas others are little more than restatements of what has been said (in condensed or briefly mentioned arguments). In some cases, they were accompanied by commentaries about the eloquence of the Advocate General, most especially in reference to Séguier,[43] or they expressed regret for not publishing further extracts of the discourse.[44]

It was common practice to mention that a judgement had been decided in conformity with (or in some rare cases, in contrast to) the conclusions of the public ministry. However, it seems that due to the probable influence of D'Aguesseau's pleadings (published between 1759 and 1789) the editor of the *Gazette des tribunaux* was driven to focus on the "defence of the law" that the king's representative offered. As a consequence of Montesquieu's praise for the public ministry, it was increasingly considered as the authorized organ of the law and perhaps the best interpreter of legal sources. In Paris, a large audience went to the *Châtelet* or to the *Parlement* to hear the Advocate General speak for many hours about the "defence of the citizen".[45]

---

[41] Ibid., vol. 4, 1777, n. 27, p. 6.

[42] Ibid., vol. 20, 1785, n. 41, p. 231; the two last ones were, during the Revolution, members of the Convention who voted the death of Louis the sixteenth.

[43] Ibid., vol. 3, 1777, n. 21, p. 321; vol. 15, 1783, n. 20, p. 324; vol. 16, 1783, n. 46, p. 306 (speaking of 30 years of triumph in the arena of Eloquence) . Also about Hérault de Séchelles and his eloquent discourses attended by a large and applauding audience, Ibid., vol. 23, 1787, p. 132.

[44] Ibid., vol. 16, 1783, n. 31, p. 74.

[45] Ibid., vol. 8, n. 37, p. 170.

In an issue of the *Gazette des tribunaux* at the beginning of 1789, it was stated that the magistrates of the public ministry were "purifying" the rights or interests of litigants, their discourses being the "consequences of laws, examined by the calm of reason".[46] Accordingly, it can be seen that when the unspoken reasons behind the judgment were assumed to adopt the conclusions of the public ministry,[47] the reasons themselves were able to be read through these conclusions: a concise and new form of analysis. This new method defined the style of the *Tribunal de cassation* from 1791 onwards: a judicial style linked with the 1790 obligation imposed upon judges to provide reasons for their decisions. The presence of many leaders of the Constituent Assembly among the lawyers whose pleadings were reported could explain the apparent ease of the transition from judgments without reasons (before 1789, or even the royal edict of May 1788 for criminal decisions) to judgments with reasons (after the clear dispositions of the laws in August 1790). We can now ask the question: was this new way of publishing judgments a hint of changes to come in legal interpretation?

Hypothesis Concerning the Conceptions About Legal Interpretation

It may seem dangerous to draw inferences from only twenty-two extracts of conclusions of the Public Ministry, which were published in the *Gazette des tribunaux* between 1776 and 1789. However, this corpus includes the opinions of nine Advocates General. Of the twenty-two extracts, nine opinions were from Séguier, while others came from Joly de Fleury, Savoye-Rollin, D'Aguesseau, Le Peletier de Saint-Fargeau, Hérault de Séchelles, Dijon de Saint-Maynard in Clermont-Ferrand, one Advocate General at the *Parlement de Toulouse* and another at the *Grand Conseil.* These authors followed the same logic as the publications of the pleadings of barristers – whether written or oral – as with the very frequent quotations of judgments decided according to (*conforme*) the conclusions of the Public Ministry. It seems unlikely that the judges would have possessed different views about legal interpretation than those developed in the extracts from barristers or the Advocates General. To illustrate, Savoye was a barrister before becoming Advocate general at Grenoble,[48] and Le Peletier de Saint-Fargeau became counsellor at the *Parlement* after his functions as Advocate General. When

---

[46]Ibid., vol. 27, 1789, n. 13, p. 196.
[47]Ibid., vol. 10, 1780, n. 31, p. 67 speaking expressly of the "reasons of the judgment".
[48]Ibid., vol. 5, 1778, n. 11 and n. 12, pp. 167 and 180–185.

the *Gazette des tribunaux* reported that the Advocate General had adopted the legal arguments of the litigants as developed by their barristers, and that the judges had followed the conclusions of the Advocate general (with some exceptions), it seems likely that all these lawyers shared the same conceptions about legal interpretation.

Furthermore, all these texts discuss, more or less, the legal interpretation of royal ordinances, customs, Roman law, canon law, precedents from the Courts, and legal *doctrine*. The first and most obvious conclusion that can be made, in accordance with the opinions of the authors of contemporary dictionaries, is that the *Parlements*, acting as "Sovereign Courts", interpreted legal texts. Moreover, there are no examples of recourse to the King, or "referee" (*référé*), ordered by the royal ordinance of 1667 in case of obscurity in the law. The *Gazette des tribunaux* also published several decisions from the Royal Council acting as a Court of cassation – with a commentary indicating that the best way to understand the case law (*la jurisprudence*) was to publish such decisions about questions of law.[49] However, these decisions did not include the reasoning behind them, and no representative of the Public Ministry came before the Royal Council. From these scarce interventions of the Royal Council, it was impossible to infer a clear policy of legal interpretation that reflected the will of the counsellors closest to the monarch. It is clearly stated in conclusions presented by the Advocate General Savoye de Rollin before the *Parlement du Dauphiné* in 1788, that the prohibition upon judicial interpretation (declared by Roman emperors) was an old prejudice and a dangerous absurdity: "We have not adopted", said Savoye de Rollin to his colleagues in the judiciary, "this strange method which meant destruction of civil liberty". On the contrary, the judiciary has the duty, according to the Advocate General, to "translate some laws through the others".[50]

There was no doubt that the *Parlements* possessed a broad power to interpret legal texts, except in rare cases of clear contravention of royal ordinances. Of course, this power was justified through the ideology of parliamentarianism, which exalted the *Parlements* as repositories of the law; as guardians, not only of the public law of the kingdom, but of the "immutability" of the law (understood as a transcendental order, in contrast to the transient will of the king).[51] Neither Domat, d'Aguesseau nor

---

[49]Ibid., vol. 21, 1786, n. 17, p. 257.

[50]Ibid., vol. 26, 1788, n. 33, pp. 58–59.

[51]Ibid., vol. 26, 1788, n. 29, pp. 37–39 with the very political discourse of Séguier (24th of September 1788) against the Lamoignon's reforms of May 1788. This discourse is very closed to the ideas developed by Montesquieu about the continuity of the legal corpus through the different reigns of the monarchs.

Ferrière expressed opposition to this recognition of sovereign interpretation in superior courts.

More generally, the twenty-two published extracts from the conclusions of the Public Ministry repeated, on several occasions, the most common opinions about legal interpretation. These opinions were primarily based on Roman maxims, and could be found in many doctrinal texts. On this subject, Ferrière noted that the law could not foresee every case, and that interpretation was necessary for almost all legal texts. In contrast, Savoye de Rollin stated in 1788 that "our clearest laws are only less obscure" and that imperfect expressions of the legislator's opinion always require interpretation.[52] Lepeltier de Saint-Fargeau adopted the same Roman formula as Ferrière – *Ubi lex non distinguit, nec nos distinguere debemus* – in relation to the interpretation of general expressions according to their commonly intended meaning.[53] A focus upon the "spirit of the law" was upheld as the primarily methodology for interpreting customs (particularly when they were silent on the discussed question) according to several approaches. For example, they could be interpreted by references to similar customs,[54] the maxims of Roman law and the principles of equity. This method of inducing the "spirit of the law" once again evokes the pages of Domat, though he is not quoted, and provides further proof of the continuity of the works of Domat and d'Aguesseau. Acts of balancing the spirit and the expression of the law were commonplace occurrences, and were also used in favour of a strict respect for the letter of the text, as well as for defending extensions or restrictions of the law.[55] The precedents of the Courts were used in the same way, in an attempt to discover and impose a reasonable authority that the judiciary should have to follow.[56] For example, Séguier noted in 1777 that "case law (*jurisprudence des arrêts*) has already made this quite natural interpretation of customs and of ordinances".[57] The prevailing view was that this method could solve questions of interpretation according to an

---

[52] Ibid., vol. 26, 1788, n. 33, p. 56.

[53] Ibid., vol. 20, 1785, n. 37, p. 170.

[54] Ibid., vol. 4, 1777, n. 34, p. 118 and, about the general customary law of France, vol. 12, 1781, n. 32, p. 83.

[55] Ibid., vol. 1, 1775, n. 5, p. 73; vol. 2, 1776, n. 31, p. 69; vol. 27, 1788, n. 16, p. 246 with the examples of the pleadings of the advocates Lacretelle, Montigny and Fossey invoking the signification of the law and the intention of the legislator.

[56] Ibid., vol. 2, 1776, n. 43, p. 264.

[57] Ibid., vol. 3, 1777, n. 23, p. 354: however, in this case, the Court did not agree with Séguier's conclusions and his "natural" interpretations of the texts.

implacable logic,[58] even in cases that were not foreseen by any law.[59] In some circumstances, this led to conclusions that "positive laws" had finally become so clear as to cut off all debate about interpretation completely.[60] Legal interpretation by the judiciary was conceived as a continuum between respect for the black letter of the law, the use of Cartesian reasoning, and recourse to the principles of Equity.

I propose that the developments requiring the strict application of the laws have to be interpreted in the same line of continuity with Domat and D'Aguesseau's works. When D'Aguesseau's grandson stated that "the law exists, and one can only require its application",[61] or when Joly de Fleury noted the imperious power of a precise law,[62] it was not the case of a new "legicentrism" linked with the Enlightenment, but was simply a further example of respect towards the traditional method of legal interpretation: a method that combined different authorities according to the motives of the judges.[63] A published conclusion from the Advocate General in Grenoble, Savoye de Rollin, supports these developments, and contains echoes of Montesquieu's famous words: "if the judge pronounces, it remains the Law which decides . . . Because the judge is the mouth which gives the oracles of the Law, one seems to have decided that his ministry is purely passive . . . but is the language of the law always so clear to offer only one meaning?"[64] This text contained no original ideas, as it was written by an Advocate General who could not lay a claim to the title of "legal theorist"; nevertheless, it can be read as proof of the questions about Montesquieu and legal interpretation that were raised in France at the end of the 18th century. The ambiguous character of the formula of the judiciary as the "mouth of the law" was well understood, but there were also doubts about the existence of *one* true meaning of a text. In this atmosphere of questioning, it is apparent that the religious debates over the biblical exegesis launched by Richard Simon at the end of the 17th century were especially influential.

---

[58] Ibid., vol. 3, 1777, n. 10, p. 149 (Séguier saying that one must understand the royal ordinance of 1670 according a clear distinction between different offences).

[59] Ibid., vol. 8, 1779, n. 27, p. 7.

[60] Ibid., vol. 12, 1781, n. 49, p. 359.

[61] Ibid., vol. 14, 1782, n. 31, p. 67.

[62] Ibid., vol. 17, 1783, n. 23, p. 357.

[63] Ibid., vol. 18, 1784, n. 38, p. 179; there is no reason to distinguish between the conclusions of the Public Ministry and a pleading from Treilhard (a future member of the revolutionary assemblies) saying that the Court had to "judge as the Law".

[64] Ibid., vol. 19, 1785, n. 14, p. 221; only the initials M. S. D. R. are indicated, but one can suppose that the Advocate General is Savoye de Rollin, whose other texts are quoted in the *Gazette des tribunaux*.

Even so, in other cases it does seem possible to deduce novel trends of legal interpretation. For example, Joly de Fleury refused to support the opinions of 16th and 17th century writers about feudal law, as he considered them ignorant of the political and social changes that had been occurring since the Middle Ages.[65] Furthermore, Savoye de Rollin expressed some criticism towards a 1731 royal ordinance about gifts, written by d'Aguesseau. Here, as an argument against the black-letter interpretation of a text coming from d'Aguesseau, a "man deprived of genius", the Advocate General Savoye promoted a progressive interpretation: an interpretation that took the effects and consequences of the law into account.[66] Based on these cases, it seems likely that some members of the new generation of Advocates General wished to appear emancipated from the authority of d'Aguesseau.

In addition, during this time the laws concerning Protestants had displayed a clear turn towards a more repressive form of legislation: a form of legislation which was no longer supported by legal practitioners. The Protestant religion had been prohibited in France since 1685, and its adherents were deprived of any civil status in absence of a Catholic marriage. In 1778, ten years after a famous pleading made by the Advocate General Servan in Grenoble in favour of a Protestant wife (married illegally "in the desert") who was claiming compensation from her adulterous husband,[67] the debate developed further before the *Parlement du Dauphiné*, and was subsequently reported in the *Gazette des tribunaux*. This development took the form of a Protestant woman's pleading (again, married "in the desert"), in which she claimed for inheritance. The barrister for the Protestant woman was Savoye, the future Advocate General in the same *Parlement*. In that case, not only did he argue for the validity of Protestant marriages according to natural laws, as Servan had done, but he rejected the use of Roman laws concerning concubines. The "chain has been broken", according to Savoye, between the laws of a "foreign people" decided 2,000 years ago and "our national laws" conceived for the French people. In his argument, the influence of Montesquieu is highly likely.[68] Savoye argued that the 1697 penal law enacted against Protestant heirs could not be extended or invoked, due to its contravention of the universal principle that everyone was free to have

---

[65] Ibid., vol. 5, 1778, n. 7, p. 98.

[66] Ibid., vol. 26, 1788, n. 33, p. 56.

[67] Joseph, Michel, Antoine Servan, *Oeuvres*, ed. X. de Portets, Paris, vol. I, 1822, pp. 13–67: these conclusions of the Public Ministry, developed in more than 50 pages, do not discuss the laws prohibiting the Protestant religion in France but invoke principles of natural law (and Pudendorf's works) about compensation of damages provoked by a fault.

[68] *Gazette des tribunaux*, vol. 5, 1778, n. 12, p. 184.

his wealth at one's disposal. He stated that "one has not to examine if the law wants for something but what it has effectively said".

The same year, the Advocate General de Cambon supported a similar point of view before the *Parlement de Toulouse*, and his conclusions were reported and praised in the *Gazette des tribunaux*. The Advocate General stated that one million Protestants were living in the South of France, and argued that Catholic magistrates should be freed from the prejudices of the past century and inspired rather by pity and enlightened reason. He pointed out that judges were subjugated to the authority of the laws from which Protestant heirs would have wished to have been distributed. These laws stated that judges must accept the legitimacy of children borne from parents enjoying a status of public possession as married people.[69] Thus, the legal argument in favour of these Protestant parents and their children was, according to de Cambon, the absence of a precise law prohibiting this status of public possession between Protestants.[70] The conclusions of the Advocate General heralded new legislation which was to be declared by the King nine years later, as in 1787 Louis XVI recognized a kind of civil marriage between Protestants. Not only this, but the Advocate General's conclusions were adopted by the judges, and corresponded with a clear change in the case law. De Cambon's statements evoked the title of the "philosophy of the century" and it seems likely that he may have been sensitive to the new climate of tolerance after Voltaire's campaign in favour of the Protestant Jean Calas (1762–1765). Other cases, such as those concerning Jewish litigants,[71] also indicate the progress of the philosophers' ideas (as well as the references to the Modern School of Natural law) among the legal practitioners.

However, one must be cautious with the use of an apparently new vocabulary. For example, even though some words in a pleading from Target – "the man is a sacred being for man"[72] – can evoke pre-revolutionary accents, the use of the expressions "light of reason", "rights of citizens", "equality before the Law" and the "sacred authority of the law" were already present in d'Aguesseau works: works which referred to an intellectual framework linked with the traditional monarchy. It would be incorrect to assume that all the Advocates General were in support of new ideas and wanted, for

---

[69] About this affair, David D. Bien, "Catholic Magistrates and Protestant Marriages in the French Enlightenment", *French Historical Studies*, vol. 2, 1962, n° 4, p. 416.

[70] Ibid., vol. 6, 1778, n. 39, p. 199. Later, in the 1828 edition of the *Répertoire universel* by Merlin (vol. 9, V° Légitimité, p. 584), the conclusions of de Cambon were lauded as a courageous act coming from a royal officer.

[71] Ibid., vol. 1, 1775, n. 5, p. 73.

[72] Ibid., vol. 6, 1778, n. 39, p. 193.

this reason, to promote a progressive interpretation of legal texts in order to adapt the laws to Enlightenment ideals. If this were the case, one cannot explain why Servan decided, in 1772, to resign from his role of Advocate General in Grenoble after his discourse about the administration of criminal justice (1766) and his failure to convince the *Parlement du Dauphiné* of his conclusions (rather influenced by sentimental pathos than by discussions about legal interpretation) in the count of Suze's affair. Another enlightened magistrate, Dupaty, who was first an Advocate General (1768), then president *à mortier* in the *Parlement de Bordeaux* (1781), was also forced to resign in front of the opposition of his colleagues.

The case of Dupaty is a prime example of the strong opposition to new ideas. In 1786–1787, three men (Lardoise, Simare and Bradier) were sentenced to death through the breaking wheel (*trois roués*). This provided the perfect opportunity for Dupaty to denounce the 1670 criminal ordinance and the procedure before the *Parlement de Paris,* by way of an anonymous memoir and a consultation from the barrister Legrand de Laleu. In this case, one judge, Fréteau – another future member of revolutionary assemblies – opposed the decision to condemn the men to death. This case also prompted many pamphlets in favour of reform (including Boncerf's plea against feudal rights at the beginning of the reign of Louis XVI). However, the Advocate General Séguier vehemently denounced Dupaty's memoir and Legrand's consultation before the *Parlement de Paris,* and required that these texts were burnt and banned. Séguier stated that he aimed to concrete "true principles, ignored in the most part by citizens of all the orders and all the ranks, to justify the legislation, and to solidify the authentic intention and meaning of the law". These conclusions were reported by the *Gazette des tribunaux* without criticism or approval. Moreover, Séguier described the reformers as: "foreigners in their own country, admiring the legislation of neighbouring countries to France ... wanting to turn upside down our laws" and regretted that the "serious tone of the bar was disappearing insensibly".[73] Finally, the Royal Council quashed the condemnation as contrary to the 1670 royal ordinance: the prestige of the statutory law was thus maintained, which satisfied both Dupaty and Séguier at the same time.

This case illustrates that it was not possible for the Advocates General to openly criticize the royal legislation as part of their function, and that the Public Ministry in Paris was divided, with the future actors of the criminal reform during the Revolution as Lepeltier de Saint-Fargeau and Hérault de Séchelles. However, the younger members of the *Parlement* remained

---

[73] Ibid., vol. 22, 1786, p. 234. About this criminal affair, Edmond Seligman, *La justice en France pendant la Révolution*, Paris, vol. 1, 1901, pp. 98–103.

silent at this time. Again, in 1788, when the *Parlement de Paris* victoriously resisted Lamoignon's reform (including in the May 1788 Edict the obligation to give reasons for criminal judgments), Séguier was alone in speaking "for the law" and defending the ideology of the members of *Parlements*.[74] One most definitely cannot say that a reformist Public Ministry, with a "pre-revolutionary" concept of legal interpretation, had already won at the eve of the French Revolution.

In conclusion, I shall attempt to summarise the various hypotheses I have presented, based on the analysis of the *Gazette des tribunaux*. The two aims of finding new ways to publish case law and of rationalizing legal interpretation were clearly linked in this review. The practice of presenting the conclusions of the Public Ministry as the "voice of the law" slowly came to be perceived in a positive light, and this in turn prepared the minds of many well-known lawyers for a new judicial style. This transformation's continuity with traditional methods of combining legal sources and interpreting legal texts (in the manner developed by Domat and d'Aguesseau), seems to be more definitive than the signs of a complete change announcing the strict legality of the French Revolution. The foundations of the legal revolution were not laid in advance. Before 1789, the future actors of the legal revolution were already present and collaborating in the same proceedings, but they did not necessarily share common ideas about law and legal interpretation. Above all, they could not foresee that the abolition of privileges on the 4th of August 1789 would sweep away the *Parlements*, the Parisian order of barristers, the feudal system, and the particular rights of the clergy and the nobility. Regardless of whether France was ripe for a uniform civil code, the new statutes were suddenly erected as the main sources of a "regenerated law" to which the king himself was subjugated. The question of legal interpretation could no longer be answered in the same way under this strict and monopolizing legality.

The story of law reports during the French Revolution is the final clue to this mixture of continuity and change. Whereas the career of the *Gazette des tribunaux* finished in October 1789 with the suppression of *Parlements*, two new reviews appeared with the new elected courts in the beginning of 1791: the *Gazette des nouveaux tribunaux* and the *Journal des tribunaux*. It is unlikely that the former barrister Mars took part in these reviews, but both used the same format and the same method of publishing periodically selected decisions of Parisian or provincial courts, and then in publishing the decisions of the new *Tribunal de cassation*. Both reviews reported pleadings and, in some cases, extracts of the conclusions of the Public Ministry, whose first incumbent in the *Tribunal de cassation* was Hérault de Séchelles.

---

[74] Ibid., vol. 26, 1788, n. 28, p. 17.

This shows a strong continuity with the actions of the *Gazette des tribunaux*. Yet, at the same time, it remained perfectly clear to the publishers of these reviews from 1791 onwards that the new judiciary had to apply new laws: laws on many subjects for which the ancient writers and precedents were irrelevant.[75] The absolute predominance of statutory law over other legal sources completely altered the structure, if not the methods, of legal interpretation.

It is also probable that the French and the German methods of legal interpretation, already different in the 18th century, diverged further with the rupture provoked by the French Revolution. The obligation imposed upon judges to provide their reasons, and the creation of the *Tribunal de cassation* – the second decision of the Constituent Assembly in 1790 – clearly displayed the will of the revolutionary deputies to strictly control a supposed "mechanical" application of legal texts by the judiciary. Despite the fact that a consensus was well established as to a restrictive interpretation of statutory texts on penal law, (most likely from the 17th century onwards), the question of civil law appeared to be more complex. In the revolutionary period, with the failure of the attempts to vote in a civil code, the *Tribunal de cassation* had great potential to develop its own case law, and to convince more and more lawyers that it was the role of the judiciary to interpret legal texts. When the Napoleonic codification was elaborated, Portalis, one of the codifiers, was able to utilise the distinction made at the end of the *Ancien Régime* between legislative interpretation (*interprétation d'autorité*) and judicial interpretation (*interprétation de doctrine*). Paradoxically, French "legicentsrism" was combined, (and perhaps remains combined in the modern day), with the marked influence of judge-made law (or, *jurisprudence*), which presumed great freedom in legal interpretation: a legacy of the Age of Enlightenment.

---

[75] *Gazette des nouveaux tribunaux*, vol. I, 1791, pp. 4–5.

Chapter 3
Legal Interpretation and the Use of Legal Literature in 18th Century Law Reports of the "Parlement" de Flandre

Serge DAUCHY

I. In his *Méthode historique appliquée aux sciences sociales* (1901), Charles Seignobos proposed to apply the historical method he had recently developed with Charles-Victor Langlois to the social sciences. This method had been formulated in a prominent work in the field of historical science: the *Introduction aux études historiques* (1897). One of the key stages of their internal critical analysis of sources (written sources in particular)[1] is defined as "interpretation criticism" – a critical process aiming at revealing the source's precise meaning or logic. Thus, in historical criticism, "interpretation" has to be understood as not only "making comprehensible" a string of words (for example by translating foreign words or by explaining technical terminology); but a good interpretation should also reveal both the author's intention and his silences.

A comparable method also grounded the "Exegetic school". The philosophy of the French Exegetic School[2] was based upon the idea that the law is to be found strictly in the Code. Thus, judges were meant to be able to discover answers to all possible situations in a completely codified law: *le juge bouche de la loi*. The assertion that the main source of law in France is legislation or statute law, and not theoretical scholarship, is without a doubt

---

[1]M. Howell and W. Prevenier, *From Reliable Sources. An Introduction to Historical Methods*, Ithaca, NY, Cornell University Press, 2001.

[2]J. Bonnecase, *L'école de l'exégèse en droit civil : Les traits distinctifs de sa doctrine et de ses méthodes d'après la profession de foi de ses plus illustres représentants*, 2e éd., Paris, 1924 (Bibliothèque de l'histoire du droit et des institutions, t. XIX). See also B. Bouckaert, *De exegetische school: een kritische studie van de rechtsbronnen en interpretatieleer bij de 19de eeuwse commentatoren van de Code civil*, Antwerp, Kluwer, 1981.

S. DAUCHY (✉)
Centre d'Histoire Judiciaire, CNRS, Lille, France
e-mail: serge.dauchy@univ-lille2.fr

MORIGIWA, Y. et al. (eds.), *Interpretation of Law in the Age of Enlightenment*, Law and Philosophy Library 95, DOI 10.1007/978-94-007-1506-6_3, © Springer Science+Business Media B.V. 2011

the result of developments in French legal thought that took place in the 16th century. In France at the time of the Ancien Régime, legal literature was primarily the work of practicing lawyers bound together by professional solidarity: a process which helped to maintain the traditional stock of juristic techniques. The French lawyer, the *avocate*, and the judge all aimed for clarity of expression, style and eloquence. This form of expression was not something purely external, but it is also structural in legal thought itself: *La forme donne l'être à la chose*. Their works, in the century of Enlightenment (and even in the 19th century) have therefore been characterized by a distaste for theoretical conceptualism and a particular distrust of conceptualistic jurisprudence, often scorned as "German quarrelling".[3] Generally, French legal thinking, from the Early Modern Period onwards, preferred a rational, almost mathematical style of reasoning, which focused on concrete problems to be solved by legal interpretation and legal argument.

II. The purpose of the present contribution is to provide some insight into how the authors of printed (and some manuscript) collections of law reports from the French *parlement* of Flanders dealt with the question of legal interpretation and the use of legal texts in the 18th century. The Spanish Low Countries – although placed (both linguistically and legally) at a crossroads between the French and German traditions – are generally considered to be anchored in the *ius commune* tradition. However, the *ius commune* tradition is no longer understood to be an all-encompassing legal system. On the contrary, legal historians emphasize a plurality of individual legal identities which arguably interact with a common legal culture – or at least a common continental heritage. For instance, particular laws differ from one region to another; within the same region, and even from one place to another.[4] Such coexistence can indeed be observed in the territories that were brought under French sovereignty in the 17th century as a result of the Devolution war.[5] Notwithstanding the change in sovereignty, Flanders's particular legal and institutional system was guaranteed by several "capitulations" which were, in effect, constitutional acts explicitly recognizing the particularities of new conquered territories and imposing formal respect of their specific legal identity. These capitulations allowed the Flemish inhabitants to continue to

---

[3] O. Jouanjan, *Une histoire de la pensée juridique en Allemagne (1800–1918) : idéalisme et conceptualisme chez les juristes allemands du XIXe siècle*, Paris, 2005.

[4] A. Wijffels, *"Orbis exiguus*. Foreign Legal Authorities in Paulus Christnaeus's Law Reports", in S. Dauchy, H. Bryson and M. Mirow (eds.), *Ratio decidendi. Guiding principles of judicial decisions*, vol. 2: *Foreign Law*, Berlin, 2010 (Comparative Studies in Continental and Anglo-American Legal History, Bd. 25/2), pp. 39–64 (pp. 40–41).

[5] V. Bufquin, *Le parlement de Flandres, la cour d'appel de Douai, le Barreau*, Douai, 1965, pp. 9–11.

enjoy their old privileges, customs, administration and justice system.[6] It was pursuant to these commitments that a high court of justice was instituted in 1668 with the title of "sovereign court",[7] to which the King granted the title of "Parlement" in 1686. Founded in Tournai[8] (Belgium), in the early 18th century, this court was transferred to Cambrai and, in 1715, to Douai.[9] Although its primary mission was to dispense justice in the name of the king, the new court was also symbolic, not only of the province's legal identity, but of respect for Flanders's particular legal traditions: it indeed appeared essential to the inhabitants of Flanders that they fell within the competence and jurisdiction of a court that was based in the province, and composed of local judges aware of its legal characteristics.[10]

III. During the first years of its existence, the new court had to deal with several difficulties: first, a moving jurisdiction due to successive international treaties; but more importantly, a feeling of legal insecurity, caused by

---

[6]See, for example, article XII of the capitulation of Lille (27th August 1667): "Que lesdites villes de Lille et châtellenie jouiront pleinement et paisiblement de tous privilèges, coutumes, usages, immunitéz, droits, libertéz, franchises, juridiction, justice, police et administration à eux accordéz tant par les rois de France par ci-devant que par les princes souverains de ce pays. . .".

[7]*Recueil des édits, déclarations, arrêts et règlements qui sont propres et particuliers aux Provinces du Ressort du parlement de Flandres, imprimés par l'ordre de Monseigneur le Chancelier*, Douai, 1730, pp. 9–11. Cf. also M. Pinault des Jaunaux, *Histoire du parlement de Tournay contenant l'établissement et les progrès de ce tribunal avec un détail des édits, ordonnances et règlements concernant la justice y envoyez*, Valenciennes, 1701.

[8]J. Lorgnier, "La justice du Roi Soleil dans les anciens Pays-Bas. Organisation de la justice dans le ressort du Conseil souverain de Tournai", in *Les juridictions supérieures*. Actes des journées de la Société d'Histoire du droit des pays flamands, picards et wallons, Nijmegen, 1994, pp. 19–52.

[9]On the court's history, see G.-M.-L. Pillot, *Histoire du parlement de Flandres*, 2 vol., Douai 1849 and the contributions published in J. Poumarède and J. Thomas (eds.), *Les parlements de province. Pouvoirs, justice et société du XVe au XVIIIe siècle*, Toulouse 1996: J. Lorgnier, "Cour souveraine et parlement de Tournai, pièce maîtresse de l'ordre judiciaire français dans les anciens Pays-Bas" (pp. 141–164) and R. Martinage, "Pouvoir royal et justice au parlement de Tournai, 1686–1709" (pp. 165–190); and, more recently, V. Demars-Sion, "Le parlement de Flandre: une institutions originale dans le paysage judiciaire français de l'Ancien Régime", in *Revue du Nord*, t. 91, n° 382, 2009, pp. 687–725 with a list of the most important royal decrees.

[10]Local particularities can be observed in different fields as the rules of civil procedure (or "style"): A. Dumées, *Traité des juridictions et de l'ordre judiciaire pour les provinces du resort du Parlement de Flandre*, Douai, 1762, *Préface*, p. VIII; criminal justice: R. Martinage, "Les singularités flamandes dans la justice criminelle du Conseil souverain de Tournai (1679–1684)", in *Revue du Nord*, op. cit., pp. 763–781; or legal professions: H. Leuwers, "Entre héritage des Pays-Bas et dynamique française: les avocats du parlement de Flandre au XVIIIe siècle", in Ibidem, pp. 783– 797.

the variety of customs of which only the most important had been officially
recorded. As a result of this, several judges started gathering short explanatory comments on the decisions of various courts. Most of these writings
could be considered as private notes for the personal use of their authors,
sometimes put at the disposal of the other members of the court. The
parlement decided upon appeal cases, and the main purpose of the explanatory notes was to avoid a large variety of legal solutions for these problems:
the explanatory comments were thus intended to prevent sudden reversals
of jurisprudence. This explains why these notes sometimes reveal the judgment's *rationes decidendi* and even the individual opinion of the judges and
the arguments they put forward to support their interpretation of the case.[11]
Practitioners, and in particular advocates, also needed to have insight into the
court's polity, not because they were interested in gathering precedents (how
could a decision be quoted as precedent without knowing the reasons given
by the judges!) but because it was important to know how the law – local
customs, statutes from the former Low Countries and royal ordinances –
had to be interpreted, at least according to the Court's general orientations.
For all of these reasons, numerous publications of judicial notes occurred.

IV. Two councilors of the court have published collections of decisions
from the Parlement of Flanders in the early years of the 18th century. The
first collection, entitled *Recueil d'arrêts notables du parlement de Tournay*
was published in Valenciennes in 1702. It is the work of Matthieu Pinault
des Jaunaux, who completed the first volume with a *Suite des arrêts notables
du parlement de Flandre* published in 1715. The second printed collection
is Jacques Pollet's *Arrêts du parlement de Flandre* published three years
after his death in 1716.[12] The first collection is classical and presents, in a
chronological order, 500 judgments pronounced by the court between 1694
and 1714. For each decision, Pinault provides general information on the
proceeding, a short comment on the legal question submitted to the court,
and the final decision. The legal problem is also summarized in the heading
of each case. Although this kind of printed collection was very common in
France as well as other European countries during the 17th century, this type

[11]S. Dauchy and V. Demars-Sion, "Argumentation et motivation dans les recueils
d'arrêts des cours souveraines de France. L'exemple du parlement de Flandre
(fin XVIIe – début XVIIIe siècle)", in A. Cordes (ed.), *Juristische Argmentation –
Argumente der Juristen*, Cologne-Weimar-Wien, 2006 (*Quellen und Forschungen zur
höchsten Gerichtsbarkeit im Alten Reich / 49*), pp. 127–152.
[12]Biographical information on both councilors can be found in P. Arabeyre, J.-L.
Halpérin et J. Krynen (dir.), *Dictionnaire historique des juristes français (XIIe–XXe
siècle)*, Paris, 2007.

of presentation and content was already on the decline by the time Pinault's law reports were published in the early 18th century.[13]

Pollet's work is more original, and representative of a new generation of law reports that appeared in France in the heart of the 17th century. It is divided into three distinctive parts. The first is composed of 38 decisions "on different noteworthy legal questions" (*Arrêts sur diverses questions notables*) that are analyzed in detail. They were also accompanied by doctrinal commentaries which emphasized the debates between legal authorities, and put forward the differences between the local, French (i.e. the Paris) and Roman point of views. The second part (*Arrêts et observations sur divers articles des coûtumes du ressort du Parlement*) is dedicated to various articles of local customs raising particular difficulties. For each of them Pollet presents one or more decisions considered to have fixed the court's interpretation of dubious customary provisions. The third part, entitled *Autres arrêts rangéz par ordre alphabétique des matières*, deals with many legal (and frequently) historical topics. In total, there are 128 topics, classified alphabetically, developed from the decisions of one or more courts.

V. With regard to the question of interpretation and the use of legal texts in the 18th century, two interesting details must be considered. First, the reasons given by authors who wished to propose a collection of commented judgments to the public; and second, the justification expressed by librarians when publishing posthumously private notes of practitioners that were never intended to be read by the broader public.[14] What was the ultimate purpose of these authors and librarians? What did they aim to achieve by publishing their reflections on a selection of judicial decisions? In his preface, Pinault des Jaunaux put forward the idea that the contribution of printed law reports was that they avoided a wide variety of legal solutions for identical legal problems, and thus reduced contradictions between judgments.[15] His work was also intended to allow practitioners a better knowledge of

---

[13]Cf. S. Dauchy and V. Demars-Sion (eds.), *Les recueils d'arrêts et dictionnaires de jurisprudence, XVIe–XVIIIe siècles*, Paris, 2005, La Mémoire du droit (collection bibliographique II), Introduction.

[14]Four collections of private Notes on court decisions, those of Dubois d'Hermaville, de Baralle, de Flines and de Blye (all of them judges of the Parlement in the late 17th century) have been gathered by a bookseller and publisher from Lille, J.-B. Henry, and printed in 1773, in two volumes, under the title *Recueils d'arrêts du Parlement de Flandres*.

[15]Au lecteur: "Ces ouvrages peuvent aussi beaucoup contribuer à empêcher la varieté & la contrarieté des arrêts, parce que rendant la jurisprudence d'une Cour supérieure plus connue dans son ressort, ils la rendent plus constante, ils en fixent les maximes & en effleurent les principes". Cf. N. Derasse, "La mise en valeur des recueils d'arrêts et

the court's jurisprudence, in order to help them prevent appeal procedures. This type of presentation insisted on the importance of a wide circulation of court's decisions among practitioners and local courts, and is typical of classical "arrestography". "Arrestography" was understood as a selection of isolated case studies (decisions from one particular or from several *parlements*) that emphasized the legal arguments of the parties in order to discover the decision's *rationes decidendi*.[16]

Jacques Pollet, on the contrary, entitled his law reports *Arrêts du parlement de Flandre sur diverses questions de droit, de coutumes et de pratique, ouvrage utile pour l'intelligence des coutumes et usages du pays.* His purpose was aimed less at fixing the court's jurisprudence, but was rather to draw general principles from the interpretation of – and confrontation between – different legal sources.[17] Also interesting from this perspective is Georges de Ghewiet's *Jurisprudence du parlement de Flandre*: a document that remained unpublished at its author's death in 1745.[18] Inspired perhaps by Brodeau's new editions of Louet's law reports,[19] de Ghewiet intended to republish Jacques Pollet's work. He did so not with the aim of completing it with new decisions from the parlement de Flandre (he was advocate for

---

des dictionnaires de jurisprudence à travers les préface", in *Les recueils d'arrêts,* op. cit. (*supra*), pp. 41–68.

[16]H. Bryson and S. Dauchy, *Ratio decidendi. Guiding principles of judicial decisions,* vol. 1: *Case Law,* Berlin, 2006 (Comparative Studies in Continental and Anglo-American Legal History, Bd. 25/1).

[17]Préface: "Quoique cette province soit d'une petite étendue, il n'y en a pourtant guerres dans le Royaume où il y ait une si grande multiplicité de loix... puisque toutes ces coutumes & ces loix subsistent ; puisque nous y sommes nécessairement assujettis, & puisqu'il est si dangereux & en même temps si aisé de donner dans des contre-sens parmi cette grande variété de règles qui expose leur "**interprétation**" à toutes les mauvaises subtilitéz de ceux qui veulent en abuser, toute nôtre application doit se réduire à en bien pénétrer l'esprit, & à en acquérir la connaissance la plus parfaite".

[18]G. de Ghewiet, *Jurisprudence du parlement de Flandre,* S. Dauchy and V. Demars-Sion (eds.), Brussels, 2008 (Commission royale pour la publication des anciennes lois et ordonnances de Belgique, Recueil de l'ancienne jurisprudence de Belgique, deuxième série). See also S. Dauchy and V. Demars-Sion, "A propos d'un 'recueil d'arrêts inédit': La jurisprudence de Flandre de Georges de Ghewiet", in *Tijdschrift voor Rechtsgeschiedenis/Legal History Review,* LXXVII (2009), pp. 157–189.

[19]*Recueil de plusieurs notables arrêts du Parlement de Paris, pris des mémoires de Monsieur Maistre Georges Loüet... avec un grand nombre d'arrêts et de notables décisions, recueillis par feu Maistre Julien Brodeau... Nouvelle et dernière édition, augmentée des plus belles décisions et des plus notables arrêts, rendus tant au Parlement de Paris, qu'aux autres cours souveraines du royaume.* Louet's *Recueils* was originally printed in 1602; Brodeau's new edition was first published in 1615.

more than 50 years) and from other high courts, but to introduce observations and doctrinal commentaries based on an important corpus of European legal literature. De Ghewiet's attention and interest went to the third part in particular, where topics were presented in an alphabetical order and introduced by one or more decisions of the court. In contrast, according to his editor, Pollet considered the second part (dedicated to the "intelligence" of the local customs) to be the most important. On one hand, there was probably less interest in local customary law due to several publications on the topic, the court's activity, and the influence of French law. On the other, law reports underwent a significant evolution in the 18th century: the traditional collections of printed decisions had adopted new concepts and a form of presentation initiated by Pierre-Jacques Brillon's *Dictionnaire des arrêts ou jurisprudence universelle des parlements de France et autres tribunaux*, published for the first time in 1711.[20] De Ghewiet's enterprise fits within that process of evolution.

VI. Pollet's and de Ghewiet's law reports further allow us to provide an account of how Flemish authors dealt with legal interpretation and how they used legal texts, and in particular, legal literature. Their work also illustrates the general features of the relationship between different legal sources from the particular vantage-point of a peripheral province at the crossroad of the Dutch and French legal cultures. Both authors, as a matter of course, refer first to the law of the Southern Netherlands as characteristic of the province's law, which they then go on to contrast with the laws of France and with learned law.[21] Although both were practitioners working in a (provincial) high court, their horizon of legal literature and legal systems went beyond the jurisdiction of the parlement of Flandres and even beyond the Netherlands and the French realm. Legal literature from the neighboring countries of continental Europe (the Dutch Provinces, Germany, Italy and to a lesser extent Spain and Portugal) was also quoted in the comments of the law reports. This occurrence highlights the broad circulation of legal books in

---

[20] J. Hilaire, "Questions autour de la jurisprudence des arrêts", in *Les recueils d'arrêts, op. cit. (supra)*, pp. 21–39.

[21] Flemish authors and practitioners insist in particular on the part played by Roman law in the legal system of the former Low Countries, e.g. G. de Ghewiet, *Institutions du droit Belgique*, Lille, 1736, part. 1, tit. 1, § 7, art. 2 (p. 13): "quoique ce pays soit un pays coutumier, le droit romain y est considéré tout autrement que dans les pays coutumiers de France, où ses principes et ses décisions ne sont pas adoptées que comme raison, au lieu que dans ce pays le droit romain est adopté comme Loi écrite". Cf. S. Dauchy and V. Demars-Sion, "Foreign Law as ratio decidendi. The 'French' Parlement of Flanders in the late 17th and early 18th centuries", in *Ratio decidendi*, vol. 2, op. cit. (note 4), pp. 65–81.

the more general context of European cross-border legal culture. Foreign legal literature – learned and customary doctrine as well as collections of foreign court's law reports – was used principally for comparative ends. It allowed practitioners (in their conclusions and written civil procedures) to put various arguments forward: arguments that showed the conformity of local law and customs with general features or, on the contrary, expressed the province's legal individuality.

In Pollet's work, citations still remain limited. On one hand he refers to the main authors of the "Belgian" territories (commentaries on customary law and law reports from the Great Council of Mechlin[22] or from the Court in Brabant[23] published during the 17th century) and, on the other hand, he quotes the major civil and canon law authorities (Azon, Accursius, Bartolus or Zypaeus. . .). Few references to foreign particular law are made directly through primary authorities, with the exception of some French authors as d'Argentré.[24] Pollet – as most of his contemporaries in the former Low Countries – had to rely on a rather narrow selection of secondary sources in order to have access to foreign primary legal sources. In that sense, Pollet's reports illustrates a highly conventional approach of legal culture in Western continental Europe during the 16th and 17th centuries, to a large extend still conceived within the traditional framework of the relationship between *ius commune* and *iura propria*. His citations of legal literature mostly appear at the end of each commented decision (or are referred to by the editor in foot-note). These citations aim to reinforce the idea of legal continuity between the former Spanish Netherlands and the new French province (and to assert its legal particularity) or to highlight principles that are considered to be observed quasi-universally throughout Europe, often against general laws applicable in the realm.

On the contrary, de Ghewiet expresses a noticeable evolution in legal interpretation and the use of legal texts, characteristic of the century (and the principles) of Enlightenment. However, it must be noted that the starting point of his own *Jurisprudence* is, as has been said previously, Pollet's printed work. Whereas Pollet cites about one hundred different references (representing approximately 80 authors), de Ghewiet refers to over 450

---

[22]In particular Rémi-Albert du Laury, *Jurisprudence des Pays-Bas autrichiens établie par les arrêts du Grand conseil de sa Majesté impériale et catholique résidant en la ville de Malines auxquels sont ajoutés quelques décrets portés au Conseil privé de sadite Majesté*, Bruxelles, 1717 and, although not published, Pierre de Cuvelier's *Arrêts du Grand conseil de Malines*.

[23]Pierre Stockmans, *Decisionum Curiæ Brabantiæ sequicenturia*, Bruxelles, 1670.

[24]Bertrand d'Argentré, *Commentarii in patrias Britonum leges, seu generales consuetudines antiquissimi ducatus Britanniæ*, Bruxelles, 1664.

printed legal books from more than 400 different authors. Several standard works on Roman law (such as Azon's *Summa aurea*, Corvinus' *Codicis methodica*, Faber's commentaries on the Institutes or Sanderus' *Ad titulum Digestor*) and others representative of late medieval and early modern *ius commune* tradition, disappear from de Ghewiet's commentaries. As one would expect from a practitioner working in the royal parlement of Flanders at the beginning of the 18th century, his commentaries refer far more than his predecessor to French authors, whether concerned with general law, local customs or specific legal topics. In particular, all titles of legal literature that associate general learned commentaries with particular law are most strongly represented throughout de Ghewiet's original developments. This genre had been developed during the late 17th and early 18th centuries and therefore, for France, already comprised a substantial body of printed legal scholarship. Finally, but also predictably, the most important collections of *Decisiones* available in print – in particular from the French parlements[25] – and legal dictionaries, receive mention in his doctrinal analyses. The greater the authority or success of a specific work (often expressed by the number of reprints), the greater the likelihood that its author (and as a matter of consequence a particular customary law or the law reports of a particular court) is more than just occasionally referred to by de Ghewiet.

One could ask whether these references have been made directly through primary sources or whether de Ghewiet relied on secondary authorities. In other words, what were the library resources he had access to? When de Ghewiet died in 1745, a librarian from Lille was asked to establish a catalogue of his personal library in order to sell his books. The catalogue[26] contains some 700 titles classified by their size (*in-folio*, *in-quarto*, in-*octavo* and *minori forma*) and, for each size, by their contents (canonists, civil law, customs, statutes, law reports and historians). This illustrates that he indeed had access to important personal library resources and that most of the authorities he referred to in his pleadings, professional statements and in his doctrinal writings could be found on his bookshelves. His personal library also shows his interest – unsurprising for an intellectual in the century of Enlightenment – for non-legal literature: history, politics, philosophy and sciences.

---

[25]There is still no exhaustive list available; the most complete one for France (and most European countries) is G. Walter's "Rechtsprechungssammlungen", in H. Coing, *Handbuch der Quellen und Literatur der neueren europäischen Privatrechtsgeschichte*, bd. 2: *Neuere Zeit (1500–1800)*, Munchen, 1976, pp. 1223–1263.

[26]Published by S. Dauchy and V. Demars-Sion, "La bibliothèque du juriste flamand Georges de Ghewiet", in *Bulletin de la Commission royale pour la publication des Anciennes Lois et Ordonnances de Belgique*, XLVIII (2007), pp. 277–320

VII. How does this literature fit into legal interpretation? For what purpose are these European authorities referred to? As noted, during the Enlightenment, French legal thought did not explore theoretical concepts. Doctrine, and in particular law reports, was more concerned with finding practical solutions to legal problems within the background of legal pluralism. According to our authors, what differentiated France was the authority afforded to Roman law when local customary law remained silent or obscure as to the legal question to be settled. Judges also had recourse to Roman law when settling dissenting opinions within the court. In other words, learned law, and in particular Roman law, was not confined to an additional role but was perceived as a formal source of law or even, as de Ghewiet calls it, the "common law" within the jurisdiction of the parlement of Flanders. For this reason, councilors (and as a matter of consequence also their law reports) were hostile or at least reserved towards French customary doctrine, and instead relied on the most renowned authorities of learned Roman and Canonical law.

De Ghewiet, for example, regularly points out that the rules and principles reported by Ferrière upon the custom of Paris are contrary to "Law". In his opinion they did not fit within the general framework of *Ius commune*. De Ghewiet adds that the role and place acknowledged to "written law" precisely distinguishes Flanders from the French *pays de coutume*. In his own words: "our references to French authors are generally used in a wrong way because we do not make the effort to examine whether our habits and customs are based on the same principles as the laws (i.e. the royal ordinances) and customs of France".[27] Legal, and in particular "foreign" legal literature was thus used to discover arguments that could justify the attachment of the Flemish judges and lawyers to the province's legal identity. Not only this, but it was also made use of to strengthen their opposition to, and refusal of, the royal efforts and attempts to centralize and uniform law and justice. This is also the reason why, when interpreting local customary law, Flemish judges and authors rather referred to law reports from the former southern Low Countries – even to decisions much later than 1668 – or to authors from other peripheral territories of the realm as Brittany.

---

[27] *Jurisprudence du parlement de Flandre*, op. cit., part III, arr. XXXVIII (n° 4 *in fine*): *A la vérité, il ÿ a quelques auteurs François qui tiennent que. . .; mais il est bon d'observer, avec M. Pollet, part. 2, arr. 36, qu'on fait souvent une mauvaise application de ce qu'on trouve dans ces auteurs, faute de se donner la peine de bien examiner si nos usages et nos coutumes sont fondées sur les mêmes principes que les coutumes et usages de France.*

VIII. As a consequence of these considerations, interpretation appears contradictory. From the point of view of contemporary practitioners, and according to the tenets of historical criticism, interpretation is to be understood as a search to discover in local customary law a legal answer to solve a particular case. It is a quest to find out – by analyzing legal texts within their environment of the former Hapsburg and Spanish Low Countries – if local customs indeed adopt the lawsuit's specific topic. In addition, it also hopes to discover how the articles concerned should be "interpreted" and understood. "Interpretation" thus also means that judges can decide whether the principles of customary law should be applied or not.

Legal pluralism does not necessary imply a strict hierarchy of norms and legal sources. On the contrary, it offers, to judges and also advocates, the opportunity to find within different legal texts the best or most suitable legal answer to a particular question, whether that answer is inspired by local customary law, royal statute law, judicial precedent, legal doctrine or even equity. In other words, when using and interpreting legal texts, judges can choose between the respective interests of the litigants, the defense of the province's legal particularity, and the acceptance of royal centralization and legal standardization. In that sense, legal literature offers a wide overview of possible solutions. It allows judges and lawyers to be informed, on a broad national or even European scale, about doctrinal disputes and arguments put forward to support an opinion. More specifically, with regard to law reports, it allows these actors to know the decisions of different high courts and the reasons for possible reversals of jurisprudence.

We should indeed not forget that, throughout the 18th century, it was not considered necessary in continental Europe to provide the reasons for a decision. Over two centuries, printed collections of *Decisiones* or law reports were successful because they proposed to reveal the *rationes decidendi* of the judicial decisions they published. Apart from the judges who had taken part in the judgment's deliberation or from lawyers who were informed by the judges, the reasons of a decision could only be inferred from an interpretation of the litigants' arguments in court, or (more likely) from the arguments of the party who had won the lawsuit.[28] Nevertheless, infering the *ratio decidendi* from the parties' legal arguments – and to thus interpret the legal value of the arguments put forward – soon appeared uncertain, and in any event did not allow the use of a court decision as

---

[28]In Flanders, the parties' arguments are included in the so-called extended decisions: S. Michel, "Les 'arrêts étendus' du parlement de Flandre, étude d'une spécificité juridique locale", in *Revue du Nord*, op. cit., pp. 745–761.

precedent, or the inference of general principles from within a single case. Therefore, traditional case law literature, known as "arrestography", became progressively obsolete.

At the end of the 17th century, we can observe – in France as well as in other neighboring countries – a slow but continuous evolution of the external presentation and content of the reports: an evolution that also seems to coincide with a new generation of authors, and lawyers specialized in editorial enterprises. This was in direct contrast to the judges who gathered notes for their own purposes, or for the internal use of the courts, both of which were only published posthumously. This evolutionary tendency became widespread on the eve of the century of Enlightenment, except for some peripheral territories. One such territory was Flanders, where the first collections of law reports appeared later, pursuant to the creation of a provincial parlement. Court decisions became gradually only a part, and sometimes even an insignificant part, of the author's developments. They formed the starting point of what should be considered as doctrinal treaties rather than as collections of printed law reports. As a consequence, the usual title of such collections *Recueils d'arrêts* was also abandoned.

In a more general way, the border between the different types of legal literature – law reports, commentaries of customary law, collections of statute law, learned doctrine – vanished, to give birth to a new kind of legal literature: dictionaries. This new terminology, typical for all fields of knowledge in the century of Enlightenment, expresses not only an encyclopedic approach to science, but also a renowned conception of interpretation. This concept was particularly noticeable in the legal sciences. The purpose of these dictionaries was to draw general principles from different legal texts *via* a process of reasoning and interpretation. Instead of presenting a catalogue of case studies and legal species insisting on the diversity of legal answers to an identical question, lawyers felt the need and necessity to pursue a more uniform jurisprudence understood as legal science.

Law reports as a matter of consequence became a substantial part of legal doctrine, fully participating in the construction of a more unified legal system by reducing contradictions between legal texts and even by reducing the weight of learned law. In 1970, Jean Carbonnier wrote a short note entitled *Note sur des notes d'arrêts,* published in the *Recueil Dalloz*, which contains the following passage: "Arrestography (as called in the 19th century) is the craftsmanship or science that suggests all possibilities and their opposite, of which each judgment is only a starting point, in order to reveal the most probable possibility. The supreme art consists in bringing together the most likely solution with the most desirable one so that jurisprudence can be orientated in that direction".[29] This is also true for legal reports in the 18th century, and could only be accomplished by interpretation of legal sources in the sense that Seignobos and Langlois understood "interpretation". This method is what the legal authors of the century of Enlightenment strived to achieve, and they thus paved the way for codification.

---

[29]Dalloz, 1970, p. 138 : "L'arrestographie, comme on disait audacieusement au siècle dernier, est l'art ou la science de suggérer tous les possibles ou leur contraire dont chaque arrêt est le point de départ, et d'en mettre un en relief comme le plus probable. L'art suprême consiste alors à faire que le probable rejoigne le souhaitable car c'est à la science de l'arrêtiste qu'il revient d'orienter la jurisprudence dans ce sens, car le commentaire d'arrêt utile, celui qui fait jurisprudence, est le commentaire qui réussit à convaincre les juges que la suite est déjà dans le précédent".

Part III
The Case of Germany

Chapter 4
The Object of Interpretation: Legislation and Competing Normative Sources of Law in Europe During the 16th to 18th Centuries

Heinz MOHNHAUPT

Introduction and Preliminary Methodological Note

Every statute – just as every normative source of law – only becomes effective, and hence enters into social consciousness, at the time when it is applied. This predominantly judicial application requires that the relevant norm be interpreted, whist at the same time amounts to the law-creating act which only at this stage enables the statute to shape social reality. Given traditional differentiations within general and specific legislation, and differentiation between statutes according to their hierarchical rankings and the different conditions for their enactment, the interpretation of these statutory sources of law always entails different tasks to which the interpreter must adapt. Within the history of legislation a differentiation is therefore drawn between differing types of legislation and statutory forms according to different canons of interpretation. This can already be observed under Roman law.[1] Rules were thus developed within theory and practice regarding the interpretation of sources of law, of which legislation and contracts are nowadays the most prominent.[2] Under the *Ancien Régime*, it was above all the

---

This is a revised version of a talk which the author gave in 2006 at the Brazilian conference of legal historians in Rio de Janeiro, soon to be published also in Portuguese in Brazil.

[1] See Gian Gualberto Archi, *Interpretatio iuris, interpretatio legis, interpretatio legum*, in: Idem, *Scritti di diritto romano*. I: *Metodologia e giurisprudenza di diritto privato*/1, Milano 1981, pp. 83–138.

[2] Fritz René Grabau, *Über die Normen zur Gesetzes- und Vertragsinterpretation* (Schriften zur Rechtstheorie, 160), Berlin 1993.

H. MOHNHAUPT (✉)
Max-Planck-Institut für europäische Rechtsgeschichte (Max-Planck-Institute for European Legal History), Frankfurt am Main, Germany
e-mail: mohnhaupt@rg.mpg.de

MORIGIWA, Y. et al. (eds.), *Interpretation of Law in the Age of Enlightenment*, Law and Philosophy Library 95, DOI 10.1007/978-94-007-1506-6_4, © Springer Science+Business Media B.V. 2011

difference between a general statute (*lex generalis*) and an individual statute in the form of a privilege (*lex singularis/privilegium*) that was significant, with particular theories of interpretation applying to the latter.[3] Accordingly, the nature of the statute is decisive in determining the canon of interpretation to be applied, and every interpretation requires a statute as the object of interpretation. Within the general spectrum of normative sources of law, this was thereafter to be regarded as a prerequisite for all interpretation.

Modern man is nowadays surrounded by an abundance of legislation intended to guide his actions, to provide him with entitlements and services from the state, to require him to refrain from acting and to punish him in the event of contravention. The modern state also gives substance to itself through legislation, and its actions are legally regulated by a constitution, provided that it is a state governed by the Rule of Law. In all states, the production of legislation is constantly on the rise because the need for regulation is ever increasing or – a scenario that must be feared – the power of conviction and the ability of legislation to enforce itself in view of diverging interpretations is ebbing away. Questions arise out of this that are to be put to the current legal system, though it is only possible to answer them by reference to the experience imparted by legal history. What are laws? Who makes them? What functions do they have? Who has authority to interpret the law? What rules are in competition with one another? What is their relationship to one another?

If we talk about legislation and laws today, then it is possible to reach agreement on an international level relatively quickly on a common basic meaning for "statute" as a type of norm, even though the concept is by no means applied uniformly everywhere[4]: thus "statute" in a material sense can be taken to refer to the abstract and general rule that is based on a specific sovereign legal system, refers to an indeterminate range of cases, is

---

[3]For example: Henning Grossen (Praeses), Interpretatio L. 16 ff. de LL ... *de jure singulari* (Respondent: Johannes Wolfgang Pfeil), Wittebergae 1630; Samuel Stryk, *Dissertatio de privilegiorum interpretatione* (Respondent: Gustav Martin), Francofurti ad Viadrum 1683.

[4]Even under the German Constitution – the "Basic Law for the Federal Republic of Germany" of 23 May 1949 – the use of the term "statute" is not uniform, since it is used partly in a material sense and partly in a formal sense; cf. on this matter the judgment of the Federal Constitutional Court of 20 March 1952, in: *Entscheidungen des Bundesverfassungsgerichts*, vol. 1, Tübingen 1952, pp. 189–195; Ernst Wolf, Der Begriff Gesetz, in: Walter G. Becker und Ludwig Schnorr von Carolsfeld (Eds.), *Sein und Werden im Recht, Festgabe für Ulrich von Lübtow*, Berlin 1970, pp. 109–135; Bernhard Diestelkamp, *Die deutsche Reichsgesetzgebung im 19. und 20. Jahrhundert*, in: *Rättshistoriska studier* (series II), vol. 7, Lund 1982, pp. 206–222 (213–221).

directed at an indeterminate number of people and contains generally bind-ing rules that may be enforced by state authorities.[5] Statutes are therefore legal instruments of control that are capable of directing people's individual and collective action.

However, the issue raises problems of presentation for historical analysis. The very broad area of research of the pan-European history of legisla-tion can be structured either according to individual states and their specific legislative histories or according to the individual structural characteristics of this type of rule. In this chapter a presentation according to the structures, criteria and elements of the species of "statute" in European legal history has been chosen, thus enabling comparisons between the various developments of legislation in different European countries.[6] In doing so, "statutes" cannot be treated in isolation as a principal source of aristocratic or state regulation according to our current understanding of legislation. Competing species of norms – such as case law, legal science, customary law and privileges – should also be considered in order to be able to throw light on the status and function of legislation. In doing so we should not focus only on competition between these types of norms, but rather also of complementary points and convergences between them.[7] I shall therefore take as a starting point the concept of a "source of law" as an over-arching umbrella concept for legal normativities, under which legislation has had the status of a primary source of law since the 16th century. When discussing the individual structural ele-ments I shall follow the classification that I have used elsewhere as the basis for the more comprehensive presentation of this problem issue.[8]

It must also be considered that the theories and practices of the best pos-sible legislative activity were always related to the theories and practices of political science as a whole, and are also still regarded as such. In this regard the liberal constitutional lawyer Carl Theodor Welcker stated in 1838 that "the theory of the preferably inner benignity of legislation coincides

---

[5]See the Article on *Gesetz* (i.e. "statute"), in: Horst Tilch und Frank Arloth (Eds.) *Deutsches Rechts-Lexikon*, vol. 2, 3rd ed., München 2001, p. 1962.

[6]See also Sten Gagnér, *Studien zur Ideengeschichte der Gesetzgebung (Acta Universitatis Upsaliensis, Studia Iuridica Upsaliensia* 1), Stockholm 1960, p. 54.

[7]See Pio Caroni, *Blicke über den Gartenzaun. Von der Beziehung der Rechtsgeschichte zu ihren historischen Nachbarwissenschaften*, in: Louis Pahlow (Ed.), *Die zeit-lose Dimension des Rechts. Historische Rechtsforschung und geschichtliche Rechtswissenschaft*, Paderborn (et al.) 2005, pp. 47–49.

[8]Heinz Mohnhaupt, *Grundlinien in der Geschichte der Gesetzgebung auf dem europäis-chen Kontinent vom 16. bis 18. Jahrhundert. Ein experimenteller Überblick*, in: *Zeitschrift für Neuere Rechtsgeschichte* (ZNR) 28 (2006), pp. 124–174.

with the theory of political science as a whole. . .".[9] Legislation amounts to a core concept for every consolidated social system, as the sole enabler of the state and stateliness.[10] In this regard legislation is a factor within the development of the state, a precursor of which is found in Aristotelian philosophy. Aristotle declared that "out of the wisdom directed at the state the leading and prominent part is however that wisdom which deals with legislation".[11] This "legislation" posited or legitimated by the ruler or by the state is the subject matter of the following reflections, in which I shall focus more on the formal criteria of legislation rather than their contents. Extralegal forms of legislation such as the laws of thought, moral laws, religious laws and above all the laws of nature will not be discussed here.

The Inter-dependency of the Sources of Law

From the 16th to the 19th century, legislation, case law and legal science constituted three sources of law with differing rule quality, which in turn were characterised by differing conditions for the creation emergence or creation of rules. Within the modern constitutional state they may also be termed the three rule-producing "branches", behind which there are authorities with varying degrees of political input within a parliamentary state governed by the rule of law. The use of the term "branches" is associated under Montesquieu's thought with the notion of the separation of these three sources of law, which had however not yet been achieved under the *Ancien Régime*. Legislation and case law – with legal science in the middle, almost as a critically attendant and conjunctive institution – are also closely related in functional terms. Within the absolutist sovereign state, such a strict separation between legislation and case law would, in constitutional law and political terms, have been tantamount to jeopardising (1) the sovereignty claim of the ruler, (2) his monopoly on law creation and (3) the emerging unity of the territorial state.[12] An absolute ruler could not let this happen. Absolutist state theory supported this practice as an expression of a process

---

[9]Carl Welcker, *Artikel Gesetz*, in: Carl von Rotteck und Carl Welcker (Eds.), *Staats-Lexikon oder Encyklopädie der Staatswissenschaften*, vol. VI, Altona 1838, p. 753.

[10]See Rolf Grawert, Artikel *Gesetz*, in: Otto Brunner, Werner Conze, Reinhart Koselleck (Eds.), *Geschichtliche Grundbegriffe*, vol. II, Stuttgart 1975, p. 863.

[11]Aristotle, Nikomachische Ethik. *Auf der Grundlage der Übersetzung von Eugen Rolfes*, ed. by Günther Bien, Hamburg 1985, VI. 8, 1141 b 20–30 (pp. 139 s.).

[12]On a systems theory interpretation of this development, see Niklas Luhmann, *Die Stellung der Gerichte im Rechtssystem,* in: *Rechtstheorie* 21 (1990), pp. 459–463.

involving the concentration of power.[13] All three elements are hallmarks of the development of the state between the 16th and 19th centuries and have repercussions on the relationship of the three sources of law with one another. In functional terms, the commonality between legislation, case law and legal science consists in the fact that they contain, or could contain, legal propositions laying down a specific "imperative order".[14] Therefore, from a functional and constitutional law perspective there is no assumption of a strict separation between the three sources of law or "branches". They have a relationship of mutual dependence on one another, which can be structured very differently according to time, place and the legal issue to be decided.[15] Consequently, the system of sources of law is not static, but rather dynamic. Even the concept of "source of law" is not unequivocal and often resembles more an instrument of argumentation rather than a basis for decision.[16] Accordingly, there is also no unitary doctrine of sources of law, but rather a variety of theories of sources of law which place the basis for validity and the form of validity at centre stage in different ways.[17] If one focuses on legal practice, it can be observed that court judgments gain normative force and the status as *vis legis* – comparable with the English case-law-system and its "binding force" – where legislation is lacking, ambiguous or incomplete. Legislation and case law thus form a mutually overlapping circle of sources of law if the people that produce them also belong to different political or constitutional institutions.

The multi-level validity of different sources of law can also lead to changes and exchanges in their hierarchical ranking. It is important to differentiate on the one hand between specific legislation applying only locally or regionally and on the other hand general legislation of general applicability. The specific sources of law with a limited extent as a matter of principle

---

[13]See Dieter Wyduckel, article *Absolutismus*, in: Werner Heun et al. (Eds.), *Evangelisches Staatslexikon*, Stuttgart 2006, col. 22.

[14]This is a distinctive term used by Eugen Huber, *System und Geschichte des Schweizerischen Privatrechts*, vol. IV, Basel 1893, p. 11.

[15]Heinz Mohnhaupt, *Rechtseinheit durch Rechtsprechung? Zu Theorie und Praxis gerichtlicher Regelbildung* im 19. Jahrhundert in Deutschland, in: Claes Peterson (Ed.), *Juristische Theoriebildung und rechtliche Einheit. Beiträge zu einem rechtshistorischen* Seminar in Stockholm im September 1992 (Rättshistoriska Studier, Nittonde Bandet), Lund 1993, pp. 125 s.

[16]See Ulfried Neumann, *Wandlungen der Rechtsquellenlehre in der neueren Rechtstheorie*, in: Lothar Philipps und Roland Wittmann (Eds.), *Rechtsentstehung und Rechtskultur*. Heinrich Scholler zum 60. Geburtstag, Heidelberg 1991, pp. 83–90.

[17]See Niklas Luhmann, *Ausdifferenzierung des Rechts. Beiträge zur Rechtssoziologie und Rechtstheorie*, Frankfurt am Main 1981, pp. 308–325 (The legal doctrine of sources of law form a sociological perspective).

took precedence over the general laws with broad validity. This multi-level operation of statutory sources of law could lead to a change in the ranking of legislation where a city or region did not have any specific laws of its own; in such cases the generally applicable Roman law – the *ius commune* – with otherwise only subsidiary validity attained the status of the dominant source of law. Legal science could in turn through its competence over interpretation achieve the status of a source of law with a similar quality, depending on the shifting demands on the legal system.[18] The three normative species of sources of law – legislation, case law and legal science – thus stood within a variable and flexible ranking system, which was not based on any self-standing source of law valid in its own right. This also has to be considered in the following reflections on "statute" and "legislation" as species of sources of law, especially since even today Germany still lacks a system of sources of law unequivocally determined under the Constitution.[19]

The Changing Ranking of Sources of Law

Since the middle of the 18th century there has been a growing awareness of the reciprocal relationship of dependency between legislation, case law and legal science. In 1749, Daniel Nettelbladt – a German Enlightenment jurist – on the one hand referred to the autonomy of the three sources of law, though on the other hand emphasised that the state of one source of law has a large influence on the state of another source.[20] In 1792 the Italian Lupi sketched out the ideal picture – *imaginem* – of the *optimi Legumlatoris, Jurisconsulti atque Judicis* by placing legislation, legal science and the judiciary alongside one another in this order of preference.[21] The task of the *Jurisconsultus* was to interpret *lex ambigua aut obscura . . . ex earum verbis*

---

[18]See also Jan Kropholler, *Die Wissenschaft als Quelle der internationalen Rechtsvereinheitlichung*, in: *Zeitschrift für vergleichende Rechtswissenschaft* 85 (1986), pp. 143–163.

[19]See Peter Landau, *Die Rechtsquellenlehre in der deutschen Rechtswissenschaft des 19. Jahrhunderts*, in: Peterson, *Juristische Theoriebildung* (as note 15), p. 89; Heinz Mohnhaupt, *Quellen, Rechtsquellen und Rechtsquellensystem. Auffassungen zu den Produktivkräften des Rechts* im 19. Jahrhundert, in: Richard H. Helmholz et al. (Eds.), *Grundlagen des Rechts. Festschrift für Peter Landau zum 65 Geburtstag*, Paderborn (et al.) 2000, pp. 814 s.

[20]Daniel Nettelbladt, *Unvorgreiffliche Gedanken von dem Zustand der bürgerlichen und natürlichen Rechtsgelahrtheit in Deutschland, derer nöthigen Verbesserung und dazu dienlichen Mitteln. Als eine Einleitung zu seinen Lehrbegriffen . . .*, Halle 1749, pp. 3 s.

[21]L. A. Lupi, *De optima condendi, interpretandi, dicundique juris ratione liber singularis*, Genuae 1792, p. 1

et ratione. Lupi assigned this interpretative task to three authorities: *Primum est Jurisconsulti, secundum Judicis, Tertium Principis.*[22] According to the doctrine of the absolutist state, the final say on interpretation thus lies with the ruler in his capacity as legislator. At the start of the 19th century the German jurist Rudhart provided the most articulate account of this recipro-cal dependency of the three sources of law and attributed them differentiated status as sources of law. Legislation took first place with the most intensive binding force and the broadest circle of addressees. What legal science has "fixed" in dogmatic terms and what which has obtained "renewed certainty through the settled uniform application by the courts" constitutes "an albeit not so abundant source of law ... as the statute book".[23] Accordingly, it is the defects or qualities of legislation that determine the ranking and func-tion of legal science and case law. Lawmakers, the courts and purveyors of legal science participate in the development and application of the system of sources of law in the same manner. In doing so a law formation process involving a division or labour and productive cooperation between all three species of rules arises.[24] This applies as a matter of principle to the English and Continental European legal system in the same way.[25] Thus a system of changing predominance of species of sources of law arises according to the principle of "communicating vessels". Writing in 1812, the German jurist Ignaz von Rudhart called this the "changing preponderance and regression of legislation, legal science and case law".[26]

The Meaning of the Common Law *ius privatum* for Legislation and the Theory of Sources of Law

This feature is the general hallmark of the legal system under the *Ancien Régime*. It is determined by the doctrine of the sources of law and the power of abstraction of Roman law, i.e. the *ius commune* of the time which charac-terised all species of law and the predominantly private law rules of which were generally decisive also for the development of the *ius publicum*. This

---

[22]Lupi, *De optima ratione* (as note 21), p. 28.

[23]Ignaz von Rudhart, *Encyclopaedie und Methodologie der Rechtswissenschaft*, Würzburg 1812, p. 66.

[24]See also Reinhard Zimmermann, *Savignys Vermächtnis*, in: Pio Caroni und Gerhard Dilcher (Eds.), *Norm und Tradition. Welche Geschichtlichkeit für die Rechtsgeschichte?*, Köln/Weimar/Wien 1998, p. 29.

[25]Raoul C. van Caenegem, Judges, Legislators and Professors. Chapters in Europaen Legal History, Cambridge 1993, pp. 67–83.

[26]Rudhart, *Encyclopaedie* (as note 23), p. 69.

ius commune system of rules made its mark on this new public law discipline that had grown out of the political science writings.[27] Within legal science, statute and legislation, which had gradually become the object of *ius publicum* since the 17th century, still remained under the influence of the doctrine of sources of law derived from the *ius commune* right into the 18th century. This applied above all to the formation of a register of statutory terminology, the systematisation of the growing bodies of rules and the ordering of sources of law amongst one another. Familiarity with the *ius civile sive Romanum privatum* was required for the *Politicus* and the representatives of the *ius publicum*.[28] In most cases, this occurred with reference to Justinian's "Institutes" in the Roman *Corpus iuris civilis, quia ius publicum, nisi cognito prius iure privato, percipi haud facile potest.*[29] Up until the 18th century the three sources of law were treated in textbooks and commentaries on the "Institutes" as elements of the system of sources of law. It is hence important to consider the sources and literature of the *ius publicum and* of the *ius privatum* when ascertaining the meaning, origin and function of statute and legislation within the general inventory of bodies of legal rules.

The Ranking of Legislation and Case Law

Today, the predominance of legislation and the legislature amongst the three "branches" is a matter of course. Originally however, it was the judiciary and not the legislature that created the first law. Indeed, the word *ius* originally referred to the places at which the law was pronounced.[30] The doctrine of sources of law in the middle ages was still also premised on a close connection between legislation and case law.[31] "To judge" and "to rule" were often

---

[27]Michael Stolleis, *Geschichte des öffentlichen Rechts in Deutschland*, vol. I: *Reichpublizistik und Policeywissenschaft* 1600–1800, München 1988, pp. 80–125.

[28]Johann Andres Bosius, *De prudentia et eloquentia civili comparanda . . .*, Jenae 1699, p. 56

[29]Johann Harpprecht, *Commentariorum . . . , in quatuor libros Institutionum iuris civilis, divi Iustiniani*, vol. I, Francofurti 1658, col. 6.

[30]Herbert Hausmaninger/Walter Selb, *Römisches Privatrecht*, 8th ed., Wien (et al.) 1997, p. 46.

[31]Bernd Kannowski, *Rechtsbegriffe im Mittelalter. Stand der Diskussion*, in: Albrecht Cordes und Bernd Kannowski (Eds.), *Rechtsbegriffe im Mittelalter*, Frankfurt am Main (et al.) 2002, pp. 5 s.

used synonymously.[32] Both legal and canon law doctrine were premised on the predominance of judicial activity. The Pope possessed legal primacy which enabled him to issue bulls, judgments, statutes, decrees and constitutions with these different statutory designations.[33] The New Testament also gives many examples of the primacy of the courts and of judges around the world.[34] For the English legal system this judicial primacy was the most important feature. In 1938 Lord Wright commented on this traditional English principle in the following terms: "The judges have made the law which used to be spoken of as a sort of entity immanent in the breast of the judges. They were law-givers, in whom was reposed the power and duty of the king as a fountain of justice".[35] On the European continent the received Statutist Doctrine grounded the original primacy of the judiciary, from which the right to issue legislation was derived. Justiciability formed an integral part of the territory, to which the right to judge applied as part of the right of sovereignty. Antonio Hespanha has written an article treating this legalistic foundation in notably succinct terms.[36] Baldus, a jurist from the middle ages, explained *quod iurisdictio ordinaria et contentiosa inhaeret territorio. ...*[37] Accordingly, the bounds of jurisdiction are determined according to the *limites territorii: ... statuta condere est iurisdictionis: quia qui statuit, ius dicit.*[38]

Alongside the writings of Jean Bodin, who enunciated the principle of sovereignty in 1576, legislation moved up to first place as a *puissance de donner loy à tous en general, et à chacun en particulier.*[39] This promotion did not occur at the same time throughout the European continent. In

---

[32]See Jürgen Weitzel, *Dinggenossenschaft und Recht. Untersuchungen zum Rechtsverständnis im fränkisch-deutschen Mittelalter*, Köln 1985, p. 767.

[33]Walter Ullmann, *Papst und König. Grundlagen des Papsttums und der englischen Verfassung im Mittelalter*, Salzburg 1966, pp. 29 s.

[34]Johannes 9, 39.

[35]Lord Wright, The Study of Law, in: The Law Quarterly Review LIV (1938), p. 185.

[36]António M. Hespanha, *L'espace politique dans l'ancien régime*, Coimbra 1983, pp. 29–34; also Dietmar Willoweit, *Rechtsgrundlagen der Territorialgewalt. Landesobrigkeit, Herrschaftsrechte und Territorium in der Rechtswissenschaft der Neuzeit*, Köln/Wien 1975, pp. 33–47, 186–190.

[37]Baldus, *In primum, secundum, et tertium Cod. Lib. Commentaria, Venetiis* 1577, p. 169 (Tit.: *Ubi et apud quem, lex* III).

[38]Baldus, *Commentaria* ad D. 1.1.9 (lex *"omnes populi"*, no. 9); see also Heinz Mohnhaupt, *Potestas legislatoria und Gesetzesbegriff im Ancien Régime*, in: *Ius Commune* 4 (1972), pp. 189 s.; *ausführlicher dazu* Mohnhaupt, Grundlinien (as note 8), pp. 133–135.

[39]Jean Bodin, *Les six livres de la république*, 3rd ed., Paris 1578, p. 161.

Portugal for example the ruler's standing was still determined primarily by judicial competence until the middle of the 18th century.[40] With the primacy of legislation the continental development parted company with the English legal system, which had largely preserved the primacy of case law. On the continent however, collections of legislation contained court judgments from the middle ages even into the modern period, thus documenting the overlaps between statutory and judicial rule systems.

"Statute" as a Problem of Definition

If the titles of the major bodies of legislation from the *Ancien Régime* in the European countries in their use of the designation *Gesetz, loix, leyes, wetten, leggi* etc. are examined, what is surprising is the almost complete absence of the term "statute" from the titles. The appellation "statute" only arises on the continent – as in England – as a non-specific umbrella term.[41] As early as 1806, the Dutch writer van Swinderen referred to the numerous *diversae significationes, quibus vocabulum lex venire solet* that were in common use in theory and practice.[42] All attempts at further specification of the term "statute" are dependent on the relevant constitutional situation and on political and constitutional theory and practice. In this respect it appears entirely impossible *per definitionem* to determine a unitary concept of statute applicable to the different eras of the history of "legislation". Nonetheless, since antiquity there has been no lack of various new attempts within European legal literature and philosophy to encapsulate the *nomos*, *lex* or "statute" within its manifestations and grounds for binding force. This is because the statute has always been considered a mandatory legal instrument for the regulation of state and society as well as for directing human conduct. The Roman Emperor Justinian expressly included statutes within the arsenal of imperial majesty.[43] In the 18th century statutes were declared to be the "soul of the state" and thus as an instrument and guarantee

---

[40]See Airton L. Cerqueira-Leite Seelaender, Polizei, *Ökonomie und Gesetzgebungslehre. Ein Beitrag zur Analyse der portugiesischen Rechtswissenschaft am Ende des 18. Jahrhunderts (Studien zu Policey und Policeywissenscchaft*, ed.. Michael Stolleis), Frankfurt am Main 2003, p. 46 s.

[41]See Mohnhaupt, *Potestas legislatoria* (as note 38), pp. 214 s.

[42]Theodorus van Swinderen, *Disputatio juridica inauguralis de legibus*, Groningae 1806, pp. 10 s.

[43]See the Prooemium to the "Institutiones" in the Roman *Corpus Iuris Civilis*.

for the "welfare and felicity of subjects".[44] Cicero still led the attempts at definition right into the 18th century: *Lex vera . . . ad iubendum et ad vetandum ratio est recta. . .*[45]; *lex est iuris atque iniuriae regula*[46]; *salus populi suprema lex esto.*[47] The definition of the Roman jurist Papinian is the most renowned: *Lex est commune praeceptum.*[48] The extensive treatise of the Roman jurist Gaius embraces the three sources of law mentioned earlier that are endowed with normative force, namely legislation, the pronouncements of expert jurists and the decisions of judges. They were described in very different terms, which at the same time indicate their differing origins; *leges, constitutiones, edicta, decreta, rescripta and response,*[49] the normative binding force of which is derived from the *vis legis* attributed to them.[50] Legislative competence was concentrated within the Roman Emperor, with the result that all of the Emperor's decisions had the status of general binding force, without thereby diminishing the variety in the names of legislative instruments. This is shown by the renowned formula of the Roman jurist Ulpian: *Quod principi placuit, habet legis vigorem.*[51] All of these Roman attempts at definition also dominate the European history of legislation into the 19th century. The Roman law designations were also used for domestic sources of law. This practice also reflects the relevant constitutional arrangements, above all where there was a need to confer legitimacy on absolutist state polities that had developed, in which the legislative branch now monopolized law creation. Writing in the 17th century, Thomas Hobbes referred to statutes as *oratio eius, qui aliquid fieri vel non fieri aliis iure imperat.*[52] This brought the absolutist imperative nature to the fore, which for Hobbes characterised legislation as an instrument for guiding conduct – as a rule and measure. The German Enlightenment jurist Samuel Pufendorf

---

[44]As e.g. for Samuel Stryk, *Specimen usus moderni pandectarum*, Francofurti 1690, p. 28.

[45]Cicero, *De legibus*, lib. II, cap. IV (n. 10).

[46]Cicero, *De legibus*, lib. I, cap. VI (n. 19).

[47]Cicero, *De legibus*, lib. III, cap. III (n. 8).

[48]D 1.3.1.: *De legibus senatusque consultis et longa consuetudine.*

[49]*Gai Institutionum Commentarius Primus*, ed. by Ferdinand Kniep, Jena 1911, pp. 2 s.

[50]See Okko Behrends, *Der römische Gesetzesbegriff und das Prinzip der Gewaltenteilung*, in: Idem and Christoph Link (Eds.), *Zum römischen und neuzeitlichen Gesetzesbegriff*, 1st Symposium of the Commission on *Die Funktion des Gesetzes in Geschichte und Gegenwart* of 26 and 27 April 1985, Göttingen 1987, p. 9.

[51]D 1.4.1.

[52]Thomas Hobbes, *Elementa philosphica* 3: De cive, Amsterodami 1647, p. 64 (cap. III, XXXIII).

referred to *lex* as *norma actionum humanarum* to ensure order and morals.[53] In his translation and commentary on Pufendorf's *De officio*, the French Enlightenment writer Barbeyrac expressly defined statutes as the *voluntas superioris* that directs all of the actions of subjects: *La règle des mouvements et de la conduite des hommes, est ce que l' on appelle Loi*.[54] The German Enlightenment philosopher and legal scholar Christian Wolff also emphasised the directive purpose of legislation in this sense: *Lex est regula, iuxta quam actiones nostras determinare obligamur*.[55] In the 18th century, the content and aim of positive legislation was to ensure the moral conduct of people – the *actus morales* – and to subject the executive action of the sovereign to the "common weal".[56] However, within the estates of the *Ancien Régime*, the nature of legislation as imperatives and requirements was not yet however endowed with the status of general validity, since the principle of equality encountered an obstacle in the unequal estate structure, and the regionally and locally differentiated sources of law. Therefore, local privileges and those of the estates – as the *ius singulare* par excellence – are counted under legislation according to the *ius commune* doctrine.[57] It therefore follows that an open or variable concept of legislation must be privileged, with the help of which the differences and shifting functionality of the species of "legislation" may be better comprehended.[58] These examples amount to stages in the development of an understanding of legislation expressed through numerous attempts at definition, the old Enlightenment elements of which were passed down in Europe into the 19th century.

---

[53]Samuel Pufendorf, *De officio hominis et civis juxta legem naturalem libri duo. Observationibus antea separatim editis … locupletati autore* Gottlieb Gerhard Titio, Lipsiae 1709, pp. 88 s. (lib. I, cap. II, §§ 1 s.).

[54]Jean Barbeyrac, *Les devoirs de l'homme, et du citoyen, tels qu'ils lui sont prescrits par la loi naturelle. Traduits du Latin … par Jean Barbeyrac. Avec quelques notes du Traducteur*, Amsterdam 1708, p. 29 (liv. I, chap. II. § 2).

[55]Christian Wolff, *Institutiones juris naturae et gentium*, Halae Magdeburgicae 1750, p. 20 (§ 39); ähnlich Christian Thomasius, *Lectiones de prudentia legislatoria, cum praefatione* Gottlieb Stollii, Francofurti et Lipsiae 1740, pp. 26 s. (§ 47): *Lex stricte dicta seu praeceptura Reipublicae est regula actuum moralium obligans subditos ….*

[56]Christian Wolff, *Vernünfftige Gedancken von dem Gesellschaftlichen Leben der Menschen Und insonderheit Dem gemeinen Wesen Zu Beförderung der Glückseligkeit des menschlichen Geschlechts*, Die vierte Auflage, Franckfurt und Leipzig 1736, pp. 435 s. (§ 420).

[57]See Heinz Mohnhaupt, *Untersuchungen zum Verhältnis Privileg und Kodifikation im 18. und 19. Jahrhundert*, in: *Ius Commune* 5 (1975), pp. 71–121 (77–91).

[58]See further Bernhard Diestelkamp, *Einige Beobachtungen zur Geschichte des Gesetzes in vorkonstitutioneller Zeit*, in: ZNR 10 (1983), pp. 385–420 (389–393).

Voluntas as the Basis for the Validity of Statutes

Will, *voluntas, la volonté, la voluntà, voluntad, arbitrio*, coercion, imperative, direction of human conduct and the general validity of legislation provide criteria for establishing the basis for the validity of statutes.[59] In the optimistic belief in the educability of people, statutes are regarded as a mechanical legal instrument, *qui appartient de nous diriger*, as the French jurist Mably stated in 1777.[60] The will of the ruler is the *causa efficiens juris scripti* par excellence.[61] Jean Bodin expressed this in the absolutist formula: *Ex quo perspicitur, leges ac mores ab eorum, qui summam in republica potestatem habent, arbitrio a voluntate pendere.*[62] A further expression of this principle of legislation is the renowned edict of Loysel of 1766: *Qui veut le Roi, si veut la Loi. C'est la première règle de notre Droit.*[63] The broad autonomy or the ruler established under this perspective brought with it the danger of absolute arbitrariness, which was to be limited by subjecting the will of the ruler to the requirement of *felicitad, ius naturale, ius divinum* and the *leges fundamentales*. Melo Freire argued in 1789, in relation to Portuguese constitutional law, that the sovereign was to direct the conduct of his subjects *ad decus et utilitatem Reipublicae.*[64] The ethical and moral purpose of legislation was increasingly overlaid during the 17th and 18th centuries by the utilitarian and political tasks of the state, which account for the political system's increased requirement for direction[65] and find their

---

[59]Confirmation in Mohnhaupt, *Potestas legislatoria* (as note 38), pp. 199–208; Jan Schröder, *Recht als Wissenschaft. Geschichte der juristischen Methode vom Humanismus bis zur Historischen Schule* (1500–1850), München 2001, pp. 97–99; concerning the first attempts at an understanding of legislation based on „voluntas" cf. Thomas Simon, "Gute Policey". *Ordnungsleitbilder und Zielvorstellungen politischen Handelns in der Frühen Neuzeit (Studien zur europäischen Rechtsgeschichte* 170), Frankfurt am Main 2004, pp. 75–89.

[60]Gabriel Bonnot de Mably, *De la legislation, ou principes des loix*, vol. I, Lausanne 1777, p. 125.

[61]Wolfgang Adam Lauterbach, *Collegii theorico-practici, a libro primo Pandectarum usque ad vigesimum pars prima, studio filii* Ulrici Thomae Lauterbach, Tubingae 1707, p. 58.

[62]Jean Bodin, *De republica libri* sex, 6 ed., Francofurti 1622, p. 242 (lib. I, cap. 10).

[63]Citing Claude-Joseph de Ferriere, *Nouvelle introduction a la pratique, contenant l' explication des termes de pratique de droit et de coutumes*, vol. III, Paris 1764, p. 188.

[64]Paschoal José de Mello Freire, *Institutiones iuris civilis Lusitani, cum publici, tum privati*, Liber I: *De iure publico*, Olisipone 1789, p. 3 (§ III).

[65]See Simon, "Gute Policey" (as note 59), pp. 246 ss., 307 ss.

expression in the numerous instances of "policy" legislation.[66] This was accompanied by a twofold differentiation between statutes that also corresponded to different legislators: God, nature, reason and the temporal ruler. Accordingly, alongside the profane *lex positiva* or *humana* we then have the supra-positive *lex naturalis* and *lex divina*: (1) positive human statutes are open to amendment, are both open to adaptation and require adaptation, and also give concrete form to the overarching natural law, which is unchangeable and eternally valid; (2) the imperative character of the positive concept of law as a matter of principle excludes legal doctrine, the opinions of teachers, contracts, advice, admonitions and moral law from the concept of statute. However, this was not undisputed, since *in scripturis dogmata saepe pro legibus sumuntur*.[67] However, according to the predominant absolutist will theory, such *dogmata, consilia, monita, pacta* remained invalid unless the majesty endowed them with binding force.[68] The Roman philosopher Seneca was still cited into the 18th century: *lex iubeat, non disputat*.[69] With the concentration of legislative powers within the will of the princes, above all expert advice and legal science doctrine were to be excluded from the category of statutes and the boundary between sovereign legislation and legal scientists was to be clearly drawn. This applied above all to the authority of the legal texts books form the middle ages and the systematic text books of Roman law, which were often used as normative texts and as the basis for judges' decisions. Law books were without doubt not legislation in a strict sense, but as authoritative texts they played a part in the history of legislation.[70] There is a certain similarity here with the "books of authority" of the English legal system, which differentiates between "persuasive" and "binding authority".[71]

However, legislation could only take effect as an instrument of direction if it was made known, in order for subjects to be able to comply with the

---

[66]Comprehensive source evidence concerning this species of legislation is contained in Karl Härter and Michael Stolleis (Eds.), *Repertorium der Policeyordnungen der Frühen Neuzeit* I-IV, Frankfurt am Main 1996 ss.; zur "Policey" als Wissenschaft cf. Stolleis, Geschichte I (as note 27), pp. 366 ss.

[67]See Thomasius, *Lectiones* (as note 55), p. 19 (§ 7).

[68]Heinrich Gottfried Scheidemantel, *Das Staatsrecht nach der Vernunft und den Sitten der vornehmsten Völker betrachtet I*, Jena 1770, p. 166.

[69]Seneca, *Ad Lucilium epistulae morales, Epistula* XCIV, n. 38, in: Seneca in ten volumes, VI, Repr. Cambridge/Mass. 1989, p. 36.

[70]See Wilhelm Ebel, *Geschichte der Gesetzgebung in Deutschland*, reprint of the 2nd ed., Göttingen 1958, ed. by Friedrich Ebel, Göttingen 1988, p. 56.

[71]See e.g. John William Salmond, Jurisprudence, 9. ed. by J. L. Parker, London 1937, pp. 195, 232 s.

requirements of the legislation and to put the courts in a position to rule according to statute.[72] The publicity of legislative intention thus became a prerequisite for its validity, because only "the sufficiently enunciated will of a ruler ... is a statute in a strict sense".[73] This resulted in the need to draw up a "dual code", namely one for the courts and legal scholars and another "for the people in general".[74]

Towards the end of the 18th century the individual will of the sovereign was replaced by the "general will" of the people. This "general will" gave rise to the "general law" of the developing bourgeois society. The political implementation of this democratic principle is made clear in Article 6 of the French Declaration of the Rights of Man and the Citizen of 26 August 1789 manifest: *La loi est l'expression de la volonté générale*. The sovereign had changed, and along with it the political will that created legislation as well as the authority to interpret legislation. A consequence of this development in France was the uniformity of the designation *loi* for all forms of legislation.[75]

Concentration and Monopolisation of the Legislative "Branch"

The derivation of legislation from the will of the lawmaker had the result that statutes came into existence and were interpreted and defined through the ruler, and not due to the content of the "posited" rules. In this regard the legislature also amounted to *première marque du prince souverain*, as Bodin declared.[76] Therefore, even without the requirement of general binding force, all enunciations made by the sovereign in its capacity as lawmaker can be statutes: ... *nam Imperator dicendo legem condit*.[77] The name given to the product of legislation played no role whatsoever in this regard. The power to issue numerous statutory provisions, their wealth of

---

[72] See in detail Clausdieter Schott, *Gesetzesadressat und Begriffsvermögen*, in: Gottfried Baumgärtel und Hans-Jürgen Becker (Eds.), *Festschrift für Heinz Hübner*, Berlin 1984, pp. 191–214.

[73] According to Carl Anton von Martini, *Allgemeines Recht der Staaten*, Wien 1788, p. 31.

[74] Carl Gottlieb Svarez, *Inwiefern können und müssen Gesetze kurz sein?* (Vorträge vor der Mittwochsgesellschaft), in: Hermann Conrad und Gerd Kleinheyer (Eds.), *Vorträge über Recht und Staat von Carl Gottlieb Svarez* (1746–1798), Köln 1960, p. 629.

[75] See Mohnhaupt, *Potestas legislatoria* (as note 38), pp. 231–233.

[76] Bodin, *Les six livres* (as note 39), p. 161.

[77] Lauterbach, *Collegii theorico practici* (as note 61), p. 65.

form and differing instrumentality were bound together into a unitary legislative power referred to as *potestas legislatoria*.[78] The Prussian jurist Carl Gottlieb Suarez stated in 1791 that "the legislative power includes the *ius leges ferendi, leges abrogandi, leges declarandi, exemptiones a legibus concedendi, Privilegia, Dispensationes*".[79] Also the *ius publicandi, interpretandi* were regarded as an integral part of the *potestas legislatoria*.[80] The bringing together of all of these legislative activities was also derived from the fundamental source of Roman law.[81] This occurred under the characteristic title *De principe legibus soluto*. Given the definition of the legislative branch in these terms, the reception and application of Roman-canonical law – the *ius commune* – became possible by basing these on a tacit decision by the *voluntas principis*.[82] The comprehensive grouping together of all legislative activities was grounded primarily on the absolutist claim by sole rulers to create law. The 1665 Danish *Lex Regia* of Fredrick III most incisively established this monopolisation of all legislative activities in the person of the ruler *suo arbitratu*.[83] Papal legislative authority also served as a paradigm for the model of legislation constructed in this manner, which embraced all rule creation including privileges, dispensations and dogma.[84]

The Variety of Names for the Products of Legislation

The lack of certainty under constitutional law led to an open terminology for the legislative acts of the legislator-sovereigns. This is particularly vividly illustrated by the Italian example: *Leggi, ordinazioni, provisioni, dichiarazioni, ordini, bandi, gride, editti, pregoni, sazioni, dispacci, lettere,*

---

[78]See Mohnhaupt, *Potestas legislatoria* (as note 38), pp. 208–214.

[79]Svarez, *Allgemeines Staatsrecht*, in: Conrad/Kleinheyer, *Vorträge* (as note 74), p. 13.

[80]According to Wiguläus Xaver Aloys von Kreittmayr, *Grundriß des Allgemeinen, Deutsch- und Bayrischen Staatsrechtes*, vol. I, 2nd ed., München 1789, p. 153.

[81]See e.g. Joannis Carolus van Wachendorff, *Dissertationum trias, Trajecti a Rhenum* 1730, pp. 104 ss.; Cicero, *Ad Atticum epistularum libri sedecim*, III, 23, in: Cicero in twenty eight volumes, XXII: Letters to Atticus, Books I–VI, Cambridge/Mass. 1980, p. 248.

[82]Carl Friedrich Häberlin, *Repertorium des Teutschen Staats- und Lehnrechts*, vol. IV, Leipzig 1795, p. 365.

[83]Petrus Höyelsinus, *Regis Christiani Quinti Leges Danicae, Hauniae* 1710, p. 1; Michael Stolleis, *Condere leges et interpretari. Gesetzgebungsmacht und Staatsbildung im 17. Jahrhundert*, in: *SZGerm* 101 (1984), pp. 89–116.

[84]Peter Landau, *Quellen und Bedeutung des Gratianischen Dekretes*, in: Giorgio Lombardi (Ed.), *Studia et Documenta Historiae et Iuris* (1986), pp. 230 s.

circolari may only attain *potere normativo* with the *placito regio*.[85] The Spanish *Novísima Recopilación* posited this legal normativity in the same way for the *pragmática, cédula, provisión, orden, edicto, pregón o bandos de las Justicias o Magistrados publios*.[86] The Portuguese history of legislation paints a similar picture to which Airton Seelaender has recently referred: *Edicta generalia, quae dicimus Cartas patentes de Leis, a Regiis Diplomatibus, Alvarás, Litteris Regis patentibus non obsignatis, Portarias, Decretis, et Regiis Resolutionibus nemo inter nos ignorat*, as stated by Mello de Freire in 1789.[87] Numerous names also appear within the German speaking area, especially for "Policy" ordinances.[88] A general perplexity may be observed within the European legal literature as to how the normativity of these laws is to be assessed. The "dreadful mixing" of types of law was objected to and led to the codification debates of the late 18th century. The following criteria serve as clarification for the plurality of names: the promulgation of statutes, general legislation (*lex generalis*) and special legislation (*lex specialis*), the statute types of Roman law and the enactment of legislation with or without the involvement of the estates.

In this way in all European states the names for legislation under the *ius commune* overlapped with those under the indigenous *ius patriae*. This also applies for the countries that were not under the sway of the reception of Roman law, such as the Kingdom of Poland and the *Copus Helveticum*.[89]

The Legislator-Sovereign and Legislation as a Hallmark of Sovereignty

Under the *Ancien Régime* legislative power was the first prerequisite of sovereignty. Legislative competence was generally speaking vested in the sovereign ruler or in the estates, or also jointly in both of these sovereign bodies. A clear description of competences came only in the constitutions

---

[85] Enrico Besta, *Fonti del diritto italiano dalla caduta dell' impero romano sino ai tempi nostri*, 2nd ed., Milano 1950, p. 171.

[86] According to the decision of Charles III of 1767 (ley 12, titulo 3), in: *Novísima Recopilación*; Antonio Xavier Perez y Lopez, *Teatro de la legislación universal de España é Indias*, Tomo XVIII, Madrid 1797, p. 108.

[87] De Mello Freire, *Institutiones juris civilis Lusitani* (as note 64), p. 6 (§ V); Seelaender, Polizei (as note 40), pp. 50–52; Raphael Ribeiro, *Historia do direito Portuguez*, Lisboa 1923, p. 538.

[88] See Mohnhaupt, *Potestas legislatoria* (as note 38), pp. 216–219;

[89] See for further detail Mohnhaupt, *Grundlinien* (as note 8), p. 150.

of the 19th century. However, there had been quasi-constitutional contracts, privileges, customary rights, *fueros* and *coutumes* since the middle ages regulating the relationship between the ruler and the estates and that granted the estates various participatory rights, from the *votum consultativum* through to the *votum decisivum* in the enactment of legislation. Although these legal bases for the participation of the estates in the enactment of legislation existed, the exercise of this "right" was however in most cases a question of the political power relations between the ruler and the estates.[90] Original participatory rights of the states in the enactment of legislation increasingly withered away in the absolutist state towards the non-binding consultation, or assemblies of the estates were simply no longer convened by the ruler.[91] However, the lack of participation by the estates meant a danger that the legislation lacked legitimacy and dignity, though absolutist rulers believed that they could do without these.[92] Specialist selected commissions, universities and courts became advisors on legislative matters. The participatory rights of the estates were undermined and circumvented in the dualist corporatist state, although not formally abolished.

Where the estates had the sole right to enact legislation, such as in the Northern provinces of the Netherlands and in the Kingdom of Poland, the *voluntas* at the same time amounted to a prerequisite for sovereignty as well as the basis for the validity of legislation. In these territories the estates stood in the position of a sole sovereign ruler and also based their legislative competence on the *Voluntas* theory.

The Legal Character of Legislation: Binding Force Under Contract or Imperatives

In order to grant a statute the highest degree of binding force and to detach it from the sole authority of the ruler, the argument that statute amounted to a contract was used repeatedly. However, this could only be established

---

[90]See Friedrich Tezner, *Technik und Geist des ständisch-monarchischen Staatsrechts*, Leipzig 1901, pp. 13 ss.

[91]As e.g. in the Kingdom of Bohemia under Ferdinand II, in Denmark under Fredrich III (1665) and in France after Louis XIV.

[92]See further in general Lothar Schilling, *Krisenbewältigung durch Verfahren? Zu den Funktionen konsensualer Gesetzgebung im Frankreich des 16. und frühen 17. Jahrhunderts*, in: Barbara Stollberg-Rilinger (Ed.), *Vormoderne politische Verfahren*, in: *Zeitschrift für historische Forschung*, Beiheft 25, München 2001, pp. 449–491 (479–484).

if the representative organs of the estates were in some way involved in the ruler's legislative procedure. These constructs based on mutual consent were grounded by reference to the commentators of the late middle ages. In this regard the renowned dictum of Baldus played a significant role: *Lex transit in contractum*.[93] That is to say, such arguments played a role in situations of crisis between the ruler and the estates, such as for example in 16th century France during the religious disturbances between the crown and the religious parties of the estates.[94]

The relevant legal status of the product of legislation follows from the differing forms of participation by the ruler and the estates in the enactment of legislation. In cases in which the monarch and the estates engaged with one another as equals – such as for example in the old German Reich – it was undisputed that imperial laws had the nature of an agreement. They were agreements between the Emperor and the Reich estates, and were designated as *pacta* or "understandings".[95] Nevertheless, on the lowest level *vis-à-vis* the subjects, these agreements had the status of an imperative in the old Reich. In the Kingdom of Poland the estates possessed a *liberum veto* with the result that a statute could only be enacted with the consent of all of the estates. The King was only the promulgator of statutes. Accordingly, the absolutist principle of legislation in Poland was the exact opposite: *Quod populo placuit . . . valeat*.[96]

Legislation: Between Consistency and Adaptation

The efficacy of every legal order depends on the extent to which legislation (1) offers calculable certainty through consistency and (2) is able to react to new requirements in state and society through its adaptability.

---

[93] See Dieter Wyduckel, *Princeps legibus solutus. Eine Untersuchung zur frühmodernen Rechts- und Staatslehre (Schriften zur Verfassungsgeschichte*, vol. 30), Berlin 1979, p. 86; Heinz Mohnhaupt, Vertragskonstruktion und fingierter *Vertrag zur Sicherung von Normativität: Gesetz, Privileg*, Verfassung, in: Jean François Kervégan und Heinz Mohnhaupt (Eds.), *Gesellschaftliche Freiheit und vertragliche Bindung in Rechtsgeschichte und Philosophie (Ius Commune, Sonderhefte* 120), Frankfurt am Main 1999, pp. 1–33 (9–15).

[94] For more detail and examples see Lothar Schilling, *Normsetzung in der Krise. Zum Gesetzgebungsverständnis im Frankreich der Religionskriege (Studien zur europäischen Rechtsgeschichte*, vol. 197), Frankfurt am Main 2005, pp. 359–370.

[95] Ebel, Geschichte (as note 70), p. 68.

[96] Cited from Hermann Vahle, *Die Rezeption römischer Staatstheorie in der zweiten Hälfte des 16. Jahrhunderts durch Jan Zamoyski*, phil. Diss., Bochum 1968, p. 37.

Case law and legal science are also to be regarded as concurrent instruments for adaptation and amendment.[97] Statutes were required to serve the *bonum publicum*, which however did not have any static content and therefore had to be reformulated through legislation from scratch each time. If the state of the "common polity" changed, then "the old statutes [could] also no longer remain on the books and ... one would likewise have to amend them".[98] Similarly, a distinction was drawn between *lex mutabilis* and *lex immutabilis*.[99] Adaptation was required in two senses: (1) statutes should be adapted to the relevant form of the state or government. According to this theory, legislation was to be formulated differently in a monarchy, an aristocracy or a democracy. This requirement was traced back to the Aristotelian doctrine of state configuration and was reinvigorated by Montesquieu and the Italian Filangieri.[100] (2) Legislation should comply with the relevant characteristics of the country and its inhabitants as well as take local and regional conditions into account. This was a requirement for the *lex mutabilis*, which had to react to the need for chancing *utilitas* and *necessitas*. These legislative environment theories, as they could be named,[101] thus contradicted a legislative order based on equality and universal application. With the assistance of various regulatory instruments of the *Potestas legislatoria*, it was possible to abide by this requirement to enact differentiated law. The adaptation of legislation in the Northern Netherlands, where legislation was corrected according to the "nature and characteristics of our country" as well as according to the "opportunity of the current times",[102] was particularly pronounced. Precisely against the backdrop of

---

[97] See the numerous examples from the history of dogma in Klaus Luig, *Historische Formen der Anpassung veralteten Gesetzesrechts*, in: Idem, *Römisches Recht, Naturrecht, Nationales Recht* (Bibliotheca eruditorum, Band 22), Goldbach 1998, pp. 173–189.

[98] Wolff, *Vernünfftige Gedancken* (as note 56), p. 429.

[99] See Thomas of Aquinas, *Das Gesetz. Summa Theologica* (Deutsche Thomas-Ausgabe, 13), Heidelberg/Graz 1977, Art. I, Quaestio 97, 1, p. 133.("de mutatione legum"); Simon, "Gute Policey" (as note 59), pp. 63–70; Gagnér, Studien (as note 6), pp. 274 s.

[100] Montesquieu, *De l' esprit des lois* (1748); Gaetano Filangieri, *La scienza della legislazione* I-VIII, Venezia 1782–1791.

[101] See Heinz Mohnhaupt, *Montesquieu und die legislatorische Milieu-Theorie während der Aufklärungszeit in Deutschland*, in: Gerhard Lingelbach und Heiner Lück (Eds.), *Deutsches Recht zwischen Sachsenspiegel und Aufklärung*. Rolf Lieberwirth zum 70. Geburtstag, Frankfurt am Main (et al.) 1991, pp. 177–191.

[102] See Anne Syberdinus de Blécourt, *Het Onzwerp-1550 van het Ommerlander Landrecht*, in: *Tijdschrift voor Rechtsgeschiedenis* (TRG) 12 (1933), pp. 346 s.; *Revision des Landrecht van Drente*, in: J.G.C. Joosting (Ed.), *Drentsch Plakkaatboek*, vol. I, Leiden 1912, p. 169.

the current tumultuous economic development and the surge in the generation of legislation, adaptation and consistency prove to be a lasting question within states that enact legislation to the present day.[103]

Generalisation and Differentiation as Alternative Models in Legislation

The generalisation and codification of law aimed to achieve unity and universality in legislation.[104] The Enlightenment 18th century and the "national" 19th century followed this trend against the backdrop of extreme legal pluralism within Europe. The Roman-canonical *ius commune* as well as the variety of individual special rights held by the estates and the *iura singularia* on the one hand overlapped with local and regional *iura particularia* on the other. Both in theory and in practice, these *iura specialia* almost always took precedence over the generally applicable sources of law.[105] A great *incertitudo iuris* arose out of this complexity in the sources of law. The "Differentien" literature as a form of comparative study sought to ascertain these differences between the two bodies of law with the purpose or harmonisation and unification. This occurred using the tools of comparative study, which focused in particular on legislation.[106]

The contrast between the general statute – the *lex generalis* – and the individual or local statute – the *leges speciales* – has pervaded the entire history of the theory of sources of law and legal practice since Roman antiquity. An expression of this tension is the legal couplet of compliance with a rule and exceptions, as represented by the *ius commune* and the *privilegium*, as well as the *dispensatio* or the *ius singulare*: *Privilegium est quod aliquem*

---

[103]See Dietrich Murswiek, *Dynamik der Technik und Anpassung des Rechts: Kreislaufgesetzgebung*, in: Burkhardt Ziemske et al. (Eds.), *Staatsphilosophie und Rechtspolitik. Festschrift für Martin Kriele*, München 1997, pp. 651–676.

[104]Hasso Hofmann, *Das Postulat der Allgemeinheit des Gesetzes*, in: Christian Starck (Ed.), Die Allgemeinheit des Gesetzes, Göttingen 1987, pp. 34 ss.

[105]See Klaus Luig, *Universales Recht und partikulares Recht in den Meditationes ad Pandectas von Augustin Leyser*, in: Idem, *Römisches Recht* (as note 97), pp. 109–132; Heinz Mohnhaupt, *Zum Verhältnis von Region und ius particulare in Europa während des 16.–18. Jahrhunderts. Historische Notizen zu einem aktuellen Thema*, in: Enzo Sciacca (Ed.), *L' Europa e le sue regioni*, Palermo 1993, pp. 226–238.

[106]Heinz Mohnhaupt, *Die Differentienliteratur als Ausdruck eines methodischen Prinzips früher Rechtsvergleichung*, in: Bernard Durand and Laurent Mayali (Eds.), *Excerptiones iuris:* Studies in Honor of André Gouron, Berkeley 2000, pp. 439–458.

a iure communi privat ....[107] The generalisation and differentiation of law accordingly represent different systemic models, i.e. also different ideals of justice and social forms. However, under the *Ancien Régime* they were not strict alternatives within law creation, but rather were often used together.[108] The enlightened Prussian Civil Code of 1794 – the "General national law for the Prussian states" – is an interesting socio-political example of this since, despite its general claim to validity, it combined and preserved the personal and individual system of privileges and the territorial principle of different provincial laws.[109] Even today, lawmakers are often forced to enact legislation applying to individual cases that neutralises the Enlightenment principle of equality and universality. However, at the end of the 18th century, the ideal of the universality and equality of the law dominated the codification debates on optimal legislation in the name of social *égalité*, of which the French "Civil Code" of 1804 provides the most important example.

On the Normativity of Case Law and Legal Science

Experience gained from the history of legislation illustrates that the "statute" cannot provide a comprehensive and definitive body of regulation, even as the dominant normative rule. Thus within the legal system there is always a need for self-correction and fine-tuning by case law and legal science. This is an enduring task of both of these competing sources of law.[110] It is also proved by legal history.

The Status of Case Law as a Source of Law

The normative proximity of statutes to judgments has always been assessed differently through the different legal eras. A binding precedental effect of a judgment cannot be inferred under Roman law, although the *mos iudiciorum*[111] suggests a paradigmatic function of judgments, i.e. that in cases in which statutes were unclear a judicial practice attained the authority of

---

[107]Ennio Cortese, *La norma giuridica* II, Milano 1964, p. 45.

[108]See Heinz Mohnhaupt, *Untersuchungen zum Verhältnis Privileg und Kodifikation im 18. und 19.* Jahrhundert, in: *Ius Commune* 5 (1975), pp. 71–121.

[109]Damiano Canale, *La costituzione delle differenze. Giusnaturalismo e codificazione del diritto civile nella* Prussia del '700, Torino 2000, pp. 29 ss.

[110]See most recently Stephan Meder, *Die Krise des Nationalstaates und ihre Folgen für das Kodifikationsprinzip*, in: *Juristenzeitung* 61 (2006), pp. 477–484 (here pp. 482 s.).

[111]Codex 2.3.14.

a *vis legis*. Roman law recognises the problem of having to obtain legal stabilisation through the practice of the courts where the statutory situation was unclear in paragraph 1.3.38 of the Digest.[112] In such cases, it could be necessary for the judge himself to create rules in order to ground his decision, which would have a certain precedental effect[113] and accordingly lead to the reciprocal overlapping of legislative and judicial rule creation.

The age of the Enlightenment, which called for the separation of these "powers", was itself all too aware of the problem of such a mixing of tasks. If the "judge were to become the lawmaker", this was seen as a danger for "bourgeois freedom" at the end of the 18th century.[114] On the European continent the legislature attempted to solve the problem through a new law of procedure – even before a reorganisation of substantive law. This occurred in Piedmont and Savoy,[115] France, Bavaria and Prussia.[116] Of course, unitary case law was not thereby brought about, since no statute is capable of formulating unequivocal and definitive rules for the new problem cases within social life that arise on a daily basis. In addition, the oft maligned *diversitas legum* hindered the development of uniform case law.[117] Hence, the degree of the normative binding force of judicial practice remained indeterminate and swayed between the status of a "guideline", a paradigm, an analogy, *vis legis* and *auctoritas*. Nonetheless, case law proved to be particularly valuable

---

[112]D. 1.3.38.: *Nam imperator noster Severus rescripsit in ambiguitatibus quae ex legibus profiscuntur consuetudinem aut rerum perpetuo similiter iudicatarum auctoritatem vim legis optinere debere.*

[113]On the system of prejudices and the much criticised system of bias see Werner Kirchner, *Generell bindende Gerichtsentscheidungen im reichsdeutschen und österreichischen Recht*, Leipzig 1932, pp. 7 ss.; Ulrike Müssig, *Geschichte des Richterrechts und der Präjudizienbindung auf dem europäischen Kontinent*, in: ZNR 28 (2006), pp. 79–106.

[114]According to Svarez, *Inwiefern können und müssen Gesetze kurz sein?* (as note 74), p. 628.

[115]See Filippo Ranieri, *Bibliographie der Gesetzgebung des Privatrechts und Prozessrechts/Italien*, in: Helmut Coing (Ed.), *Handbuch der Quellen und Literatur der neueren europäischen Privatrechtsgeschichte*, II 2, München 1976, pp. 146 s., with regard to the 1651 *Nuovi ordini* of Emanuele Filiberto.

[116]*Project des Codici Fridericiani Marchici, oder eine, nach Sr. Königl. Majestät von Preussen Selbst vorgeschriebenen Plan entworfene Cammergerichts-Ordnung, nach welcher alle Processe in einem Jahr durch drey Instantzen zum Ende gebracht werden sollen und müssen*, Berlin 1748 (reproduced with an introduction by Heinz Mohnhaupt, Milano 2000).

[117]Peter Oestmann, *Rechtsvielfalt vor Gericht. Rechtsanwendung und Partikularrecht im Alten Reich* (Rechtsprechung. Materialien und Studien, vol. 18), Frankfurt am Main 2002.

as a guide to orienting legal practice, which was documented through the publication of collections of judgments throughout Europe.[118] In this regard, in 1702 Pinault for example established the great utility of collections of judgments, since they could contribute to avoiding contradictory judgments: *parce que rendant la Jurisprudence dúne Cour supérieure plus connue dans son Ressort, ils la rendent plus constante, ils en fixent les maximes et en assurent les principes.*[119] The following examples of the statutory binding force of court judgments in Europe are worthy of mention: the *decreta communia* of the Imperial Chamber Court [*Reichskammergericht*],[120] the *assentos* of the *Casa da Supliçãcao do Cível* in Portugal,[121] the French *arrêts de règlements des Cours souveraines . . . pour être observées comme loix*[122] and the Spanish *autos acortados*, which acquired the force of law as judicial interpretative decisions if they were promulgated by the King.[123] Such judicial decisions were also legitimised under customary law as *stylus curiae*.

The Status of Legal Science as a Source of Law

Legal science was directly linked to the primary source of "statutes" and the unstable source of "case law". However, the question as to its status as a source of law arises in an entirely different way. It may even be doubtful whether the notion of source of law may be applied at all to "legal science", because even the *communis opinio doctorum* which acted as the basis for a doctrine endorsed by the majority of legal scientists from the middle ages into the 18th century would according to our current understanding have to be regarded more as an "argument" than as a "source". Nonetheless, it is beyond dispute that legal science participated in the formation of rules

---

[118]See the collections of case law and "consilia" in: Coing, Handbuch II 2 (as note 115), pp. 1113–1445.

[119]Matthieu Pinault, *Recueils d' Arrêts notables du Parlement de Tournay*, vol. I, *Valenciennes* 1702, Au Lecteur, s.p. (p. III).

[120]See Nicolaus Hieronymus Gundling, *Ausführliche und gründliche Discourse über Die sämtlichen* Pandecten, Franckfurt 1739, p. 37.

[121]Paschoal José de Mello Freire, *Historiae juris civilis Lusitani liber singularis*, 4th ed., Olisipone 1806, pp. 154 s.

[122]See Claude-Joseph de Ferriere, *Dictionnaire de droit et de pratique*, vol. I, Paris 1762, p. 121.

[123]Alfonso Garcia Gallo, *Curso de historia del derecho Español*, vol. I, 5th ed., Madrid 1950, p. 354.

for the application of law – above all during eras in which there was a clear dogmatic legal science, though on the other hand no sufficient body of legislation. There are maxims, principles and legal rules that are not based on a statute but nonetheless impliedly have binding force. Gustav Hugo stated in this regard that "statutes are not the only source of legal truths".[124] This occurred against the backdrop of the Roman law that applied in Germany, as interpreted by the Historical School of Law. In this regard the *ius commune* in Germany prior to the entry into force of the German Civil Code (1.1.1900) can, as regards its effect, be regarded as law without legislation.[125] As a rule statute law is systematically processed, moderated and – as in the case of the *ius commune* – possibly also replaced by legal science.[126] This can already be ascertained from the glosses of the middle ages, in the Glossators, the Commentators and their significance for judicial practice. In 1809 the German philosopher and jurist Feuerbach spoke of the scientific construction of legislation, stating that: "Where legislation ends, doctrine starts, which is different from it but in direct contact with it". This was an issue especially in 19th century Germany.[127] Accordingly, within the history of law there appears to be a ranking order of the sources of law with statutes at the pinnacle, as an expression of unstable criteria for appraisal, to which legal science was also subordinate.

Criticism of the State of Law

Criticism of the state of law is long-standing. It relates to all three types of source of law, although predominantly to legislation and hence to the uncertainty of the statutory basis for the courts' decisions. Criticism was initially sparked off by the complexity of the pluralism of sources of law

---

[124]Gustav Hugo, *Die Gesetze sind nicht die einzige Quelle der juristischen Wahrheiten*, in: Idem, Civilistisches Magazin, vol. 4, Berlin 1815, pp. 89–134 (94, 114).

[125]See Hans-Peter Haferkamp, Der Jurist, das Recht und das Leben, in: *Fakultätsspiegel Sommersemester 2005 (Universität Köln; Veröffentlichung des Vereins zur Förderung der Rechtswissenschaft* n. F. 3), ed. by the Verein zur Förderung der Rechtswissenschaft, Köln 2005, p. 87.

[126]For this function of legal science see e.g. Walter Jellinek, *Schöpferische Rechtswissenschaft*. Inaugural lecture by the rector of the Christian- Albrechts-Universität on 5 March 1928, Kiel 1928, where he also refers to the "great affinity" between the legal scholar "and the judge" (p. 15).

[127]See Haferkamp, Der Jurist (as note 125), pp. 83–98.

– i.e. the *incertitudo iuris* – [128] and above all by Roman law and its mixture of valid and obsolete bodies of rules. This resulted in a major need for interpretation and adaptation through legal science, which only further raised the uncertainty. In the optimistic belief in the normative omnipotence of the legislature, the remedy to the solution was seen in legislation. The *référé législatif* in France and the requirement for a reference of all *casus dubii* and *dubia iuris* for decision by the legislature served this purpose in the 17th and 18th centuries.[129] The ideal of the *ius certum* became a much considered topic in discussions on legislation during the Enlightenment. The *Ius Romanum* was designated as an *amplissimum et vastum Oceanum iuris*.[130] The Italian Muratori expressly discussed the *difetti della Giurisprudenza* in a special book with the same title.[131] In Portugal in 1747, Luis Antonio Verney criticised this state of affairs as representative of the European legal situation in his *Verdadeiro Método de estudar*. After listing all the *difeitos*, he called for a clear system of the sources of law, new tasks for legislation and the removal of legal uncertainty, namely a *cienca certa de toda a justicia* and *leis certas e breves*.[132] These were pan-European claims which were aimed at systematic codification in individual countries. In Spain for example, the European Enlightenment basis for legislation ran: *Felicidad, rigorosa etica, sumo bien*. In conclusion, a brief reference has to be made to two points of view which are significant for the European history of legislation.

---

[128]This was a much discussed issue; see e.g. Michael Heinrich Gribner (Praeses), *De iure incerto ex dubia legum, quibus utimur, auctoritate oriundo dissertatio* (respondens: August Garlichs), Wittenberg 1715; Rudolph Johann Ernestus, *Dissertatio iuridica de iuris incertitudine*, Altdorf 1718; Johann Friedrich Boeckelmann (Praeses), *De incertitudine iuris et remediis adversus eam* (repondens: Magnus von Wedderkopf), Heidelberg 1664.

[129]Examples in Johann Jacob Moser, *Von der Landeshoheit in Regierungssachen überhaupt* (Neues teutsches Staatsrecht, vol. 16,1), Franckfurt und Leipzig 1772, pp. 321–323.

[130]Giacomo Antonio Marta, *Compilatio totius iuris controversi ex omnibus decisionibus universi orbis, quae hucusque extant impressae*, Venetiis 1620, Praefatio.

[131]Lodovico Antonio Muratori, *Dei difetti della giurisprudenza*, 2nd ed., in Venezia 1743.

[132]Luis Antonio Verney, *Verdadeiro método de estudar para ser util à republica*, 1747, here cited according to the edition by Antonio Salgado, vol. IV, Lisboa 1952, pp. 188, 191, 224.

Comparative Observation of Legislation and Conditions of Law

During the 18th century, the work of legislation was accompanied by a comparative observation of law and legislation. Comparison was adopted in all sciences as a means of obtaining knowledge – including for legislation.[133] Rules and exceptions, the general and the particular, equality and difference, as well as similarity and analogies were thereby determined. The "Differentien" literature provides an early example of this approach.[134] The field of investigation for comparative observation was to be Europe. One of the basic questions during the Enlightenment age was to what extent general equality was possible through legislation, and a whether a differentiation of individual law was necessary.[135] The cosmopolitan Enlightenment conceptual trend called for a "universal history of legislation", in order "to expand and improve our insights into the field of legislation [through] comparisons ... of different legislation" and hence to be able to discern the reciprocal influences of the statutes of different peoples on one another.[136] In doing so it was also possible to rely on Aristotle.[137] The Portuguese minister Pombal declared in this regard in 1768 that the lawmaker in the enlightened era of reform was no longer able to change the form and constitution of war-torn states through the force of his genius alone.[138] The scrutiny of other European statutes and lawmakers was indispensable for this. This pragmatic, far-reaching and even conceptionless "comparison" amounted to an attempt to order the much discussed parlous bodies of sources of law in a straightforward manner and to introduce systematic codification.

---

[133] Overview in Heinz Mohnhaupt, *Historische Vergleichung im Bereich von Staat und Recht vom späten 18. Jahrhundert bis zur Mitte des 19. Jahrhunderts, Beobachtungen zur deutschen Bezugnahme auf Italien*, in: Aldo Mazzacane und Reiner Schulze (Eds.), *Die deutsche und italienische Rechtskultur im Zeitalter der Vergleichung* (Schriften zur Europäischen Rechts- und Verfassungsgeschichte, vol. 15), Berlin 1995, pp. 31–62; Idem, *Vergleichende Beobachtung von Staat, Gesellschaft und Recht im 18. Jahrhundert als Vorform der modernen Rechtsvergleichung*, in: Comparative Law (Nihon University), vol. 14, Tokyo 1997, pp. 1–24.

[134] Mohnhaupt, *Die Differentienliteratur* (as note 106).

[135] See further above in Section about „Generalisation".

[136] According to Johann Friedrich Reitemeier, *Encyclopädie und Geschichte der Rechte in Deutschland. Zum Gebrauch akademischer Vorlesungen*, Göttingen 1785, Vorrede p. XXIII.

[137] Aristotle, *Politics*, book 4 (1288 b-1289 a); on the comparison between legislation: book 7 (1324 b).

[138] Here citing from Heinrich Schäfer, *Geschichte von Portugal*, Band V, Gotha 1854, pp. 378 s.

Codification as an Idea and Form for Legislation During the Enlightenment Era

The Enlightenment criticism of legal conditions was intended to reorder the law and hence also reorder society. An end was to be put to the above all oft bemoaned "dreadful mixing" of the individual fields of "national law" [*Landrecht*], the "political Codex" and the "Polity Codex".[139] Private law should above all receive unequivocal consent in a new form, as a comprehensive and systematic code through the elimination or reformation of Roman law. The term "codification" was to be used for such a statute developed out of the spirit of Enlightenment rationalism,[140] even though this concept is used today with little reflection for almost every historical product of legislation and legislative projects. The codifications of the Enlightenment era were authoritatively prepared from the legal science of the *ius commune*. The early Enlightenment writings on *Prudentia Legislatoria* can serve as an example of this.[141] "Every codification is a work of science".[142] This did not however deprive legal science of the possibility or requirement for it to develop its nature as a source of law in those cases in which codification did not meet the expectations placed in it, also because it could not fulfil them. However, the Enlightenment codifications adopted the optimistic and idealistic view that legal science could be turned into an indispensable competing source through codification. This was furthered by the prohibition stated in the "General national law for the Prussian states" (1794) and in the Austrian "General Civil Code" (1811) on interpreting the code in a generally binding manner through case law and legal science. In this way the 18th century prohibition on interpretation of the Regent according to the Roman paradigm in Justinian's *Corpus iuris civilis* was expanded into a general prohibition on commentary, in order to render impossible any law creating power other than codification.[143] However, the experiences of the modern history of

---

[139]See Friedrich Philipp Karl Boell, *Journal der Gesetzgebung des achtzehnten Jahrhunderts*, 1st issue, Frankfurt und Leipzig 1786, Vorbericht s.p. (p. V)

[140]For a historical overview summarising the concept of codification, see Barbara Dölemeyer, article on *Kodifizierung/Kodifikation*, in: *Der Neue Pauly. Enzyklopädie der Antike*, vol. XIV, Stuttgart/Weimar 2000, col. 1003–1009.

[141]Range and compilation in: Heinz Mohnhaupt (Ed.), *Prudentia Legislatoria. Fünf Schriften über die Gesetzgebungsklugheit aus dem 17. und 18. Jahrhundert*, München 2003.

[142]As correctly pointed out by Pio Caroni, *Das entzauberte Gesetzbuch*, in: Idem, *Gesetz und Gesetzbuch. Beiträge zu einer Kodifikationsgeschichte*, Basel/Genf/München 2003, p. 132, with reference to Peter Liver.

[143]See Mohnhaupt, *Potestas legislatoria* (as note 38), pp. 226–230.

legislation repeatedly show that even the best codification cannot secure a monopoly on law creation by the legislature and the *ius certum* sought by it. Along with their competence over interpretation, legal science and case law are nowadays competitors or assistants in the legislative process, with differing law creating powers, whilst of course the Constitution has now taken on an overriding leadership and control function in the creation of law. Confronted with an over-abundance of legislation in constitutional states determined by shifting political forces and an increasing flood of individual legislation, the resigned slogan is now for "de-codification"[144] along with the "disenchanted statute book", as Caroni has aptly put it.[145] Therefore, the need has arisen for a larger space in order to interpret legislation and the increasing number of statutes.

---

[144]Natalino Irti, *L'età della decodificazione*, 4th ed., Milano 1999.
[145]Caroni, *Das entzauberte Gesetzbuch* (as note 142), pp. 125–163.

Chapter 5
The Concept and Means of Legal Interpretation in the 18th Century

Jan SCHRÖDER

In this chapter I would like to present some characteristics of the *theory* of legal (statutory) interpretation in the 18th century.[1] As these characteristics emerge more clearly when compared with older theories, I will also make reference to the early modern period, beginning with the year 1500. I will concentrate on the German-speaking area of Europe and on two questions in particular: first, how did the *concept* of legal interpretation develop in the period between 1500 and 1800? Second, how did the *means* of interpretation develop throughout this time? Thus, we shall be dealing with the comprehensiveness of statutory interpretation on the one hand and the content of interpretation on the other; that is to say, we will first examine the quantity and then the quality of interpretation. I will show that in relation to the concept of interpretation, the developmental trend was towards a restrictive approach, i.e., towards a reduction of the interpretational tolerance afforded to the judiciary. With regard to the means of interpretation, the trend was towards the advancement of empirical elements in interpretive methods – towards a "devaluation" or "positivisation" of the interpretive process. Then, in the section "Background: The Modification of the Concept of Law in

---

[1] See generally Vogenauer, Stefan: *Die Auslegung von Gesetzen in England und auf dem Kontinent. Eine vergleichende Untersuchung der Rechtsprechung und ihrer historischen Grundlagen*, Tübingen 2001, pp. 430 sqq., 669 sqq.; Schröder, Jan: *Recht als Wissenschaft. Geschichte der juristischen Methode vom Humanismus bis zur historischen Schule (1500–1850)*, München 2001, pp. 48 sqq., 130 sqq.; idem (ed.): *Theorie der Interpretation vom Humanismus bis zur Romantik – Rechtswissenschaft, Philosophie, Theologie*, Stuttgart 2001 (papers on legal interpretation by Maximiliane Kriechbaum, p. 47 sqq., Klaus Luig, p. 133 sqq., Gerhard Otte, p. 191 sqq., Joachim Hruschka, p. 203 sqq., Joachim Rückert, p. 287 sqq.).

J. SCHRÖDER (✉)
Faculty of Law, University of Tübingen, Geschwister-Scholl-Platz, D-72076, Tübingen
e-mail: jan.schroeder@jura.uni-tuebingen.de; ejschroeder@web.de

MORIGIWA, Y. et al. (eds.), *Interpretation of Law in the Age of Enlightenment*, Law and Philosophy Library 95,
DOI 10.1007/978-94-007-1506-6_5, © Springer Science+Business Media B.V. 2011

the Early Modern Period" of this chapter, I will describe the background for these observations, and some concluding remarks will follow (section "Concluding Remarks").

The Concept of Statutory Interpretation

Sixteenth and Early Seventeenth Century

What did one understand by the term "statutory interpretation" in the 16th and early 17th centuries? Based on a modern legal understanding, one would most likely define it as the determination of the meaning of any given law. In the early modern period, however, no such completely standardised notion of interpretation existed, and the term was understood in a much broader sense. In fact, several authors did not limit their understanding of interpretation to the determination of the meaning of legal texts alone. Rather, they extended it to nearly every legal activity including, therefore, public legal education.[2] Although these authors represented the extreme end of the interpretive scale, they also constituted a minority in this debate.

In opposition to these minority voices, the most prevalent opinion throughout the 16th century was that interpretation was only concerned with the correct understanding of individual statutes. However, this "narrow" understanding of interpretation was also accompanied by the expectation that judges would exercise a broad discretion: a discretion which included processes that today would be considered as developing the law. This narrow interpretation was based primarily on the apostil from the 13th century on the word *interpretationem* in D.1, 2, 1, which states that *interpretatio* describes the obvious meaning of a word (*vocabuli apertam significationem*). However, from the commentary on the Digest, it is clear that "interpretation" was also understood in a broader sense to include the correction, restriction and expansion of the law (*pro correctione, arctatione et prorogatione*). Even so, all authors agreed that "interpretation" included

---

[2]See e.g. Hotomanus, Franciscus: *Iurisconsultus, sive de optimo genere iuris interpretandi*, Basel 1559 (grammatical, dialectical and juridical interpretation, dialectical interpretation concerns the scientifical order, p. 63 sqq.); Forster, Valentin Wilhelm: *Interpres, sive de interpretatione juris libri duo*, Wittenberg 1613, ed. Otto, Everardus: *Thesaurus iuris Romani*, II, Leiden 1726, col. 945–1068, lib. 1, cap. 1, nr. 5, col. 956 (*Breviter, dicimus interpretationem juris, eorum quae in jure continentur, rectam & artificiosam explanationem aut explicationem, & expositionem*); Placcius, Vincentius: *De jurisconsulto perfecto, sive interpretatione legum in genere*, Stockholm and Hamburg 1693, pp. 53, 186 sqq.

both of these elements; indeed, both factors are part of interpretation, and all treatises pertaining to statutory interpretation include both factors.[3]

With respect to the extent of interpretation, this implies that the interpreter was entitled not only to determine the literal meaning of a law but also to restrict or extend the law according to its *mens* or "ratio". Indeed, this does not come as a surprise to the modern-day lawyer. Nevertheless, it is important to note that by employing a broad interpretation, the interpreter not only exceeds the literal wording of the statute but also its *mens* and *ratio*. Therefore, they not only accept an expansion of the limits of the statute in a situation where the particular "ratio" is broader than its literal meaning, but also if a merely similar, more remote "ratio" applies to the specific case.[4] Hence, in the hierarchy of specific and more general reasons which may lie beneath a statute, the more general reasons can also be used to expand the statute's meaning. I will attempt to demonstrate this by way of an example: namely, the so-called *laesio enormis*. This term describes the infringement (*laesio*) of one party's rights, where a considerable disparity exists between performance and consideration in a reciprocal contract.[5] The only legal provision governing this issue at the time was the well-known norm of the *Codex Iustinianus*, the imperial law from the 3rd century AD (C. 4, 44, 2). This norm remained in force in Germany until well into the 19th century.

---

[3]The broader concept is preferred by Rogerius, Constantius: *Singul.(aris?) tractatus de iuris interpretatione*, Lugduni et Taurini 1550, pp. 33–35, especially nr. 4–6; Caepolla, Bartholomaeus: *De interpretatione legis extensiva*, Venice 1557, fol. 8v, nr. 17; Alciatus, Andreas: *De verborum significatione libri quatuor*, Lyon 1530, col. 1, 48. The narrower concept is preferred by Phedericis, Stephanus de*: De interpretatione iuris commentarii IV*, Lyon 1536, Praefatio, p. 8 sq.; Everardus a Middelburg, Nicolaus: *Loci argumentorum legales*, Lyon 1579, loc. 79, nr. 4, p. 437; Forster, V. W. (n. 1), lib. 2, cap. 4, nr. 1; Suarez, Franciscus: *Tractatus de legibus ac deo legislatore* (1612) = *Opera omnia*, ed. Berton, C., VI, Paris 1856, lib. 6, cap. 2, nr. 1, p. 8.

[4]Forster, V. W. (n. 2), lib. 2, cap. 2, § 1, nr. 21, col. 1012 (extension "propter similitudinem et paritatem rationis. Nam si ratio est eadem, tunc non est tam extensio quam comprehensio"), see also § 3, nr. 11, col. 1023. Cf. also Rogerius, C. (n. 3), p. 92; Caepolla, B. (n. 3), fol. 17v, nr. 124; Phedericis, S. de (n. 3), p. 15; Lagus, Conrad: *Iuris utriusque methodica traditio...*, Frankfurt 1543, fol. 12v.

[5]See generally Ziegler, K.-H.: Laesio enormis, *Handwörterbuch zur deutschen Rechtsgeschichte*, ed. Erler, A. and Kaufmann, E., vol. 2, 1978, col. 1350 sq.; Schulze, Wolfgang Georg: *Die laesio enormis in der deutschen Privatrechtsgeschichte*, Diss. iur. Münster 1973; Luig, Klaus: Vertragsfreiheit und Äquivalenzprinzip im gemeinen Recht und im BGB, *Aspekte europäischer Rechtsgeschichte. Festgabe für Helmut Coing zum 70.Geburtstag*, ed. Bergfeld, C. et al., Frankfurt am Main 1982, p. 171 sqq.; Becker, Christoph: *Die Lehre von der laesio enormis in der Sicht der heutigen Wucherproblematik*, Köln etc. 1993.

The relevant passage from the Codex states the following: if a vendor of a piece of immovable property obtains as a purchase price less than half of the true value of the property in question, he can dissolve the contract or demand that the purchase price be increased. What is the "ratio" of this statute? We know very little about the specific, special "ratio", i.e. the legislator's direct intention. On one hand, the intention may have been to protect land owners from being forced to sell their land at a low price in times of economic hardship. This particular "ratio" – the protection from compulsory selling due to necessity – could perhaps justify the application of the statute to all objects of purchase, that is to say, to apply it to all movable property also. On the other hand, there may also be another, more general, somewhat more remote "ratio" that can be discovered in this particular statute: namely, the idea of contractual equity. This would require that in all reciprocal contracts, performance and consideration be proportionate to one another. If one also takes this more remote or (in the phrasing of the 16th century) "similar" "ratio" into account, the law can be extended even further. In that case, the law must also apply to the benefit of the *vendee* if *he* is disadvantaged, i.e. if he must pay more than double the true value of the piece of land. Furthermore, it must also be applied to any other non-gratuitous contracts such as service contracts or rental and leasing agreements. In fact, the "ratio" of the statute requires that it must apply to the benefit of one party as well as the other party, depending on which of the parties is subject to any disadvantage. From the time of the Middle Ages until well into the 17th century these incremental expansions of the law were, in fact, considered to be permissible.[6] They represented little more than a broad interpretation based on the more remote, yet "similar" ratio: an action which was considered by most to be unobjectionable.

Late 17th and 18th Century

In the following period, the concept of interpretation became increasingly narrower. According to the well-known definition postulated by Christian Thomasius in 1691, both legal and non-legal interpretations aimed to discover explanations for the text that illustrated both *was ein anderer in seinen Schrifften hat verstehen wollen/ und welches zu verstehen etwas schwer oder dunckel ist* (what someone intended to say; and that which was obscure and

---

[6]For example, in the 16th century Everardus a Middelburg, N. (n. 3). loc. 79, nr. 77 sq., p. 480 sq.

not easily understood without further consideration).[7] Attempts were made to deduce the intention of the author of the statute – according to a distinction introduced by Thomasius – either *aus den dunklen Worten* (from the obscure wording: the grammatical interpretation) or *aus anderen Umständen* (from other circumstances: the logical interpretation).[8] Therefore, statutory interpretation, whether logical or grammatical, only consisted of identifying the intention of the legislator: an intention which was strongly identified with the purpose of the law itself. This perception can also be found in the work of other authoritative authors of the period, for example, as early as Pufendorf (1673), who discussed the process of ascertaining the *genuinus sensus* of the text[9] and, as late as Thibaut (1806), who argued that one ought to also be concerned with determining the purpose of the statute.[10]

This new concept of interpretation as a means of determining the purpose of a statute no longer resonated with the old idea of a broad interpretation, which permitted the expansion of a law for a "similar" reason. This "similar" reason was no longer the purpose of the statute, and nor could it be said to comprise the intention of the legislator. Thus, almost all legal scholars of this period vehemently repudiated the old idea of an extended interpretation for a "similar" reason. As Pufendorf said: "for the expansion of a statute, it does not suffice that there is a similar ratio in a particular case, rather, the ratio must be completely the same".[11] Moreover, in 1806 Thibaut stated that there is *nicht leicht eine mißlichere, für die Rechtsverfassung gefährlichere Theorie* (seldom a more troublesome opinion more dangerous for the rule of law) than that of the expansion of any given law for a "similar" reason.[12] This method of developing the law by interpretation was now beyond the accepted understanding of the concept of interpretation. Nevertheless, the

---

[7]Thomasius, Christian: *Ausübung der Vernunft-Lehre*, Halle 1691, 3. Hauptstück, nr. 25, p. 163 sq.

[8]Thomasius, C. (n. 7), 3. Hauptstück, nr. 34, p. 166.

[9]Pufendorf, Samuel: *De iure naturae et gentium libri VIII* (1672), *Gesammelte Werke*, IV, ed. Böhling, Frank, Berlin 1998, lib. 5, cap. 12, § 1, p. 524.

[10]Thibaut, Anton Friedrich Justus: *Theorie der logischen Auslegung des römischen Rechts*, 2nd ed., Altona 1806, p. 11. See also the quotations in Schröder, J. (n. 1), pp. 138, 143.

[11]Pufendorf, S. (n. 9), lib. 5, cap. 12, § 17, p. 535. "Neque sufficit extendendae v. g. legi alicui, si in aliquem casum quadret ratio, similis illi, quae in ista lege est; sed oportet, ut ratio sit eadem". See also Thomasius, Christian: *Institutionum jurisprudentiae divinae libri III* (1688), 7th ed., Halle 1730, lib. 2, cap. 12, nr. 89, p. 238; Glück, Christian Friedrich: *Vollständige Erläuterung der Pandekten nach Hellfeld. Ein Commentar*, 1. Theil, 2nd ed., Erlangen 1797, § 36, p. 259 sq.

[12]Thibaut, A. F. J. (n. 10), p. 71. Also see the quotations in Schröder, J. (n. 1), pp. 139, 155.

fact remained that any given interpretation may still have exceeded, or fell short of, the possible grammatical meaning of the law.

This can once again be shown by way of the *laesio enormis* example. From the late 17th century onwards, the older, broad interpretation of the *Codex Iustinianus* (C. 4, 44, 2) became subject to increased criticism. This was without doubt due in part to substantive legal reasons. Gradually, the notion of freedom of contract had begun to arise, which replaced the old principle of contractual equity. Notwithstanding this development, forms of broad interpretation were also criticised on the basis of methodological considerations. For example, Thomasius and the Saxon legal scholar Johann Lorenz Holderrieder emphasised that not even the narrow "ratio" of this *laesio enormis* provision was known.[13] It was not known to whom the imperial re-script was addressed and it may have been possible that the Emperor may not have made a mistake at all. The legitimacy of an expansion of this law based on a more remote "ratio" became doubtful.

By way of an initial summary we can conclude that two major steps were made in the development of the concept of legal interpretation between 1500 and 1800. Initially, the interpreter was entitled to not only exceed the literal meaning, but he was also entitled to exceed the intention and purpose of the legislator by drawing upon a more remote "ratio". However, by the 18th century the interpreter could step outside the boundaries of the literal meaning only. A third possibility, in which the literal meaning of the statute could not be overstepped at all, had not yet been considered. This third option appeared for the first time in the early 19th century.

Means of Legal Interpretation

Sixteenth and Early Seventeenth Century

What are the means of statutory interpretation? In modern German legal theory it is well established that there are four "elements" of interpretation: textual, systematic, historical and teleological. This cannot, however, be stated as a matter of course in respect of all periods. Both the textual and contextual elements were in fact deemed necessary at all times, but the importance of the other elements fluctuated depending on the influence of prevailing contemporary theories of interpretation. With regard to the

---

[13]Thomasius, Christian: *De aequitate cerebrina: l. 2 c. de rescind. vendit. et ejus usu practico* (1706), Halle 1713; Holderrieder, Johannes Laurentius: *Dissertatio iuridica inauguralis De principiis interpretationis legum adaequatis*, Leipzig 1736, S. 49.

earliest stage of the early modern period, it is apparent that considerable importance was placed upon the concept of the "ratio". While the interpreter's primary role was to determine the *mens* of the statute (its purpose), in the 16th century the *mens* of a statute was considered to be identical with its "ratio": an association that was scarcely debated.[14] For instance, the Dutch legal scholar Nikolaus Everardus von Middelburg stated that the "ratio" and *mens* of a statute appeared to be one and the same.[15] The "ratio", however, is not simply the legislator's neutral and impartial purpose; rather, it is always a reasonable, or at least functional, reason of the legislator.[16]

In accordance with the ideas prevalent at that time, the contemporary literature of the 16th and 17th centuries provided primarily "rational" methods of determining the *mens*. Aside from obvious methods such as referring to the literal meaning and the context of the statute, there were other means of interpretation. For example, one could examine the subject matter of the statute, try to ensure that absurdity was avoided, or apply the usual or common understanding of the law. One could also obey the rules of *aequitas* (equity), and, in cases of doubt, could follow the principle that the most benevolent result ought to be achieved.[17] Furthermore, contemporary theories of argument were deemed necessary to apply regarding any interpretation, so the purpose of a statute could also be derived by utilising

---

[14]Cf. Piano Mortari, Vincenzo: *Ricerche sulla teoria dell' interpretazione del diritto nel secolo XVI. I: Le premesse*, Milano 1956, pp. 63 sqq., 100 sqq.; Maclean, Ian: *Interpretation and meaning in the Renaissance. The case of law*, p. 142 sqq.; Raisch, Peter: *Juristische Methoden. Vom antiken Rom bis zur Gegenwart*, Heidelberg 1995, S. 26 f.; Schröder, J.: *Recht als Wissenschaft* (n. 1), p. 59 sq.

[15]Everardus a Middelburg, N. (n. 3), loc. 79, nr. 18/19, p. 445 ("ratio enim legis et mens legis idem esse videntur"). See also Rogerius, C. (n. 3), S. 17, nr. 17 ("ratio legis nihil aliud est, quam mens legis"); Caepolla, B. (n. 3), fol. 17v, nr. 126/127 ("mens legis nihil aliud est, quam anima legis. . . quia mens et ratio legis ab ipsa non differt"), fol. 18v, nr. 135 ("mens legis colligitur ex ratione legis"); Zasius, Ulrich: *In Digestum vetus*, zu D. 1, 3, 17 nr. 18, Sp. 377, *Opera omnia* I, Lyon 1550, p. 191: the "mens" will be concluded from the "ratio"; Donellus, Hugo: *Commentarii de iure civili* (1589), 6th ed., I, Nürnberg 1801, lib. 1, cap. 13, § 9, p. 89 ("ratio nihil est, nisi voluntas legis"); Forster, V. W. (n. 2), lib. 2, cap. 2, nr. 2, Sp. 1006 ("ratio seu mens legis").

[16]Derrer, Sebastian: *Jurisprudentiae liber primus, instar disciplinae institutus et axiomatibus magna ex parte conscriptus. . .*, Lyon 1540, lib. 1, tit. 7, nr. 19/20. See also Piano Mortari, V. (n. 14), p. 32; Schröder, J. (n. 1), p. 60.

[17]See the partly different catalogues of means at Donellus, H. (n. 15), lib. 1, cap. 13, § 6, p. 88, cap. 15, §§ 6–9, pp. 122–126; Forster, V. W. (n. 2), lib. 2, cap. 3, nr. 7, 19, col. 1029, 1032, lib. 2, cap. 4, nr. 19–22, col. 1039 (cf. also lib. 1, cap. 2, nr. 36–41, col. 967); Grotius, Hugo: *De iure belli ac pacis libri III* (1625), ed. de Kanter-van Hettinga Tromp, B. J. A., Leiden 1939, new edition with annotations by R. Feenstra et al., Aalen 1993, lib. 2, cap. 16, §§ 5–8, p. 410 sq.

dialectic topoi such as the statute's similarities, dichotomies, or interdependency with other statutes.[18] Empirical means, in particular the statute's history, played next to no role whatsoever. This seems somewhat surprising for the modern lawyer, but historical facts were deemed unimportant during this stage of the early modern period; rather, it was the statute's "ratio" – its reason – which was sought after. This issue of rationality was decisive in determining whether a statute could be interpreted contrary to its literal wording. Consequently, "rational" laws, such as the *ius commune* were generally open to expansion; however, laws that were exorbitant, punitive or odious were not, unless the expansion thereof would lead to a reasonable result. This is the basis for the rule that statutes (including local and territorial law, but not common law) were to be interpreted narrowly by lower-ranked legislators, who were generally suspected of being unreasonable.[19]

An explanatory example may also be helpful on this point. For instance, a law prohibits the export of grain. Does the prohibition also extend to flour? This case seems to refer to a statute from Padua, which was most likely first discussed in the late 13th century by the Italian legal scholar Albertus Gandinus.[20] Gandinus stated that the statute could not be applied to flour. Despite dissenting beliefs, Gandinus's ideas seemed to be the opinion held by the majority of jurists in the late Middle Ages and throughout the 16th century. For example, Dinus Mugellanus and Baldus were also vehemently against the extension of this law and, in the 15th and 16th centuries, Cepolla and Federici followed the same line of reasoning.[21] The reason against the expansion of this statute, first provided by Gandinus, is that the statute contravenes *ius commune*, the Roman common law. Such a statute could not be capable of being extended, as the *ius commune* was regarded by the legal scholars of the Middle Ages as identical with legal reason *per se*. Any prohibition to export grain was, therefore, not only "absurd", but would also

---

[18] Phedericis, S. de (n. 3), p. 16 sq.; Forster, V. W. (n. 2), lib. 2, cap. 2, § 1, nr. 1–17, col. 1009 sqq.

[19] Caepolla, B. (n. 3), fol. 44r, nr. 141; Phedericis, S. de (n. 3), S. 163, 174; Alciatus, A. (n. 3), col. 59; Forster, V. W. (n. 2), lib. 2, cap. 2, § 3, nr. 6, col. 1021 f.; Donellus, H. (n. 15), lib. 1, cap. 14, § 9, p. 115 sq. See also Schröder, J. (n. 1), p. 70 sq.

[20] Kantorowicz, Hermann: *Albertus Gandinus und das Strafrecht der Scholastik*, vol. 2, Berlin and Leipzig 1926 (= critical edition of Gandinus' "Tractatus de maleficiis"), p. 374 sq. See also Vogenauer, S. (n. 1), Teil 1, 4. Kap., p. 561 sq.

[21] Baldus: *Commentaria in primam Digesti veteris partem*, Lyon 1585, at D. 1, 3, 39, fol 28v; Dinus (quoted by Bartolus, at D. 32, 1, 78, 4); Phedericis, S. de (n. 3), S. 174; Caepolla, B. (n. 3), fol. 44r, nr. 141. The opposite opinion is held by Bartolus and Alciatus, A. (n. 3), col. 60.

violate natural law: it was irrational. This law could be said to be binding merely by virtue of it being the will of the legislator, and this will of the legislator alone could never justify the statute's extension.[22]

Late 17th and 18th Century

In the second half of the 17th century, the theory of legal interpretation began to demonstrate increasingly clear positivistic traits. Namely, it was thought that the interpreter now ought to begin to explore the legislator's intention. Hence, the old connection between "purpose" and "ratio" crumbled. Pufendorf stated as early as 1672 that anyone who considered *mens* and "ratio" as being identical erred gravely; the "ratio" was only a means of determining the purpose of a statute.[23] At the same time, the notion of "ratio" also became more positivistic. It was now deemed to coincide with the motivation and intended purpose of the legislator: it was believed to be the reason which moved the legislator to enact the statute (Pufendorf).[24] It could nonetheless be completely absent from any given law as well, as the legislator's will alone was sufficient to enact a law.[25]

   The tendency, therefore, was towards a de-rationalisation of the statute and towards a positivisation of the "ratio". Along this line of reasoning, the importance of using empirical means to determine a statute's meaning increased, especially with relation to the statute's background and the history of its origin.[26] In the 16th and early 17th centuries, a statute's history was, at most, taken into account to determine its literal meaning only.[27]

---

[22]Phedericis, S. (n. 21): "Nam quoniam eae leges non vi rationis, sed voluntate tantum superioris nos obligant, non videntur offendi, nisi in eo in quo verbis expressae sunt", Caepolla, B. (n. 21).

[23]Pufendorf, S. (n. 9), lib. 5, cap. 12, § 10, p. 531.

[24]Pufendorf, S. (n. 23); Thomasius, C.: *Jurisprudentia divina* (n. 11), lib. 2, cap. 12, nr. 69, p. 235; Eckhard, Christian Heinrich: *Hermeneutica iuris* (1750), new edition by Walch, Karl Wilhelm, Leipzig 1802, lib. 1, cap. 1, § 33, p. 28; Thibaut, A. F. J. (n. 10), p. 12 ("Gründe, worauf seine Vorschrift beruht").

[25]Pufendorf, S. (n. 23): there is only required the legislator's will; Holderrieder, J. L. (n. 13), p. 40.

[26]Cf. Schröder, Jan: Zur Geschichte der historischen Gesetzesauslegung, *Der praktische Nutzen der Rechtsgeschichte. Hans Hattenhauer zum 8. September 2001*, ed. Eckert, Jörn, Heidelberg 2003, p. 481–495 (also in Schröder, Jan: *Rechtswissenschaft in der Neuzeit*, Tübingen 2010, pp. 143–158).

[27]Hotomanus, F. (n. 2), p. 61 sq. (grammatical interpretation); Hopper, Joachim: *Seduardus seu De Vera Juris prudentia* (1590), in: Hermann Conring: *Opera,* ed. Goebel, Johann Wilhelm, VI, Braunschweig 1730, Reprint Aalen 1973, p. 37 sqq., lib. 4, tit.

Nonetheless, by the end of the 17th century at the latest, it began to appear as a general means of interpretation employed by several authors. Reference is made to this concept by Johannes von Felde in 1689, by Vincenz Placcius in 1693 and, once again, most notably by Thomasius.[28] As early as 1688, in his monography on *Institutionen des Naturrechts* (The Institutions of Natural Law), Thomasius proposed that one could draw upon history to elucidate the *ratio legis*. He continued to advance this theory in *Ausübung der Vernunftlehre* (The Exercise of the Theory of Reason) from 1691. Pursuant to this, it became a widely-accepted practice to place the historical development of a statute alongside the methods commonly applied to determine its meaning, such as its context, subject material, its effect (i.e., avoidance of absurd results) and the *ratio legis*.[29] This development was inevitable: if the interpreter was to identify the legislator's intention, he must at least possess knowledge of the historical context surrounding it.

In accordance with these developments, the case concerning grain and flour discussed in the example above would now be resolved in a considerably different manner to that of the 16th century. The intrinsic purpose of statute law was no longer decisive in determining its meaning, and the historical intention of the legislator took centre stage. If the legislator, by enacting this prohibition on the export of grain, wished to prevent a shortage of bread, his intention had to be realised by applying a broad interpretation which also encompassed the export of flour. From the late 17th century onwards, the grain and flour case became the quintessential example of a legitimate broad interpretation. Thomasius regarded the extension of the prohibition on exporting flour as so obvious that he even used the case as support for his arguments in favour of the general extension of "odious", exceptional and penal laws.[30] The acceptance of interpretive extension seems to have occurred without any great controversy in the late 17th and 18th centuries. It

---

16, p. 45 (historical interpretation); Forster, V. W. (n. 2), lib. 1, cap. 5: "*De Historica Interpretandi ratione*" (col. 975–984).

[28] Von Felde, Johannes: *Scientia interpretandi*, Helmstedt 1689, p. 1062, examples pp. 1063–1065; Placcius, V. (n. 2), p. 105 sq. (several kinds of *causae* of a statute, which can only be explored historically); Thomasius, C.: *Jurispr. Divina* (n. 11), lib. 2, cap. 12, nr. 83, 84, p. 237 (the "ratio" of contracts has to be investigated *ex lectione diligent historiarum*), Thomasius, C.: *Ausübung* (n. 7), 3. Hauptstück, nr. 85, p. 195 sq. (politics and other means).

[29] Holderrieder, J. L. (n. 13), § 13, p. 33 (history is one of five means of interpretation); Eckhard, C. H. (n. 24), lib. 1, cap. 1, § 35, p. 30 (the "ratio legis" can be found out by history); Glück, C. F. (Fn. 11), 1.Buch. 1. Titel, § 29, p. 206 sq., § 36, p. 246 sq. (history is necessary to find out the will of the legislator and the *ratio legis*). But see also the critical remarks by Thibaut, A. F. J. (n. 10), p. 29 sq.

[30] Thomasius, C.: *Ausübung* (n. 7), 3. Hauptstück, nr. 123, p. 213 sq.

can be found in annotations to Pufendorf's Natural Law[31] and in the writings of the Bavarian statutory drafter Kreittmayr in the late 18th century, which stated: . . .*wenn zum Beispiel die Holz- oder Getreide-Ausfuhr bestraft wird, so trifft diese Strafe auch denjenigen, der Mehl oder Kohlen ausführt* (if, for example, the export of wood or grain would be punished, this punishment also applies to those who are exporting flour or coal).[32] The fact that such an interpretation might be unreasonable, and may restrict the citizens' freedom was no longer of any consequence.

In summary, one can say that interpretation became historicised. Whereas in the 16th and early 17th centuries the reason behind any given law was determinative, in the late 17th and 18th centuries the focus had shifted to place greater importance upon the historical intention of the legislator. The interpretive result could not only be a more restrictive interpretation than in the 16th century, but also a more extensive one if – like in the grain and flour case – the legislator's intention, which stepped outside the literal wording, could be historically determined.

Background: The Modification of the Concept of Law in the Early Modern Period

What is the background of the narrowing of the concept of interpretation and the historicization of statutory interpretation during the Enlightenment period? I would like to point to one major driving force that was present in this background: the changing of the *concept of law* during the 17th century.[33] According to the traditional view, law was necessarily just and reasonable. Thomas Aquinas had defined it as *quaedam rationis ordinatio ad bonum commune* – an order of reason for the common good.[34] This definition endured, and as late as the 16th century, law was described as a "general, just and good order of a higher power" (Franciscus Connanus, 1550); a "moral regulation by the legitimate authority" (Matthäus Wesenbeck, 1582);

---

[31] Pufendorf, S. (n. 9), lib. 5, cap. 12, § 17, annotation (a) ed. Hert, J. N., Frankfurt am Main 1716, S. 770. See also Holderrieder, J. L. (n. 13), p. 41; Ritter, Carl August: *Regulae interpretationis juridicae praestantiores*, Leipzig 1740, p. 6.

[32] von Kreittmayr, Wigulaeus Aloys Xaver: *Anmerkungen über den Codicem Maximilianeum Bavaricum civilem* (1758 sqq.), new ed. 1821, 1.Theil, 1. Kap., § 10, p. 17.

[33] A historical survey is given by Schröder, Jan: Zur Entwicklung des Rechtsbegriffs in der Neuzeit, *Gedächtnisschrift für Jörn Eckert*, ed. Hoyer, Andreas et al., Baden-Baden 2008, pp. 835–845.

[34] Thomas Aquinas: *Summa Theologiae*, II 1, quaest. 90, art. 4 ad 1.

and as a "decree ordering or permitting that which is right" – and that which is right is just and beneficial (Hugo Donellus, 1589).[35] No differentiation was made between positive law and Natural Law. In Ulrich Zasius's words, positive law is merely *ius naturale formatissimum*, the most defined form of Natural Law.[36]

However, throughout the 16th century, doubts began to arise concerning this moral concept of law. In 1576, Jean Bodin described law as being merely the order of the sovereign.[37] Furthermore, in 1588, in the third volume of his essays, Michel de Montaigne stated with some regret that laws were "obeyed, not because they are just, but because they are laws".[38] These concerns intensified until the middle of the 17th century and an empirical value-free notion of law ultimately triumphed. The connection between the dissolution of the morality-based system of law brought about by religious and civil wars, and the 17th century empirical "revolution of the natural sciences", is clear. Thomas Hobbes' statements of 1642 and 1651 were widely quoted: in particular, that a statute is simply an "order" by the most superior authority; and that "authority and not the truth" made the law.[39] In Germany, similar statements were made by Samuel Pufendorf (1672),[40] who openly declared that a law could also correspond to the legislator's "naked arbitrariness".[41] Furthermore, in 1792, Kant described the complete set of positive law as *aus dem Willen eines Gesetzgebers hervor geht* (arising from

---

[35]Connanus, Franciscus: *Commentariorum iuris civilis libri X*, Basel 1562, lib. 1, cap. 8, nr. 7, p. 44; Wesenbeck, Matthaeus: *In Pandectas iuris civilis et Codicis Iustiniani lib. IIX commentarii*, Basel 1582, lib. 1, tit. 3, nr. 2 ("honestum legitimate potestatis decretum"); Donellus, H. (n. 15), lib. 1, cap. 5, §§ 1, 2, p. 25 ("constitutio omnis iubens in publicum, permittensve, quae recta sunt, prohibens que contraria"), idem, lib. 1, cap. 5, § 6, p. 28: "recta sunt, quae honesta et aequa per sese, aut quae omnibus vel pluribus in eadem civitate utilia".

[36]Zasius, Ulrich: *In titulos aliquot Digesti veteris commentaria*, ad D. 1,1,1, § "Huius studii", nr. 41, *Opera omnia* (n. 15) I, p. 128.

[37]Bodin, Jean: *Les six livres de la république*, Paris 1583, I, 8, p. 131.

[38]Montaigne, Michel de: *Essais*, livre 3, chap. 13 (1588), German edition by Lüthy, Herbert, Zürich 1953, p. 851.

[39]Hobbes, Thomas: *De cive* (1642), cap. 6, nr. 9: "Leges civiles... nihil aliud sunt, quam ejus, qui in civitate summa potestate praeditus est, de civium futuris actionibus mandata (= idem; *Opera philosophica quae latine scripsit omnia*, ed. Molesworth, William [1839–1845], vol. 2, p. 222; idem: *Leviathan* (1651) (= idem, *Opera...*, vol. 3, cap. 26, p. 202, "autoritas, non veritas, facit legem").

[40]Pufendorf, Samuel: *De officio hominis et civis juxta legem naturalem libri duo* (1673), lib. 2, cap. 12, § 1 = *Gesammelte Werke*, vol. 2, ed. Hartung, Gerald, Berlin 1997, p. 80 ("decreta summi imperantis civilis").

[41]Pufendorf, S. (n. 9), lib. 2, cap. 3, § 24, p. 163 ("ex nudo legislatoris arbitrio").

a legislator's intention).[42] Under the influence of Pufendorf and Kant, by the turn of the century this had become the common view in German natural law and in the legal literature on positive law.[43] The previous notion of the law as an embodiment of morality was completely replaced by a neutral notion according to which a statute represented nothing more than the intention of a legislator.

I propose that the restrictions on the concept of interpretation, and the historicization of interpretation in the late 17th and 18th centuries, were connected to these changes in the concept of law. It seems apparent that interpretation cannot be viewed as independent from its object. The way in which law is understood affects both the concept of interpretation and its means. In relation to the concept of interpretation, if law was taken to be always just and reasonable – as was the case in the 16th century – the interpreter was permitted to transgress not only its literal wording, but also the legislator's purpose for the sake of ensuring reasonable results. If, however, law was simply an expression of the legislator's intention – as was the case since the late 17th century – interpretation could make reference to this intention alone; the notion of interpretation had become restricted. With regard to the means: to determine what was reasonable – as in the 16th century – no historical means were needed. Reason governed the means of interpretation, and reason is timeless. However, if one wished to determine the intention of the legislator in the method of the late 17th century onwards, the history of that intention was required in certain circumstances. Thus, in my view, the modification of the concept of law was mirrored in the changes in interpretational theory.

Concluding Remarks

To conclude, I would like to summarise my arguments briefly. Two developmental tendencies from the 16th to the 18th centuries are apparent: first, the concept of interpretation became more restricted as interpretation came to consist only of determining the meaning of a law; of identifying the legislator's intention. Interpretation no longer allowed the reasonable development of law by applying the remoter "ratio" of a statute. Second, the means of

---

[42]Kant, Immanuel: *Die Metaphysik der Sitten, 1. Theil: Metaphysische Anfänge der Rechtslehre*, 2nd ed., Königsberg 1798, p. 44 (B 1).

[43]For example, Wolff, Christian: *Institutiones juris naturae et gentium*, Halle 1750, § 1068, p. 664, cf. also § 39; Böhmer, Justus Henning: *Introductio in ius Digestorum* (1704), I, 9th ed., Halle 1756, lib. 1, tit. 1, § 14, p. 10. Further quotations in Schröder, J. (n. 1), p. 98.

interpretation were extended by including the history of the statute as a means of determining the legislator's intention. Both factors are easily comprehensible when one considers the modification of the concept of law in the 17th century. Law was no longer perceived as necessarily a reasonable decree; rather, it was merely an expression of the legislator's intention. During the 16th and early 17th centuries, interpretation depended on a reasonable result; during the late 17th and 18th centuries, it depended on the order of the legislator: not truth, but authority made the law.

This result – the narrowing and historicization of interpretation in the 18th century – may sound somewhat surprising. Indeed, we have known for a long time that in the 18th century interest in history was gaining importance. However, the era of Enlightenment is also the era of reason. It would most certainly be an anomaly if the rational element were to have completely vanished from the interpretational theory. Yet, I believe that it remained prevalent, but simply changed its position within the system. Rationality was no longer the primary goal of interpretation; nonetheless, it remained important as an (alternative) presumption of rationality. If the purpose and ratio of a statute could not be determined historically, the interpreter could assume a reasonable ratio. As Thibaut stated, *[es muß] doch wohl demjenigen Grundsatz der Vorzug eingeräumt werden, welcher, wenn sonst nichts im Wege steht, bey gleichen Möglichkeiten der vernünftigste ist* (It goes without saying that the principle which is most reasonable in the circumstances must be preferred if nothing else speaks against it).[44] This principle, however, only possesses subsidiary validity – in the same way that natural law is subsidiary to positive law. The historical determination of the legislator's intention still took priority; but if this should fail, one could still fall back on presumptions of rationality.

Upon examining these factors, an important distinction in relation to modern interpretational theory becomes apparent. In the 18th century, rationality was a genuine factor of interpretation, and could be determined objectively. It was firmly rooted in natural law, and its existence and validity as a subsidiary source of law was rarely questioned. In the present day, we have lost this conviction and no longer accept the tenets of natural law. From the late 19th century onwards, presumptions of rationality have been suspected of

---

[44]Thibaut, Anton Friedrich Justus: *Über den Einfluß der Philosophie auf die Auslegung der positiven Gesetze*, idem: *Versuche über einzelne Theile der Theorie des Rechts* (1798), 2nd ed., Jena 1817, p. 173. See Schröder, J. (n. 1), pp. 148–150.

being merely subjective "value judgments",[45] and even of being class- or society-specific pronouncements of morality. This is one of the origins upon which the plight of modern interpretational theory is founded. Even so, I have shown that in the 18th century at least, the historical and rational elements remained finely balanced; both still valid approaches to interpreting the law.

---

[45]Rümelin, Gustav: *Werturteile und Willensentscheidungen im Civilrecht*, Freiburg im Breisgau 1891, p. 6. Summarizing Schröder, Jan: *Zur Theorie der Gesetzesinterpretation am Anfang des 20. Jahrhunderts* (forthcoming).

Chapter 6
"Needs" – Pandectists Between Norm and Reality

Hans-Peter HAFERKAMP

Introduction

The history of legal interpretation between 1500 and 1850 has been aptly described by Jan Schröder as a progressive loss of interpretational freedom. He states: "At first, it was possible for an interpreter to go beyond the realm of the legislator's words as well as his will and purpose. Later on he was merely allowed to exceed the words, and subsequently he was denied even this freedom".[1] Around 1800, juridical interpretation appears to have gradually lost touch with contemporary concerns. Legal documents were perceived as little more than historical texts dating from another time, and there was a growing awareness of the difficulties associated with placing oneself in the time and position of the author.

During this period, the method of legal interpretation changed from a reasonable, "logical" approach to a method of "reconstruction". In my field of study, 19th century Pandectism, this transition seems to have increased the authority of antique legal texts. This also corresponds with the view legal historians allotted to Pandectism for a long period of time. Pandectism held a reputation of being entirely concerned with antique sources, and was thus perceived to ignore contemporary social issues and the Industrial Revolution.[2] This discontinuity resulted in a reduction of the scope of interpretational freedom between the concept of enlightenment hermeneutics and the romantic hermeneutic concepts of Schlegel and Schleiermacher. In the

---

[1] J. Schröder, „Entwicklungen der juristischen Interpretationstheorie von 1500 bis 1850", ZNR (2002) 56.

[2] Franz Wieacker, *Privatrechtsgeschichte der Neuzeit*, 1st ed. (1952) 253.

H.-P. HAFERKAMP (✉)
Institut für Neuere Privatrechtsgeschichte, Deutsche und Rheinische Rechtsgeschichte,
Universität zu Köln, 50923 Köln, Deutschland
e-mail: Hans-Peter.Haferkamp@uni-koeln.de

MORIGIWA, Y. et al. (eds.), *Interpretation of Law in the Age*
of Enlightenment, Law and Philosophy Library 95,
DOI 10.1007/978-94-007-1506-6_6, © Springer Science+Business Media B.V. 2011

following discussion I will examine this development from a new perspective, and analyze one particular argument from the Pandectists' 19th century interpretational repertoire. This argument serves as a link between the close commitment to antique texts and the "reality" of the 19th century. With regard to the 18th century, I would like to show that the traditional labels of "practical" law in the 18th century and "theoretical" law in the 19th century are inconsistent. The concepts of "practicability" or "reality" were simply approached in different ways. Thus, I hope that an examination of the 19th century will in turn promote a greater understanding of the 18th century.

I will begin my consideration with a term Georg Friedrich Puchta introduced into the doctrine of the Historical School of Law,[3] but which was in fact coined by Savigny in 1814: the *Volksgeist*. When relating to the historical and dynamical moral code of a people as the primary source of just law, the interpretational system of Pandectism found itself in conflict: on the one hand, the intention was to reconstruct a norm of Roman law in its historical meaning; the result, on the other hand, had to correspond to a contemporary set of values. Thus, *Volksgeist* confronted the antique law with reality – but what kind of reality? When approaching the concept of *Volksgeist*, one comes across a term used by Savigny which has so far been mostly neglected in academic studies, but which articulates more precisely Savigny's understanding of *Volksgeist*.[4] This term, "needs" (*Bedürfnisse*), shall mark the starting point for my considerations.

In 1814, Savigny did not speak of a *Volksgeist* but a "common consciousness of the people".[5] He explained the origin of such a common conviction as a "recurring need".[6] The term "need" was not used coincidentally, and 25 years later in 1839, Savigny continued to speak of a "legal consciousness" existing as an "unsatisfied need".[7] What did he mean by this?

---

[3]For the first time in Georg Friedrich Puchta, rec. Eduard Gans: *Das Erbrecht in weltgeschichtlicher Entwicklung*, part 1 (1824), part 2 (1825), in: Friedrich Christoph Karl Schunck (ed.), *Erlanger Jahrbücher der gesamten deutschen juristischen Literatur 1* (1826) 14.

[4]To this Hans-Peter Haferkamp, *rec. Horst Heinrich Jakobs, Georg Friedrich Puchta. Briefe an Gustav Hugo*, in: SZ GA 127, 762 ff.

[5]Friedrich Carl v. Savigny, *Vom Beruf unsrer Zeit für Gesetzgebung und Rechtswissenschaft* (1814) 13.

[6]Id., *Vom Beruf unsrer Zeit für Gesetzgebung und Rechtswissenschaft* (1814) 13.

[7]Savigny, *§ 52*, Bl. 224, 6 (This text is based on the (unprinted) discussion by letter about § 52 of Savigny's System. The text can be found on the following webpage: http://savigny.ub.uni-marburg.de/. A debate about this text in: Hans-Peter Haferkamp, *Die Bedeutung der Willensfreiheit für die Historische Rechtsschule*, in: Ernst-Joachim Lampe (ed.), Michael Pauen (ed.), Gerhard Roth (ed.), Willensfreiheit und rechtliche Ordnung (2008) 196 ff.

In 1815, Savigny had expressed his ideas more precisely: law originated from "nature, destiny and the people's needs".[8] The term *Volksgeist*, therefore, combined "nature" – the national character – with "destiny", and a certain legal "reality" or "need". Savigny viewed this "destiny" as the development of a nation, and he increasingly understood it in a religious way. One could also say "reality" was incorporated into the origin of law, and "need" bridged norms and reality. "Need" was a crucial element in legal development and Savigny was convinced that a "practical need would find its own way to satisfaction".[9]

Jhering's famous critique of 1865 was essentially a repetition of Savigny's argument. He accused the Pandectists of believing in an "illusion of juridical logic", and pointed out that legal norms changed "with the needs of life".[10] Thus, instead of describing the well-known change in Jhering's basic assumptions as a development from a "jurisprudence of construction to the needs of real life" (as Regina Ogorek has done),[11] should we not speak of a "return to Savigny"? Then again, one could also speak of Jhering's "return to Jhering himself". In 1844, a time in which Jhering – as he himself later described – was imprisoned by the jurisprudence of concepts (*Begriffsjurisprudenz*), he had declared: "Academic interest should not impede a norm which has been a practical need".[12]

Savigny and Jhering were not alone in using the term "need". If one takes into consideration the writings of other Pandectists, it becomes evident that between 1814 and 1880, even supposing *Begriffsjuristen*, several authors constantly emphasized the importance of "needs" in the genesis and knowledge of law. In 1827, Johann Christian Hasse criticized "academic pretentiousness" and demanded an a priori consideration of "practical needs in general".[13] Also in 1827, Georg Friedrich Puchta defined "a jurist's

---

[8]Friedrich Carl v. Savigny, *rec. of N. Th. v. Gönner, Über Gesetzgebung und Rechtswissenschaft in unserer Zeit* (1815); here quoted from a reprint in: Savigny, *Vermischte Schriften*, vol. 5 (1850), reprint (1981) 141.

[9]Id, *Geschichte des Römischen Rechts im Mittelalter*, vol. 3, 2nd ed. (1834) 84.

[10]Rudolf v. Jhering, G*eist des römischen Rechts auf den verschiedenen Stufen seiner Entwicklung*, vol. III (1865) § 59, 314.

[11]Regina Ogorek, *Richterkönig oder Subsumtionsautomat?* (1986) 219 ff.

[12]Rudolf v. Jhering, *Die Lehre von der hereditas jacens: I. Standpunkt der Betrachtung*, in: id., *Abhandlungen aus dem Römischen Recht* (1844) 153 f. note 1.

[13]Johann Christian Hasse, *Von der Bestellung der Servituten durch simple Verträge und Stipulationen*, in: Rheinisches Museum für Jurisprudenz, Philologie, Geschichte und griechische Philosophie, vol. 1 (1827) 92.

business" as the task of "giving a need a certain legal shape".[14] In the same year, Eduard Gans described juridical customs as a set of rules in which "the particularity of needs itself [. . .] constitutes law".[15] Concerning the law of succession, Christian Friedrich Mühlenbruch asked in 1833 whether there had been "a practical need".[16] In 1839, Theodor Marezoll stated that bourgeois "need" would lead to the creation of new law.[17] In the same year, Johann Christian Kierulff announced: "Real law is the satisfied need".[18] Karl Adolph von Vangerow agreed in 1851, stating that "practical need" leads to corresponding rules of law.[19] As a final example, I refer to Bernhard Windscheid's 1884 statement, in which he described jurisprudence as being guided by "practical needs".[20]

Is this a refutation of my opening thesis? If Pandectism was close to life, would it not be better to speak of a "jurisprudence of needs" instead of a "jurisprudence of constructs", *Begriffsjurisprudenz*? This would be much too simple. As is generally known, it is difficult to decide whether law is actually close to life, or only claims to be so. One could, in a Kantian view, refuse an answer in order to avoid a naturalistic fallacy. But if one accepts the question, the difficulty still remains of how to "measure" a result and to define how close the law is to "life" – furthermore: which "life"? But if one asks in a specific historical manner, another issue is raised: What did the term "need" mean to the Pandectists? What was the contemporary notion of that term?

When trying to reconstruct the history of the term "need", it becomes evident that we are dealing with an "Archimedean" term.[21] Around the year 1780, consistent with Koselleck's notion of a semantic "saddle period", "need" or *Bedürfnis* was subjected to a semantic shift. The older

---

[14]Georg Friedrich Puchta, *Über die Negatorienklage*, in: Rheinisches Museum für Jurisprudenz, Philologie, Geschichte und griechische Philosophie, vol. 1 (1827) 163 f.

[15]Eduard Gans, *System des Römischen Civilrechts* (1827) 182, 184.

[16]Christian Friedrich Mühlenbruch, in: Christian Friedrich v. Glück, *Pandecten*, vol. 36 (1833) 179.

[17]Theodor Marezoll, *Lehrbuch der Institutionen des Römischen Rechts* (1839) 11.

[18]Johann Friedrich Martin Kierulff, *Theorie des Gemeinen Civilrechts* (1839) 1.

[19]Karl Adolph v. Vangerow, *Pandekten I 1*, 6th ed. (1851) 1018.

[20]Bernhard Windscheid, *Die Aufgaben der Rechtswissenschaft (Leipziger Rektoratsrede vom 31. Oktober 1884)*, in: Paul Oertmann (ed.), *Bernhard Windscheid. Gesammelte Reden und Abhandlungen* (1904) 109.

[21]Margit Szöllösi-Janze, *Nothdurft – Bedürfnis. Historische Dimension eines Begriffswandels*, in: Michael Prinz (ed.), *Der lange Weg in den Überfluss* (2003); Johann Baptist Müller, *Bedürfnis und Gesellschaft. Bedürfnis als Grundkategorie im Liberalismus, Konservativismus und Sozialismus* (1971) 10 f.

term *Nothdurft* (*indigentia* in Latin) was replaced by "need".[22] Whereas *Nothdurft* emphasized the physical needs of a human being, the term "need" included a spiritual connotation: it denoted ambition and desire, the driving forces behind individuals and society. Needs were viewed as "the foundation of social life and the initiation of bourgeois society".[23] At the same time, "needs" are subject to historical changes, and they also act as a catalyst of change in human society. In the 19th and 20th centuries, "need" became a central term in economics, sociology and psychology, especially in the works of Karl Marx and Siegmund Freud. Thus "need" also had linguistic connections to two other terms used by jurists in the 19th century: "development" and "spirit". "Need" represented the natural development of individuals and society; the law and the state could not counteract this development without suffering damage: in the words of Anselm Feuerbach: "With the rise of needs [...] the law itself grows and builds large and complex interwoven webs which can neither be shortened at will nor can their fine strings be interchanged with bigger ones without thus interfering with the conditions of life themselves".[24]

The following considerations are intended to show that Pandectists used the term "need" to address fundamental issues of their science. At the same time, this term was closely related to the question of how to merge Roman law and 19th century reality into a modern Pandectism. This was the central question for a jurisprudence concerned with ancient texts. I would like to approach this subject from two different angles. First, I will introduce "needs" as a problem of knowledge. The jurist had to identify "needs" in order to work with them. There was no measure of consensus among Pandectists as to how a jurist was supposed to work with these "needs". Subsequently, I will distinguish between three approaches discussed by the Pandectists in the 19th century: an "intuitive" approach, a "real" approach, and a "rational" approach. Second, I will address the question: in which part of contemporary theories of law can this argument be located? Is it part

---

[22]Uta Kim-Wawrzinek, Johann Baptist Müller, *Bedürfnis*, in: Otto Brunner, Werner Conze, Reinhart Koselleck (ed.), *Geschichtliche Grundbegriffe – Historisches Lexikon zur politisch -sozialen Sprache in Deutschland*, vol. 1 (1972) 440 ff.

[23]*Art. Bedürfnisse (politisch)*, in: Deutsche Encyclopädie, Bd. 3, S. 157 f.; see Margit Szöllösi-Janze, *Nothdurft – Bedürfnis. Historische Dimension eines Begriffswandels*, in: Michael Prinz (ed.), *Der lange Weg in den Überfluss* (2003); Johann Baptist Müller, *Bedürfnis und Gesellschaft. Bedürfnis als Grundkategorie im Liberalismus, Konservativismus und Sozialismus* (1971) 10 f.

[24]Anselm v. Feuerbach, *Betrachtungen über die Öffentlichkeit und Mündlichkeit der Gerechtigkeitspflege* (1821) 153.

of interpretational theory, part of the sources of law, or something entirely different altogether?

"Needs" as a Problem of Knowledge

Let me begin with my first question: How should jurists identify "needs"?

"Intuitive" Need

In Savigny's circle, a consensus existed that it was necessary for needs to be experienced as an individual's intuitive participation in a general sense of values. Needs were expressions of legal consciousness. Savigny's scholar, Georg Friedrich Puchta, spoke of a "natural sense of equity which a jurist [...] must not ignore".[25] In a similar fashion, Johann Friedrich Martin Kierulff called for a "satisfaction of the felt need".[26]

Consequently, needs could not be identified using any kind of empiricism; instead, a jurist had to be a part of collective values, the *Volksgeist*. The path to comprehension was through sensitivity and intuition. A jurist had to feel the people's needs; he had to be their representative. How could this be achieved? To quote Savigny: "The main requirement of this task is a pure, unprejudiced sense of truth".[27] As a protection against untruth "a quiet humble heart" was needed, "faithful love to truth and a heartfelt prayer [...] because in the end it is the simple childlike mind to which alone the truth will be revealed".[28] The truth was revealed, but by whom? Savigny suggested that "God's will" was "the deeper cause of morality and the law".[29] Savigny's close friend, Moritz August von Bethmann-Hollweg, agreed, and stated that a jurist could only guard himself against mere "speculation" "if

---

[25]Georg Friedrich Puchta, *Über die Negatorienklage*, in: Georg Friedrich Puchta, et al. (ed.), *Rheinisches Museum für Jurisprudenz, Philosophie, Geschichte und griechische Philosophie*, vol. 1 (1827) 163 f.

[26]Johann Friedrich Martin Kierulff, *Theorie des Gemeinen Civilrechts* (1839) 2.

[27]Friedrich Carl v. Savigny, *System des heutigen Römischen Rechts*, vol. 1 (1840) 94; for Savignys hermeneutical thoughts regarding this see Stephan Meder, *Missverstehen und Verstehen. Savignys Grundlegung der juristischen Hermeneutik* (2004) 85 ff. and passim.

[28]Adolf Stoll, *Friedrich Karl v. Savigny – Ein Bild seines Lebens mit einer Sammlung seiner Briefe, vol. II – Professorenjahre in Berlin 1810–1842 (1929)*, no. 338, 239; see also Dieter Nörr, *Savignys philosophische Lehrjahre – Ein Versuch* (1994) 263.

[29]Savigny, *§ 52, Bl. 224, 6.*

he finds that other humble path, the path of faith, on which he is guided by a superior light, which, by capturing, regenerating and reviving his whole being, gives a new push to every force in himself. What he longs to behold there, he will receive here – the eternal law, the divine law. Not merely as an obscure idea, but as an enlightened innermost force in his soul".[30] *Deus in nobis*: law is the work of man, but God is always acting inside of us.

The Pandectists' writing was thus intended to negotiate between legal consciousness, historical sources and the academic demand to understand law as a system. In 1844 (that is, in his supposed phase of *Begriffsjurisprudenz*), Jhering stated: "Academic interest [...] should not impede a norm [...] which has been a practical need, but it should be a legislator's goal to satisfy them both".[31] Jhering followed the direction of Puchta, who had demanded that jurists "express a need in a certain juridical form [...] and to elevate the demands of equity and of the non-juridical consciousness to genuine legal norms by linking them to the existent legal system".[32]

I will now go on to the Pandectists' second approach to indentify "needs": the "real" approach.

"Real" Need

In 1879, Bernhard Windscheid praised Savigny for demonstrating the German jurisprudence that "every code [...] is nothing else than an outcome of people's needs and interests which it satisfies and advances. Therefore these needs and interests are the basic principles, if the code is to be recognized in its actual meaning".[33] Even earlier, Windscheid had referred to "needs" in his dogmatic program, and in 1853 he had dealt with the assignment of claims in a well renowned article. He emphasized that the "need

---

[30]Moritz August v. Bethmann-Hollweg, *Grundriß zu Vorlesungen über den gemeinen und Preußischen Civilprozeß*, 3rd ed. (1832) XIV; in 1837, with regards to Savigny, he expressed this a little more neutrally. On the one hand he spoke of a "sincerity and love, to which alone the true nature of all things will be revealed" and on the other hand of a complete penetration of the subject "and his relation to the totality of knowledge", see Moritz August v. Bethmann-Hollweg, *rec. Savignys Recht des Besitzes*, 6th ed., in: Jahrbücher für wissenschaftliche Kritik 12 (1838) 265 ff., 267.

[31]Rudolf v. Jhering, *Die Lehre von der hereditas jacens: I. Standpunkt der Betrachtung*, in: id., *Abhandlungen aus dem Römischen Recht* (1844) 153 f. note 1.

[32]Georg Friedrich Puchta, *Über die Negatorienklage* (1827) 163 f.

[33]Bernhard Windscheid, *Festrede zum Gedächtnis an Savigny* (1879) 84, for the consideration of needs by Windscheid see Ulrich Falk, *Ein Gelehrter wie Windscheid*, 2nd ed. (1999) 133 ff., 158 ff., 176 ff., for this citation see 178.

of legal relations" demanded the legitimacy of such an institution and that the "legal consciousness of the people" accepted "this need". "Needs" were representatives of economical and ethical purposes. Windscheid explained that even if Roman law did not allow an assignment of claims, it was necessary to "accentuate our legal consciousness even against the Roman Law".[34] Although these terms were reminiscent of Savigny, in 1853 Windscheid found himself at a *turning point of jurisprudence*.[35] Under this banner, Johannes Emil Kuntze summed up a new literature of reform in 1856. He saw "symptoms of a crisis"[36] that unified a new generation of Pandectists everywhere. Kuntze summarized these tendencies as: stronger references to real life, the emancipation of legal history from dogmatics, the pursuit of the refinement of legal dogmatics, and an emphasis on a national perspective. These proposals all had a certain tension in common. Their authors wished to leave the domination of ancient texts behind, but the resulting focus on the present was not intended to result in deficits in rationality. Almost everyone was horrified at the thought of a jurisprudence arguing freely with its sense of justice. Thus, the authors tried to satisfy the present pressure of modernization by continuing to utilise the ancient legal texts. As exemplified by an illustration by Leist, a child will not "let go of its mother's guiding hand before it feels safe standing on its own feet".[37] The main problem was the search for possible ways in which one could adjust the law beyond the ancient texts in a scientifically controlled way. The term frequently used for this adaptation to reality was again "needs".

This conceptual continuity was accompanied by a new semantic shift in the idea of "need". Needs should be – in accordance with the natural sciences – increasingly recognized, and not only felt.

Volksgeist was now more and more perceived as "mysticism".[38] The concept of "people" was no longer understood as a metaphysical-cultural unity but as a network of real interests. In 1865, Wilhelm Arnold began

---

[34]Bernhard Windscheid, *Die Singularsuccession in Obligationen*, in: Kritische Überschau I (1853) 40, 42.

[35]Id., *Die Singularsuccession in Obligationen*, in: Kritische Überschau I (1853) 27.

[36]Johannes Emil Kuntze, *Der Wendepunkt der Rechtswissenschaft* (1856) 4; earlier id., *Das römische Recht in der Gegenwart und die Aufgabe der modernen Rechtswissenschaft in der Zukunft (Besprechung von Jhering, Schmidt, Lenz und Esmarch)*, in: Kritische Überschau 2 (1855) 173 ff.

[37]Burkard Wilhelm Leist, *Civilistische Studien auf dem Gebiete dogmatischer Analyse. Erstes Heft: Über die dogmatische Analyse Römischer Rechtsinstitute* (1854) 10.

[38]Rudolf Stammler, *Über die Methode der geschichtlichen Rechtstheorie* (1888) 6; concerning Ernst Zitelmann, *Gewohnheitsrecht und Irrtum*, in: Archiv für civilistische Praxis, vol. 66 (1883) 323 ff.

to split *Volksgeist* into its real components,[39] which he identified as: language, art, science, custom, economy, law, and state. Many authors could not resort to their own sense of justice anymore without a feeling of discomfort. They tried to understand the structure of law which before, as an "organism", had been left to autonomous, uncontrolled development.[40] Jhering explained in 1865 that: "The science of law does not state organisms, just as organic chemistry does not – it dissolves them".[41] In 1854, Burkhard Wilhelm Leist called for an autonomous "analysis of the existing legal institutions".[42] In the same year, Reinhold Schmid created a theory of law to "[not] be completely dependent on an uncertain sense of law".[43] In 1858, Jhering developed his natural-historical method to "put an end to the dominance of sense".[44] From this point onwards, references to a sense of law were perceived to be unscientific".

There was now a much stronger demand for empirical evidence in order to identify needs. The "practical needs" or the "needs of life" were increasingly understood as the "needs of legal practice" or the "needs of commerce": a much more realistic understanding. As early as 1843, Georg Beseler proposed to uncover the needs of life by studying them "in a natural scientist's way".[45] Legal practice, in particular, seemed to be an appropriate subject from which one could gain a detailed view of legal reality and its needs. Then again, deriving arguments from the courts' legal practice had had a bad reputation for some time. In 1846, Savigny repeatedly complained about inconsistent "pretences about the status of recent legal practice".[46] Savigny himself was dependant on mail correspondence with judges he

---

[39]Wilhelm Arnold, *Cultur und Rechtsleben* (1865); later on id., *Cultur und Recht der Römer* (1868).

[40]"We must not try to achieve something by using slogans like ‚Volksgeist' and organism. They are empty phrases and by using them we push our problems aside instead of solving them". Wilhelm Arnold, *Cultur und Rechtsleben* (1865) 9; in 1876 Adolf Merkel said, the "perception of all people as an organism" shall "from now on be subject to a special consideration and examination", Adolf Merkel, *Über den Begriff der Entwicklung in seiner Anwendung auf Recht und Gesellschaft*, in: Grünhuts Zeitschrift (1876), reprinted in: Adolf Merkel, *Hinterlassene Fragmente und Gesammelte Abhandlungen* (1898) 59.

[41]Rudolf v. Jhering, *Geist des römischen Rechts, vol. III 2, § 39*, 4th ed. (1884) 351.

[42]Burkard Wilhelm Leist, *Ueber die dogmatische Analyse Römischer Rechtsinstitute* (1854) 5.

[43]Reinhold Schmid, *Theorie und Methodik des bürgerlichen Rechts* (1848) 251.

[44]Rudolf v. Jhering, *Geist des römischen Rechts, vol. III 2, § 39*, 2nd ed. (1871) 332.

[45]Georg Beseler, *Volksrecht und Juristenrecht* (1843) 58, 109.

[46]Letter to Blume, reproduced in: Dieter Strauch, *Friedrich Carl von Savigny. Briefwechsel mit Friedrich Bluhme 1820–1860* (1962) 311 *(Brief vom 5. 9. 1846)*.

was friendly with to be informed about legal practice.[47] Even Windscheid, who usually argued vehemently for a consideration of legal reality, warned against "this often mentioned, yet frequently untraceable legal practice" in 1862.[48] Slowly, publications of case collections occurred. Not until 1847 did Seufferts Archiv begin to republish cases systematically.[49] Collections of court decisions had so far only appeared sporadically.[50] With Windscheid's first volume of his pandect textbook in 1862, the persistent consideration of legal practice slowly began.

Court decisions were one way of becoming acquainted with legal practice. By studying cases, one could become acquainted with the legal reality. However, as long as a theory about the raising and changing of needs was missing, one could say little about fundamental "needs". Without such a theory, one could not distinguish phenomena of legal reality from "real needs".

This leads us to the third approach of identifying "needs" – the "rational" approach:

Rational Need

To develop a theory of needs, both the sociology of law (which was of little importance before 1900), as well as Freud's psycho-analysis, were not

---

[47] See for instance Blume, see also Heinz Mohnhaupt, *Richter und Rechtsprechung im Werk Savignys*, in: Walter Wilhelm (ed.), *Studien zur europäischen Rechtsgeschichte* (1972) 262 f.

[48] Windscheid, *Lehrbuch des Pandektenrechts*, 1st ed. (1862), preface.

[49] Johann Adam Seuffert (ed.), *Archiv für Entscheidungen der obersten Gerichte in den deutschen Staaten* (beginning with vol. 9: *Seufferts Archiv für Entscheidungen*) (1847 ff.).

[50] One of the first collections: Oberhofgericht Mannheim, *Jahrbücher des Großherzoglichen Badischen Ober- Hofgerichts zu Mannheim, I–VII. Gesammelt und mit Genehmigung des Großherzoglichen obersten Justizdepartements herausgegeben vom Staatsrath von Hohnhorst, Kanzler des Oberhofgerichts* (1824–1832); also Oberappellationsgericht Wiesbaden, *Sammlung der merkwürdigeren Entscheidungen des Herzöglich Nassauischen Oberappellations-Gerichts zu Wiesbaden. Herausgegeben von W. von der Nahmer (Advokat und Procurator bei dem Herzöglichen Oberappellations-Gerichte, so wie bei dem Herzöglichen Hof- und Appellations-Gerichte in Wiesbaden), I–II* (1824–1825); Oberappellationsgericht Lübeck, *Juristische Abhandlungen mit Entscheidungen des Oberappellationsgerichts der vier freien Städte Deutschlands. Von A. Heise (Präsidenten) und F. Cropp (Rath bei dem Oberappellationsgerichte) I–II* (1827–1830); Obertribunal in Berlin, *Entscheidungen des Königlich Geheimen Ober-Tribunals, herausgegeben im amtlichen Auftrage von A. H. Simon (geheimer Ober-Justiz- und Revisions-Rathe), und H. L. von Strampff (Kammergerichts-Rathe, I–LXXXIII* (1837–1879).

considered, and Marx's writing was refused for political reasons. A "view behind the scenes" could very well have been inspired by Hegel, as his theory of bourgeois society (which he had developed in his 1821 legal philosophy) was founded on a "system of needs" as a mediation between the satisfaction of individual and collective needs.[51] Hegel thus concluded that protection of property by the judicature was necessary in order to maintain the momentum of the (mediated) needs.[52]

Eduard Gans designed the idea of a universal legal history, in which he observed the development of the concept of law during the reign of different *Volksgeister* in history. He did not need to resort to needs as an engine of civil society and law because, following Hegel, he focused on legislation, and thus denied an immediate influence of need on the law.[53] Lorenz von Stein went even further. In 1841, Stein wrote a long review of Savigny's "System", where he discussed the question of which pieces of Roman law were still applicable. According to Stein, the law in its essence is subordinated to the state-being and its "basic ideas and specifics".[54] To evaluate this, one had to face "reality and its scientific and practical need".[55] From this perspective, the next step was obvious: to turn one's sight to society itself; the jurist had to become a social scientist. Parallel to the mentioned critique, Stein worked on a historic analysis of French society from 1789 till 1830. In his famous *Begriff der Gesellschaft* of 1842, he described human society – in line with Hegel – as set in motion by the system of needs.[56] He deciphered the main

---

[51] For an introduction see Rolf Peter Horstmann, in: Ludwig Siep (ed.), *G.W.F. Hegel, Grundlinien der Philosophie des Rechts* (1997) 193 ff., 200, 206 ff.

[52] Georg Wilhelm Friedrich Hegel, *Grundlinien der Philosophie des Rechts*, in: Johannes Hofmeister (ed.), *Sämtliche Werke Bd. XIII* 4th ed. (1955) § 188.

[53] See for instance id., *rec. Friedrich von Raumer, Über die Preußische Städteordnung*, in: id., *Vermischte Schriften* (1834) 136; Lawmaking brought about legislators "according to their knowledge and needs". Need as a guideline for good legislation is emphasized for instance in Eduard Gans, *Das Erbrecht in weltgeschichtlicher Entwicklung* vol. 3 (1829) 49, 65, vol. 4 (1835) 19, 68, 107, 251. For a universal history by Gans see Heinz Mohnhaupt, *Universalgeschichte und Vergleichung bei Eduard Gans*, in: Reinhard Blänkner et al., *Eduard Gans (1797–1839). Politischer Professor zwischen Restauration und Vormärz* (2002) 339 ff.; for the system of needs as a motor for civil society see (in close accordance with Hegel) Gans, *Naturrecht und Universalrechtsgeschichte* (1981) 82 ff (introducing the term „Nationalökonomie" („national economy")).

[54] Lorenz v. Stein, *Zur Charakteristik der heutigen Rechtswissenschaft*, in: *Deutsche Jahrbücher für Wissenschaft und Kunst* (1841) 365–366, 369–370, 373–374, 377–387, 389–391, 393–399, 377.

[55] Id., *Zur Charakteristik der heutigen Rechtswissenschaft*, in: *Deutsche Jahrbücher für Wissenschaft und Kunst* (1841) 383.

[56] Gottfried Salomon (ed.), *Lorenz von Stein, Der Begriff der Gesellschaft und die soziale Geschichte der französischen Revolution bis zum Jahr 1830* (1921) 29.

needs using history and historical teleology. In doing so, he parted from his Pandectist roots.

Despite a focus on history as a method of gaining insight into the law, and despite the fascination for natural sciences, there were no Pandectists who sought to follow a social theory of this kind. The Historical School of Law opposed Hegel and heavily criticized the evolutionary theory of law presented by Gans in his book on inheritance law.[57] After 1860, not even Darwin's theory of evolution could convince the jurists of its usefulness.[58] Consequently, the Pandectists used the term "need" without having a clear theoretical concept. It remained a popular argument for suggesting a closeness to practice. Its persuasive power did not lie in proving an existing "need", but rather in proving an allegation of it to others. Thus, the concept of "needs" remained unsophisticated and obvious to all.

Theoretical Classification of the Argument

This leads us to the question: what does this have to do with juristic interpretation? In considering this question, I move to my second perspective: what did "needs" mean as an argument in the legal theory of the Pandectists? In the 19th century, this question had no unanimous answer.

For Savigny, "needs" were part of the *Volksgeist*. His doctrine concerning legal relationships, *Rechtsverhältnisse*, served as an intersection between legal norms and *Volksgeist*. Savigny used this doctrine to trace the rights back to the condition of the law "the way it surrounds us in real life".[59] At the same time, these legal conditions, in their system of mutual references, guaranteed the organic coherence of the law. For Savigny, academic-juridical interpretation meant in part a retracing of needs in *Ius Commune* texts, be they antique texts or later interpretations. The Jurist had to purge "the present state of law from all its elements that [...] have been created without a genuinely practical need".[60] For Savigny, intuition as a part of his hermeneutics was combined with a taxonomist's work. In particular, he displayed a tendency to read contemporary desired results into historical

---

[57] Georg Friedrich Puchta, rec. Eduard Gans: *Das Erbrecht in weltgeschichtlicher Entwicklung*, part 1 (1824), part 2 (1825), in: Friedrich Christoph Karl Schunck (ed.), *Erlanger Jahrbücher der gesamten deutschen juristischen Literatur 1* (1826) 14.

[58] Hans-Peter Haferkamp, *Darwinrezeptionen in der Rechtsgeschichtswissenschaft*, will be published in Ludwig Siep (ed.), *Evolution und Kultur*.

[59] Friedrich Carl v. Savigny, *System des heutigen Römischen Rechts*, vol. 1 (1840) 7.

[60] Friedrich Carl v. Savigny, *Vom Beruf unsrer Zeit für Gesetzgebung und Rechtswissenschaft* (1814) 119.

sources. For example, he held that the Romans had already known (juridical) representation even though a multitude of antique texts contradicted this.[61] This combination of intuition and scientific knowledge had already been rejected by Puchta.[62] In interpretation, he demanded a stricter faithfulness to the actual words. If this led to a conclusion in Roman law that was no longer appropriate, the only remaining possibility was to state a negation of this norm by customary law. He held that in the persistent exercise of an aberrant rule by courts or by jurisprudence a practical need could become evident. Need was no argument in interpretational theory but a legal source for customary law.

The development of this kind of customary law made by jurists and especially the courts was, according to Puchta, an intuitive process and, as such, it had to be strictly distinguished from the logical methods of finding the law employed by the legal sciences. The systematic work of jurists could not make use of "needs". Thus, it was not possible to trace the norms back to the *Volksgeist* found with this method. Scientific method and practical needs were separated. Between 1856 and 1858, Jhering developed this argument further. In his natural-historical method, Jhering created a world of "legal bodies" – "needs".[63] This realm of legal bodies, which had to be constructed, relied, according to Jhering, "entirely on itself"[64] without being driven by the demands of reality. A norm thus found existed "because it cannot not exist", even if this norm "could never hope to be of any practical use".[65] Consequently, Jhering's natural-historic method considered itself as "jurisprudence's emancipation from the coincidence of the immediate need".[66] Need was no longer a juridical argument. Legal science created the law, but legal reality decided whether there was a practical need for it.

Alas, Jhering's argument remained widely unheard. After 1848, despite the fact that many Pandectists still referred to "needs", most of them no longer regarded them as a source of law. Using the sources of law to create a demanded law, replaced the idea of the *Volksgeist* step by step. It became clearer that law was made and not so much found. "Needs" served as a scientific falsification to verify the practicability of the created law. A debate

---

[61] See Franz Josel Hölzl, *Friedrich Carl von Savigny Lehre von der Stellvertretung* (2003).

[62] To the following see Hans-Peter Haferkamp, *Georg Friedrich Puchta und die Begriffsjurisprudenz* (2004) p. 371 ff.

[63] Rudolf v. Jhering, *Geist des römischen Rechts*, vol. III 2, § 41 (1871) 343.

[64] Id., *Unsere Aufgabe*, JhJb 1 (1867) 19.

[65] Id., *Unsere Aufgabe*, JhJb 1 (1867) 18.

[66] Id. *Geist des römischen Rechts*, vol. III 2, § 41 (1871) 369.

between Windscheid and Justice Otto Bähr in a time before the codification of the German Civil Code (BGB) exemplifies this. In one particular matter, which is of no further interest here, a number of Pandectists referred to practical needs in order to justify their views. Among them was Otto Bähr. Bernhard Windscheid disagreed with him, but in accordance with Bähr, he argued that the law did not exist for its own sake, but much rather to satisfy "human needs". He concluded however: "Practical needs are not a source of law".[67] Otto Bähr replied that even if "practical needs" may not be an immediate source of law, they still were "a source of our sources of law" and, therefore, "indispensable for understanding and applying the law".[68] To show said practical need, he used a decision of the Supreme Court of the German Reich, which reflected his own point of view. The decision, he argued, contained the "answer of legal practice" and, therefore, the "rebuttal of Windscheid's argument".[69] By deducing the practical needs from court decisions, legal science as a matter of fact becomes bound by precedent. For the judge, Otto Bähr, this was much less a problem than for the Professor, Bernhard Windscheid, who countered Bähr in 1887 and stated: what "satisfies the practical needs is disputable. It is not important what we think, it is important what the legislator had in mind".[70]

With the above arguments and views in mind, we can conclude as follows.

Summary

Pandectism in the 19th century was confronted with the old problem of how to obtain or create law from ancient Roman law that was applicable in the present. One label Pandectists used to describe the relationship between law and reality was "needs". Before 1848, the focus lay on "practical needs", but later shifted to the more empirical "needs of legal relations" or "legal practice". The main question was how to discover these said needs as a jurist. In respect of this, Savigny in particular pointed out the intuitive participation of all jurists in the body of values, the *Volksgeist*. After 1848, under the influence of natural sciences, it became surrounded by the atmosphere of not living up to scientific standards. "Needs" had to be identified precisely. How that could be achieved however, remained unclear. One attempt was to give

---

[67] Bernhard Windscheid, *Wille und Willenserklärung*, in: AcP 63 (1880) 78, 81.

[68] Otto Bähr, *Urteile des Reichsgerichts mit Besprechungen* (1883) 14.

[69] Id., *Urteile des Reichsgerichts mit Besprechungen* (1883) 5, 8.

[70] Bernhard Windscheid, *Lehrbuch des Pandektenrechts I*, 6th ed. (1887) § 22 note 8; generally ulrich Falk, *Ein Gelehrter wie Windscheid*, 2. ed. (1999) 34.

more weight to court decisions. In numerous other attempts "needs" were simply claimed. Accordingly, a consensus of where to place the argument in legal history could not be found. To Savigny, needs became a part of legal interpretation. Puchta regarded it as a source of customary law, and Jhering as no legal argument at all. To most Pandectists, needs served rather as a control mechanism of those rules which had been crafted quite freely from ancient sources. Which needs actually existed and how they functioned in reality also remained unclear. Thus, it can be seen that the Pandectists most definitely did not develop a complete theory of needs. Jhering's attempt to disenchant the concept of a sense of justice or Stein's attempt to understand the driving powers of society were only the initial stages of this. In the end, to claim that something would satisfy a need remained a hidden judgment, and a mere allegation that a "need" related to reality. The question of whether or not Pandectists were detached from the real world cannot be answered by analyzing the concept of "needs"; however, it can be concluded though, that they did not wish to be.

Part IV
The Nature of Legal Interpretation

Chapter 7
Interpretation by Another Name

The Function of *Rechtsfindung* in the Modern State

Morigiwa Yasutomo

What is loosely known as the "interpretation of law" is an aspect of legal practice that is fundamentally inescapable for the jurist. Although an emperor, a king, and a Napoleon attempted to establish a legal code that rendered interpretation redundant, none succeeded. Interpretation does indeed seem to be an integral part of the life of law: the law evolves through interpretation. However, until very recently, the term "evolution of the law" was spoken of only metaphorically or in pseudo-scientific terms. This has changed in the past few decades; with a focus on the fact that interpretation is Janus-faced, various analyses of interpretation have emerged.[1] These analyses note that law is forward-looking and backward-looking at the same time. In order to speak of evolution seriously, one must be able to explain what this means and how interpretation works. It is only when the identity of the law is preserved that the particular law can evolve. The situation is the same for all forms of development. In order for a company S to develop, it must still be company S when it has grown many times its size, and perhaps metamorphosed into something quite unrecognizable to someone who knew only of its early days. Development is the changing of something constant, and if change is forward-looking and the constant element is perceived when looking backwards, we may say we have a Janus-faced entity.

We should now ask the question: what, in particular, makes the classical issue of identity and change special in law? As will be explained later, that which makes the identity of the object of legal interpretation possible, gives authority to the law; that which makes change possible in law brings about justice according to the law. The coexistence of identity and change is

---

[1] Exemplified by Joseph Raz, "Why Interpret?" in Raz (2009, 223–240).

Morigiwa Y. (✉)
Graduate School of Law, Nagoya University, Nagoya 464-8601, Japan
e-mail: morigiwa@nagoya-u.jp

Morigiwa, Y. et al. (eds.), *Interpretation of Law in the Age of Enlightenment*, Law and Philosophy Library 95,
DOI 10.1007/978-94-007-1506-6_7, © Springer Science+Business Media B.V. 2011

overlaid with the coexistence of authority and justice. This makes the issue at hand unique. The compatibility of authority and justice, and the simultaneous realization of both is a blessing for public decision-making, and a treasure that makes the rule of law reality.

How is this brought about? There are many elements of governance involved. As this conference focuses on the role of the courts in the Age of Enlightenment, we shall focus on the function of the judiciary in bringing this about. As we are dealing with the interpretation of the law in a period when judges were increasingly restrained by decrees and statutes, we shall focus on the role the judges play in the emerging relationship between the sovereign authority of the state *vis-à-vis* the citizen.

In civil courts, judges are required to solve the problems brought about by conflicts between citizens in an authoritative way. They are to give the final word on the conflict that citizens themselves could not put to an end. The opposing parties would not resort to violence and murder, as among other things, the cost involved is prohibitively high. It is also likely that none of the parties could come up with a knock-down argument. The court nevertheless is asked to decide one way or the other, not arbitrarily but by providing such persuasive public reason justifying the decision that it would be irrational for the losing party to complain. As my colleagues have amply demonstrated, the courts managed to do this in an unassailable way. The court is the mouth of the law, and hence, the decision is the *voice* of the law. The justifying reason behind judicial decisions is that it is the law: *Gesetz ist Gesetz;* the court is merely applying the *Gesetz.*

However, if there were a statute or other source of law that manifestly applied to the case at hand, the parties would probably never have taken the time and trouble to come to court. Indeed, it was the lack of such clear-cut arguments that brought them to court in the first place. What was it that the judges were able to do that the ordinary citizen could not, in finding the applicable law? What is it that allows them to come up with a truly persuasive argument, which in the quarters of philosophy is sometimes called an exclusionary reason? The answer is most aptly put in the German term: *Rechtsfindung. Rechtsfindung* is finding the law in a case. What is finding the law in a case? This is the particular sense of judicial interpretation that I will explore in this chapter.

To begin, I have a broad framework in which I propose to work out a theory of *Rechtsfindung.* To this end, I shall attempt to produce a "sketch" of what the framework looks like. In order to do this, I shall discuss two "small" questions. First, what is interpretation? Second, what is judicial interpretation? In this brief discussion of interpretation, it is my hope that many of the conceptions of interpretation presupposed by historians in this volume can be taken into account.

Interpretation

I propose, for the reasons given below, that interpretation is best understood as constituting an important element in the process of augmenting knowledge. Modern man is said to have free will, and is thus free from physical laws in a sense. Hence, he is transcendent from physical objects. We do what we do because we decide to do so, not because we are predetermined to do so through a chain reaction of cause and effect. One may doubt whether we can, in fact, make sense of free will. However, the claim here is merely that concerning important ethical issues such as what constitutes informed consent, free will is presupposed.

If we claim that there is good reason for this presumption, then we ought to know what we are doing when we consent, when we make a decision or do other things with our free will. This creates a "minor" epistemological problem: do we really know what we are doing? This problem is sometimes called the "aporia of modern philosophy". The question was posed most notably by Kant: how is experience possible? In a wider sense, how is knowledge in general possible?

To illustrate: I am a subject that can "know" a given thing, and this book on the table is the object that is to be known. In the typical scheme of thinking about knowledge, I, the knowing subject, would know that there is a book on the table if and only if there is in my consciousness the recognition that "there is a book on the table" is true. In order for the sentence "there is a book on the table" to be true, I must be able to provide proof that there indeed is a book on the table, and the proof must be either evident or rational. This proof is intended to be irrefutable, though in fact it is falsifiable. This is a very stringent condition, but nonetheless it is what is asked of us, when we are claiming not just belief, but knowledge.

If so, is knowledge really possible? Let us say the transcendent subject attempts to find out everything about the book, a transcendent object, and the conditions for the proposition "there is a book on the table" to be true are fulfilled, and so proven by the knowing subject. If it is the case that then and only then would the knowing subject be able to say that "I *know* that there is a book on the table", then knowledge may well be impossible.

By definition, transcendence means that a complete grasp of the book itself is not possible. There would always be properties that the subject was unaware of, and the subject would have to check whether that property was indeed there for the proposition "there is a book on the table" to be true. This process can go on *ad infinitum*, and therefore the subject could never reach a stage where he or she could say conclusively that he or she knows that there is a book on the table. If the epistemic problem of being able to prove is included as a condition of knowledge, then what is practically impossible makes the theory impossible. The aporia of modern philosophy is the problem of explaining how knowledge is possible, thereby justifying knowledge. The above is merely one facet of describing the "minor" issues involved in the modern enterprise of explaining and justifying knowledge.

In order to design and live a life that is free, the modern man with free will would necessarily have to have the power of knowledge. Unless the independent subject is able to know that there is a book on the table – and more important things – he cannot plan and live a life according to his will. If he cannot answer the question of knowledge conclusively, then the modern man is in a predicament: he is unable to explain and justify a fundamental tenet the modern man presupposes: living a life of free choice.

Just as many people are happy to ride a bicycle without being able to explain how it is possible, being unable to explain is, in itself, not life-threatening. However, we would be left in a position in which we would have to admit that one of the things we think most important in life is yet unexplained. As a result of this, even if life does not become meaningless, it may now seem rather insecure. At least for peace of mind, explaining and justifying our claim to knowledge seems worthwhile. Many philosophers have attempted to discover ways in which they can state that knowledge is indeed possible. Typically, as in the case of Descartes, it is not easy: one tends to fall into solipsism, if not into skepticism. These dark conclusions are the usual end of these philosophical endeavors, unless one can discover more worthwhile things to pursue in life, thus enabling oneself to leave the issue behind altogether.

In early 20th century, a philosophical movement called "phenomenology" raised hopes for knowledge. However, as far as Edmund Husserl is concerned, the jury is still out and it has been three quarters of a century since. Have things changed since then? Yes. Martin Heidegger appeared to have found a way out. I must admit that I am not very interested in Heidegger, and know little about him. Therefore, I merely claim that if Heidegger says things in line with what I now propose, then he most likely is correct.

How can we escape this situation? How shall we deal with the aporia? Something must be wrong with this schema. I propose to examine the aporia, and find out what it is. First, we shall turn to the main conditions that make up the schema. The knowing subject and the object to be known are transcendent to each other. How can one know something about that which is transcendent to you? Even if this were to be possible, how can you be certain that you know? You cannot do this without examining, from a bird's eye or a god's eye view, the correspondence between the proposition in your head that you believe is true and the state of affairs in the real world that the proposition describes. You are unable to do such a thing, precisely because you are not a bird in this imaginary situation or a god. You are not outside the world, but inside it. Your vision is limited to that of the knowing subject. No matter how you describe it, the vision is limited both physically and mentally. Therefore, as long as one thinks in terms of the schema, one is searching for the impossible.

If that is the case, we, as good philosophers, should raise doubts as to each of the assumptions that make up the schema. Am I transcendent? If I am not transcendent and if I do not possess free will, there is little motivation to explain and attempt to justify knowledge. This is one potential path by which our concerns can be laid to rest. However, can we actually do so? I would suggest that few would give up so easily. Perhaps instead we could suggest that the book is not transcendent. If it isn't, and the book is in some sense an inherent part of the knowing subject, then again knowledge is not really a serious question. Thus, if there is good reason to believe that we are all one in a metaphysical sense, we would want to take this path. However, this is little more than asking the same question as the former, and it is unlikely that one would want to conclude that we are not transcendent. So, let us maintain: the book is not a part of the subject.

Then are we stuck with the aporia? As far as the assumptions are concerned, we are unlikely to surrender them. Thus, it appears that we are trapped; but are we really? I propose to undertake further questioning, by examining the situation in the following way. It is not what is presented here that is the problem; it is what is missing from this scheme: the two-termed relation between the subject and the object. What, besides the knowing self and the known object, is absent? It is yet invisible, but with the following example, it may be made apparent.

While observing the book on the table, I state "there is a hook on the table". However, what is on the table is not a 'hook', it's a book. I have intentionally made a mistake in using the word. This example should demonstrate what was missing from the two-termed relationship between the subject and the object: language. Language was transparent until this point, yet it was there all along. We even talked about sentences and propositions being true. Nevertheless, language remained invisible because there was no need to be conscious of our using language. Indeed, it was most desirable that language did not interrupt, thus allowing us to concentrate on what we wanted to know.

How was it possible for language to be invisible, unobtrusive? We were acting upon the presupposition that there were no mistakes in my pronunciation, no use of inappropriate words, and no infelicities in my speech acts. However, once there *is* a mistake, language no longer remains transparent. It was this absence of mistakes and hitches that allowed us to forget about language. In order for this to happen, we must have a mastery of language. Among other conditions, I must not be intoxicated; I must be sober enough to speak correctly. When the required conditions are present, language remains invisible. Invisibility means, in this context, that language functions without our conscious operation of it; the things we use language for can usually be done more effectively if we are not conscious of the language we use in doing those things (cf. Austin 1976).

This conclusion also means that there is always a background presence of language and the use thereof, which exists as the third term in the schema of knowledge. However, because it is presupposed that there will be no mistakes in the use of language, it is inconspicuous, hence transparent. As is well known, this presupposition does not always hold when words are used. There are instances when language is intentionally made opaque; for example when reading poetry, or practicing a foreign language. When one is in the theatre enjoying a Shakespearean play, one is fully aware of the words spoken. There are instances when language becomes opaque against our wishes. We are all familiar with instances in which we find ourselves saying what we did not intend, or feeling tongue-tied.

Once we are aware of the existence and the transparent character of language, I argue that a three-termed system of knowledge should be preferred, with language as the third term. I propose that this formulation results in a much better chance of escaping the aporia. Even so, I must admit that there is no decisive argument that explains how this three-termed system operates. Nonetheless, early on last century it was perceived as an entirely liberating way of looking at the problem of knowledge. Eventually, this point of view came to be described as the "linguistic turn".

Let us explore this new way of looking at the situation and see how it might lead us out of the aporia. Say that the letter L symbolizes language, O the object to be known and S the knowing subject. What must S do in order to establish knowledge? S must first be able to put this state of affairs (the established facts about O) into words in L that are communicable to others. These others must be those with whom you want to communicate, and the state of affairs must be expressed without mistakes. To do so, one would first encounter the dimension of syntax, where S uses the terms and grammar of a language correctly. Second, the dimension of semantics, where S uses meaningful expressions about O. Third, one encounters the dimension of pragmatics, where S uses correctly the expressions of L in the appropriate circumstances. These three-dimensions of using language, i.e., in its relation to other signs, objects and people, are usually called the three branches of semiotics. This is one way of classifying what is involved in the statement: "there is a book on the table". The problem of knowledge becomes the problem of the use of language: the formulation of information to oneself and others, transmission of the information to others, and all three dimensions involve the ability to use language well.

How can one use a language well? Let me begin with the wrong way of looking at the problem. Wittgenstein experimented with the concept of private language, and attempted to show that there can be no such thing as a private language. (Wittgenstein 2009, sections 243–315). This was most salutary. Wittgenstein tried to demonstrate the absurdity of a private language through conceivably the most paradoxical thought experiment concerning language. In order for there to be a speech act, conventions must exist that make the speech act of saying "there is a book on the table" meaningful. Social conventions are usually customary, arising through tacit understanding between members of society. A private language by definition does not presuppose the existence of other members of society that speak the same language. Therefore, from this way of looking at language, as a system of conventions, a private language would be an offshoot from ordinary inter-personal language at best. It cannot explain language, but instead presupposes the societal use of language. This seems clear enough. However, as the literature and discussion on the subject illustrate, being able to adopt this way of looking at language is not easy at all if you have been entrenched in the two-termed way of perceiving the relationship between the self and the world.

Let us go on to what I propose to be the more appropriate approach. The three-term schema presupposes that there is someone to whom you speak about the object in question. This means that there are at least two people in the world. Thus, we are already out of the snare of solipsism. From the philosopher's point of view, this is a particularly liberating outlook.

Understanding, or the acquiring of knowledge, is not a two-term activity, with one term as the knowing subject and the other, the object. Rather, it is a three-termed relationship consisting of the person communicating to another one's understanding of the object to which both refer. The speaker cannot avoid affecting the understanding of the listener. The listener cannot help asking questions stimulated by the influence. In responding to the questions, the understanding one has of the object in question develops through testing and defending one's interpretation with the listener. Through this exchange, when what seems foreign becomes something one can relate to, we have a fusion of two understandings. This is what Hans-Georg Gadamer (Gadamer 1990) called *Horizontsverschmelzung*, or the fusion of the horizon.

The process of better understanding the object of interpretation is not a once-and-for-all, one-time event. This process is based on a communal concentration on the object of interpretation. It is a repeated, continually-developing process in which we come to better understand ourselves and the world. Hence, the term: the *hermeneutischer Zirkel* or the hermeneutic circularity. It is a spiraling and never-ending process.

Interpretation is never-ending, due to the peculiar property of the medium in which understanding is cultivated: language. In order to use language, we focus on that which we are discussing, and not the particular words that we use. The sign, or the aspect of language which represents any given thing or idea, is transparent when what is represented is present in our consciousness. When what is represented is not clear, the sign is no longer transparent and presents itself as an enigma requiring interpretation. Interpretation thus initiates the augmentation of knowledge. It therefore follows that the interpretive process of reason-giving is the search for knowledge. When norms and reasons give *public validity* to a claim, we have knowledge, and the sign becomes transparent once again. It is precisely this power of language to change between transparency and opacity that makes knowledge possible. This power of language, through active and passive processes, reveals a hidden infinity of what can be known.[2] If the number of possible signs are infinite, the process of knowing is an infinite one. Knowledge, i.e., the grasping of the truth, is a never-ending spiraling process, as what is to be known can only become an object of knowledge when what is not to be known is rendered unproblematic by an infinite possible concatenation of signs.

Thus, the problem of knowledge becomes a problem of communicability, and in order for communication to become possible, language must be possible. In order for language to be possible, one cannot be alone. In fact, there must be a society, a dynamic, developing society: one needs not only the good will and the effort of others, but also substantial investment. Building a conventional institution incurs substantial cost and time, and is successful only when there is resource enough for publicity and education, along with its regulation and continuance. Only with these conditions, for example, could the French language become the language of France. This is what the French government attempted to do in forming its nation state, and succeeded. In contrast, among the intelligentsia of Kazakhstan, the majority of the people speak Russian. They cannot speak their own Kazakh language. This effectively illustrates how difficult and significant it is to be able to nurture one's own language.

Hence, after habitual use and a fair amount of social effort, the public good of a national language is produced, and only when this exists do we have the foundation for a sound communal, system of knowledge. This is

---

[2]The sign hides itself in its transparent mode, thus making what it represents unproblematic, and when it shows itself by becoming opaque, makes problematic what it represents by making apparent that it is hiding what is represented.

because knowledge in the three-term schema is centered upon the communicability of information. The linguistic turn is thus geared towards solving the problem of the aporia of knowledge.

Judicial Interpretation

Interpretation is a method of augmenting knowledge. In law, interpretation becomes even more accurate and precise as a method of augmentation. In German, finding the facts of a case is called *Tatsachenfeststellung*, and if one is a good lawyer, one has to be skilled not only in statutory interpretation but also in *Tatsachenfeststellung*. All good judges will tell you that in most cases *Tatsachenfeststellung* is more important than statutory interpretation; one seldom has to engage in such interpretation, as the applicable statute is not contested.

The art of *Tatsachenfeststellung* and that of legal interpretation together comprise the art of *Rechtsfindung*. *Rechtsfindung* is the type of interpretation in which we engage when finding the law in a case. It is a more precise and artificial version of the three-termed schema of communicating information or acquiring knowledge.

In order for there to be language, the interpretation of which is not contested at every step, there must be a valid authority that produces the final judgment on an interpretive question. Is such a system possible? It is my argument that it is, and as to the question of how, social recognition of a professor of truth is usually the answer. Truth serves as a regulative idea that regiments the use of language, and thus can define abuses thereof. For example, someone insists that "two plus two is five". A professor responds that "no, two plus two is four. Five wrong; it's not true". You may disagree with using the term "truth" in arithmetic, regarding it as an analytic enterprise rather than a synthetic one. If problems with the foundation of arithmetic make things too complicated, instead take the example of the law of gravity. If someone states that the law of gravity does not hold in this room, the physics professor would say "you're wrong, the law of gravity does indeed hold in this room". If the person insists, "no, no, my interpretation is different", to that we do not say, "oh, yes, we all have freedom of interpretation". Rather, we believe in the authority of the professor saying, "no, you are wrong, what you are saying is not true, it's false". Thus, one can see that truth and falsehood (and a valid authority thereof) possess a monopolizing power in deciding what a correct interpretation is.

I stated earlier that interpretation is a process that augments knowledge. If we regard the practice of law as an enterprise for learning, then interpretation in law should try to be as close to the general model of interpretation above as possible. We should respect truth in law as much as possible, especially in the finding of facts. However, because we are operating within a world of value judgments, we require a regulative ideal that is fit for the world of values, and functions as truth does in ordinary parlance or in the sciences.

What can we find in law that acts as the functional equivalent of the concept of truth that I have just illustrated? Many people, who like to connect logic and law, believe in an internal connection between logic and law. I do not believe that any such connection exists. Then, what is the functional equivalent that we wish to find? To answer this question, let us examine once more the function that truth plays. It locks in one interpretation and allows no other. Functionally speaking, this means that truth demands absolute authority and as a result we have stability in interpretation. Therefore, what one must try to discover is a comparable concept that works in the legal field; a concept that brings about absolute authority that promises stability of the law.

Joseph Raz in his inspiring essay titled "Why interpret?" has illustrated that there are two moments in interpretation, or two different types of processes at play when we are interpreting the law. First, we engage in processes that answer the question, why interpret; second, we engage in processes that respond to the question, how should we interpret. When one thinks about interpretation, the processes tend to mix with one another, and produce a confused idea of what interpretation is. Raz was able to avoid this mistake by dividing interpretation into the two different functions. Thus, let us ask the first question: why do we want to interpret in the first place? Both Friedrich the Great and Napoleon tried to prevent the interpretation of their codes. However, it was not long before commentaries were produced. A common understanding is that prohibiting interpretation is not practical; interpretation is inevitable. However, this is not satisfactory for our current purposes. Rather, we should say: "we should interpret". But then, why should we interpret?

Raz argues that the reason we interpret is to bring about authority and stability. This is the type of explanation we seek to clarify the function of interpretation. Why does interpretation bring about such functionality? It is because interpretation is not the changing of a norm; it is merely an interpretation thereof: the norm retains its original authority.

One could argue that the present situation is much like the relationship between a "concept" and a "conception" of the concept. It can be said that the *concept* of the good remains the same at all times, while each individual possesses different interpretations or *conceptions* of what the good is. These conceptions compete with each other, with the protagonist of each conception providing the best set of reasons conceivable for the adoption of her particular preference. The consequence is that the concept of the good becomes enriched and deepened, the more we discuss and reflect upon it. This is what we are doing when engaging in moral philosophy.

I propose to examine the problem at hand in the same manner. To illustrate, imagine a norm. This norm commands the authority and validity that any good norm should have in a given system. If the system is a kingdom, the norm is authoritative and valid because it was issued in the name of the king; or in a liberal democracy, it was issued in the name of the people in accordance with the constitution. No matter what scheme or polity is in question, legal authority exists in virtue of the source of supreme authority in that system. Hence, to justify the validity of a legal norm, one always refers to the source of legal authority of that system. We say that judges merely produce new interpretations that do not affect the norm itself. In this way, the authority and stability of norms remain. This is why the judges must interpret rather than change the law, the legal authority for which the judge does not have. Thus, the use of the words "judge-made law" should be prohibited if possible. A more precise way of describing the phenomenon is "judge-interpreted law".

I shall now go on to discuss "how to interpret", not "why interpret". We shall discuss the part that conception, not the concept, plays in this system. In the case of a legal norm, the counterpart of the conception of a concept is the interpretation thereof. When a judge interprets the law, does she think conservatively and attempt to retain the authority of that norm? The judge must keep this in mind, but it certainly cannot be the *only* function of interpretation. There is a further element driving the interpretation. She must distinguish the "how" from the "why" question and move on to the "how".

In many cases people and judges alike are driven to use interpretive techniques, because they find that a norm, if applied mechanically, provides a bad solution to a problem. The most evident case is when the application would go against the interest of both parties in a civil suit. If by a simple act of interpretation the situation can be turned into a win-win game, why not do so? I propose that this is the driving motivation behind judicial interpretation in an uncorrupted system. I will remind the reader at this point that I am attempting to provide a type of legal philosophy that can be of help to judges and practicing lawyers. This is my aim in discussing interpretation in this fashion.

Thus, how should a judge interpret the content of a norm? She should be focused upon justice and the public good that can be produced by that interpretation. Therefore, it will tend to be a public-reasoned, justice-oriented type of interpretation. Justice in law is the functional equivalent of truth. Justice is what is sought after in law, to take the place of truth in the sciences. If we think of justice as totally unrelated to law, in a positivistic way, then this makes little sense. However, I shall now attempt to explain this idea in such a way that it is accessible to a staunch positivist.

Let us go back to the common person or the practicing lawyer. We know that as a practicing lawyer, if one does not have a sense of justice, or an understanding of the moral values involved in a judicial decision, one does not belong in the legal profession. The same applies if you have no respect for the facts of the case. Calling oneself a positivist or an anti-positivist is meaningless in this context. One must always have respect for both the value of justice and the facts in order to be a decent practicing member of the legal profession.

As a consequence, how should one think about justice? Justice should be thought of not as a concept detached from its context, but only as it works within society: within an institution that can produce and reproduce justice. John Rawls in his theory of justice[3] demonstrates how this can be done. Rawls does not speak merely of the concept of justice; he speaks mainly of a basic structure of society that inevitably produces justice. Justice in this sense is a public good, just as clean air, water, roads, and airports are. Safety provided by the military and the police, and justice provided by the court, are two of the most important public goods that the artificial state can provide, as social contract theorists have so dramatically described.

Thus, when it comes to the second question of "how to interpret", we should be interpreting in such a way that there will be as much justice as is possible within the framework of law. We should interpret the case so that when it becomes a precedent, it would form an institution where it would produce as much justice as possible.

Of course the conceptions of justice in law have been, and will be discussed and refined. Fortunately, for countries such as Germany, France or Japan, which have more than one century of jurisprudence since codification, the wheel does not have to be reinvented. All that one need do is look at the casebooks to discover discussions on what justice demands, what the law ought to be in a particular type of case. This is precisely what casebooks do. They provide a reservoir, a repository of public reasons, which establish a certain conception of justice. This is why one can refer to positive justice in the practice of law.

Law is a method of providing positive justice in society, and in that sense law and justice are related to each other. I believe even the starkest positivist would allow this. This is the common ground where practicing lawyers,

---

[3]Cf. not only his *Theory of Justice* (Rawls 1971) and *Restatement* (Rawls 2001) but also his influential articles in *Collected Papers* (Rawls 1999).

judges, professors of the black letter law and more theoretical professors can engage in fruitful dialogue with one another.

In answering the earlier question of "why interpret", I have been careful to keep discussions of "how to interpret" from seeping in, and was focused on attaining authority and stability. In looking at the issue of "how to interpret", the same consideration applies. I have distinguished the issue from that of "why interpret" and referred to justice and the realization of the public good of justice as the basic aim of interpretation. In justice, we have found a surrogate for truth. Thus, identity *and* change are both realized in law.

I must admit, that here, instead of the universality of a law of nature such as gravity, what we can ask for at best is generality. In order to attain this generality, the type of reasons that need to be given to justify one's decision and one's outlook must have the property of *Öeffentlichkeit*, or public openness. It must be noted that the proposition "two plus two equals four" or "the law of gravity holds in this room" does have this type of *Öeffentlichkeit*. It is a proposition that is public in a broad sense; it is valid anywhere, and at any time. It can withstand attempts at refutation, criticisms of all kinds and maintain its truth value. Then, if one is a rational being, one cannot say that it does not hold. This is the type of statement that must be aimed for in legal decisions, and in ascertaining the "correct" interpretation of a legal norm until further interpretive development occurs. Of course, this is not an easy task: however, it is what the jurist should strive for. Justice is a regulative ideal; interpretation of law should strive for justice as much as possible within the constraints that the art and technology of interpretation create.

When a legal system has enough experience and enough jurisprudence to engage in such interpretation, then a system of law is produced in which the rule of law *actually* exists. This system is what we are trying to realize in developing countries, and the type of system that we work to enrich in developed countries.

Thus, *Rechtsfindung* is one answer to the question: what is another name for interpretation. *Rechtsfindung* provides us with interpretations of the law, which in turn means that it provides us with the public good of authority *and* justice.

Bibliography

Austin, John Langshaw. 1976. *How to Do Things with Words,* Second Edition. Edited by J. O. Urmson and Marina Sbisà. Cambridge, MA: Harvard University Press.
Gadamer, Hans-Georg. 1990. *Wahrheit und Methode: Grundzüge einer philosophischen Hermeneutik*, Tübingen, Mohr: 1960. 6. Auflage, 1990.
Rawls, John. 1971. *A Theory of Justice*. Cambridge, MA: Harvard University Press. Revised edition, 1999.

Rawls, John. 1993. *Political Liberalism.* New York, NY: Columbia University Press. Second edition, 2005.

Rawls, John. 1999. *Collected Papers.* Edited by S. Freeman. Cambridge, MA: Harvard University Press.

Rawls, John. 2001. *Justice as Fairness: A Restatement.* Edited by E. Kelly. Cambridge, MA: Harvard University Press.

Raz, Joseph. 2009. *Between Authority and Interpretation. On the Theory of Law and Practical Reason.* Oxford and New York: Oxford University Press.

Wittgenstein, Ludwig. 2009. *Philosophical Investigations*, 4th edition. 1st edition translated by G. E. M. Anscombe, revised 4th edition by P. M. S. Hacker and Joachim Schulte. Wiley-Blackwell.

Chapter 8
What Is Interpretation of the Law for the French Judge?

Michel TROPER

The question "What is interpretation of the law for the French judge?" can have several meanings, and can relate to both empirical questions and normative problems. For instance, consider the following questions:

(a) How does the French Judge interpret the law?
(b) How does the French Judge describe the way in which he interprets the law?
(c) How should the French Judge interpret the law?

This third question, which is the normative question, can itself be understood in different ways. We could ask either "How should the French Judge interpret the law according to French legal doctrine?" or "How should the French Judge interpret the law according to the lawmaker?" Legal scholars and the lawmaker may possess differing views on how judges should interpret the law; the lawmaker may expect literal interpretation, whereas legal scholars may prefer a more functional interpretation.

However, the normative and the descriptive questions are all interrelated – more importantly, they are all related to some more general questions, such as the nature and scope of the judicial function, or the views prevailing in the French legal culture on the judiciary and its relation to legislation. In fact, in France – and this is also true of other European countries – we have two competing ideas of the judicial function. The first was inherited from the Enlightenment, and the second developed after the Second World War under the influence of both the Common Law, and a revival of natural law theories.

Allow me to describe them in turn.

M. TROPER (✉)
Centre de Théorie et Analyse du Droit, Université de Paris Ouest – Nanterre,
Paris, France
e-mail: troper@u-paris10.fr

MORIGIWA, Y. et al. (eds.), *Interpretation of Law in the Age of Enlightenment*, Law and Philosophy Library 95,
DOI 10.1007/978-94-007-1506-6_8, © Springer Science+Business Media B.V. 2011

I.

Since the Revolution, French Legal culture has been dominated by the idea that the judiciary is entirely subordinate to other governmental powers. This view comes from Montesquieu's vision of the separation of powers (Troper 2010; Eisenmann 1933). Montesquieu wrote that of the three powers in the State the judiciary "is in some way null" because the judge is only the mouth that speaks the words of the law, but is incapable of creating rules himself (Montesquieu 1748, Bk XI, chap. VI). Montesquieu's theory of the judicial function was famously expanded by Beccaria, who was the first to compare a judgment to a syllogism where the law – meaning statutory law – is the major premise, the facts are the minor premise, and the sentence is the mere conclusion (Beccaria 1764). The two premises are given to the judge (the former by the lawmaker, the latter by a jury) and the conclusion logically follows: thus, the judge is left with no discretion, and ideally could be replaced by a robot.

This view was almost unanimously accepted at the time of the French Revolution. The reason why revolutionaries found it so appealing was not their love for Montesquieu, whom they had many reasons to reject, but the fact that it fully met their needs. One should keep in mind that in pre-revolutionary France, courts were extremely powerful and posed a great obstacle to reforms. There were "Parliaments", completely different from our modern legislatures, that acted as supreme courts of appeal. There were several of these Parliaments in the country. They had the power to devise the laws that they intended to apply, and claimed a veto power over legislation enacted by the king (Hanley 1983). Indeed, the main source of law was judge-made law. This conflicted with the new concept of freedom, which was understood as the right to be governed by statutes only, as statutes are the expression of the will of the people. Thus, when men obey a statute they are only submitting to themselves.

As a consequence, in 1790 the National Assembly passed a law that prohibited judges (under very severe penalties) from creating legal rules, and restricted them to the mechanical application of pre-existing statutes. It was implied that several codes would be issued: codes that would be clear, complete and coherent, so that for every case judges would find a precise statutory rule to apply. Coherence meant that the codes would be without contradictions, completeness meant that there would be no gaps, and clarity meant that there would be no need for interpretation, according to the famous Latin maxim that *in claris non est interpretandum* (what is clear must not be interpreted).

Let us focus our attention on the third quality of the law. For the revolutionaries, clarity was an ideal that they wished to achieve for two main reasons. First, clarity was prized, as it was considered to be a prerequisite to the citizen's freedom. If the law is clear, then everyone knows what the consequences of his actions will be. Thus, he will be able to proceed or refrain from acting. The second reason was the idea that the power to interpret a law amounts to the power to legislate. Therefore, the power of interpretation was to be reserved to the lawmaker, according to another famous maxim *ejus est interpretari legem cujus est condere*. It follows that interpretation was strictly forbidden to judges, and was punished exactly by the same penalties as an attempt to enact a general rule.

Nevertheless, the revolutionaries were not dim on this matter. They were aware that judges would inevitably encounter difficulties in the application of the law. If judges were not permitted to interpret the law they would be unable to decide certain cases. On the other hand, granting permission to interpret the law would amount to giving them a form of legislative power. The solution to this dilemma was found in a distinction between interpretation *in abstracto* and interpretation *in concreto*. The former was equivalent to legislation and was strictly forbidden: when judges found it difficult in the abstract to understand the meaning of a statute they were required to turn to the lawmaker and ask for an abstract and general interpretation. But if in a concrete case they found a similar difficulty, they were under an obligation to make a decision.

However, the decision was not considered to be interpretation, but the mere application of the law. Naturally, the decision could always be appealed and if that occurred, the grounds for appeal would not be that it was a wrongful interpretation, but an incorrect application of the law. The place where the appeal was heard was at a tribunal of cassation, established *alongside the legislature* (Halpérin 1987). The tribunal was not a supreme court of appeal. It did not examine the facts, but only the law. It did not decide the case, but only confirmed or overturned the decision of the court of appeal. If it overturned the decision because the law had been wrongly applied, the case was sent to another court of appeal. Even so, this other court could very well come to the same decision as the previous court, and disagree with the tribunal of cassation. The new decision could also be appealed, but if the third court of appeal was still in disagreement with the tribunal of cassation on the correct application of the law, this created a presumption that the law was not clear and that there was a need for interpretation, i.e. an act of legislation. Thus, the matter had to be referred to the legislature, which then issued an interpretation *in abstracto*.

It was thus an agreed theory that there was no such thing as judicial power. Even the current and relatively recent French constitution does not mention a judicial power but only a judicial "authority".

However, it does not follow that judges should not be independent. On the contrary, the revolutionaries based the necessity of judicial independence on the very principle of the separation of powers. If judges were dependent on either the legislature or the executive they would not apply a general and antecedent law, nor the will of the people, but the particular will of the law-makers or that of the executive. Citizens would not be able to predict the consequences of their actions and – as we have seen – they would lose their freedom. Independence of the judiciary has the same purpose as the limitation of its role. It is a guarantee that citizens will be submitted to general laws only and not to the whims of the men who happen to be in power.

This same general idea of the limited role of the judiciary was also present in the civil code, and was dominant until very recent years. This is the reason why although we can find in the code several provisions on the interpretation of contracts, there are none that deal with the interpretation of statutes. This view also holds many consequences for the organization of the judiciary, the status of the judges, the style of opinions, the doctrine of the sources of law or the basic conception of fundamental rights.

What does it imply for judicial ethics? Let us stress the first and most obvious implication, namely that judges may not interpret the law. However, the idea that they can apply it without interpretation is perfectly untenable, and reinforces the power of judges instead of restraining it. Of course, judges cannot avoid interpreting statutes. Nonetheless, the attitude that they are constrained to adopt is the following: there is no need for interpretation when the law is clear, and the law we have to apply clearly has meaning. However, this declaration that the law clearly has meaning and therefore does not require interpretation is itself obviously the result of an interpretation.

Thus, the whole idea does not limit the power to interpret the law, but on the contrary expands it, because interpretation does not appear as such. Rather, it is clothed as "application" and never justified. Opinions are extremely brief, only a few lines and always with the same syllogistic structure:

(1) the law says that if A then B,
(2) we found that A has taken place
(3) therefore B.

In practice, the distinction between abstract and concrete interpretation collapses, because after a decision of a lower court based on an interpretation of the law has been challenged before the Court of Cassation (the name it received after 1828), the final interpretation of the court is *de facto* binding on all the lower courts. It is *de facto,* because everyone knows that all other interpretations will be overruled. Thus the law applies to all similar cases as interpreted by the Court of Cassation, which means that the interpretation is perfectly abstract (Troper and Grzegorczyk 1997).

Second, as the interpretation given by the court cannot be appealed and cannot be overruled, except by way of an entirely new law, the statute means what the court has said it means. There is no "true" meaning of the law that could be opposed to the court. Thus in the exercise of that power the court enjoys complete discretion. Thus, what the revolutionaries feared has indeed been made possible: the court has exercised legislative power. Indeed it is a well known fact that, for instance, the whole body of the law of liability was created by the Court of Cassation throughout the 19th century, stemming from five articles of the civil code.

Third, this power is augmented enormously, as courts are not bound to justify their interpretation and are not bound by precedents.

Fourth, it is reinforced by the prevailing idea that judges do not express their own will and that their decisions do not correspond to their own political or moral preferences. Rather, their decisions are merely the application of pre-existing law. Although this view is false it has been widely professed. Court decisions enjoy what Max Weber calls "rational legitimacy".

Nevertheless, this huge power has been exercised with considerable restraint and we must now turn to the causes of this restraint. Why is it that although one hears complaints that judges are politically too conservative or (more rarely) too progressive, there is no claim that they are despotic or that what they do goes beyond a conservative or a progressive application of the law? It is a fact that many sincerely believe that the judges are subordinate to the law, and that they merely apply it. Another way of framing the question would be: "why do judges profess a view of a subordinate judiciary that is false, and do not act according to a better theory that recognizes the extent of their power?"

One very obvious answer would be: because judges share a system of ethics, and view themselves not as the masters of the law that they are, but as the servants that they are not. This is undoubtedly true but misses an important point: how does one know that judges abide by these ethics, rather than believing, for instance, that they ought to do what is best for society or do justice, irrespective of what a particular law says?

The choice of a system of ethics depends logically on meta-ethics but also reflects some empirical constraints. Since the meta-ethics of the French judges are not specific, let us focus on the empirical constraints. In addition to the fact that judges have – as we have seen – a strong interest in professing the concept of a subordinate judiciary, an idea that does not diminish but rather increases their real power, there are several factors that encourage them to sincerely believe in it.

(a) The first lies in the mode of education. Judges have been trained since the beginning of the 19th century in law schools, and have been taught the prevailing ideology of a subordinate judicial function. These schools were organized on the margins of the universities as technical schools, where critical thinking was not a priority. They were called "schools" rather than "faculties". Moreover, students and professors alike came from the same social groups as lawmakers, and had no immediate interest or even desire to distort the law. The prevailing ideology was submission to the lawmaker, because the lawmaker was believed either to have superior wisdom as in the case of Napoleon, or to express the will of the people in democratic times. From this idea followed the privileged method of interpretation aimed at the discovery of the intention of the lawmaker, i.e. literal interpretation known as exegesis. One should add that this method of interpretation of statutes coincided with the method used in the catholic religion for biblical interpretation.

(b) Secondly, the mode of selection and promotion of judges has always been that of the civil service. Recruitment was – and still is – by way of a competitive examination. Judges are awarded grades by their superiors and can be promoted to a higher position according to those grades. Until recently, promotions were decided by the Minister of Justice. A *Conseil Supérieur de la Magistrature* has been created in 1958. It has the power to discipline judges and must consent to their promotions. Elected judges, although they do not hold the majority[1] have a large number of seats. The Conseil does not always share the Minister's views, but its very existence makes it extremely difficult for a judge whose views would be too marginal to be promoted. A successful career largely depends on general conformity with prevailing ethical views.

(c) A third factor is the procedural situations of judges that determine their specific constraints. In the case of lower court judges their situation is quite simple. If they wish to avoid being overruled they must follow very closely the jurisprudence of the court of appeal that is above them, and that of the Court of Cassation. Their personal careers depend in part on the proportion of their decisions that have been overruled.

---

[1] Since the constitutional amendment of 2008.

The real problem is restraint by the Court of Cassation. In addition to the fact that members of the court share a prevailing ideology, one should also take into account the fact that the lawmaker – or even the constituent power – can always enact a new law if they dislike the rule created by the court. This happens rarely, but the very possibility of such a reaction acts as a very powerful constraint. One way of presenting the ideal of interpretation (as focused on the lawmaker's intention) is to say that it is not the original lawmaker's intention that matters, but rather the present lawmaker's.

On the other hand, even when there is little probability that its decisions will be overruled, a supreme court enjoys more power when its jurisprudence is relatively stable, rather than changing at whim according to the personality of plaintiffs or to the circumstances. With the latter attitude, the court's decision only binds the parties to the case, but other citizens are unable to predict what the court's attitude would be in another case, even if that case was similar to the first. On the contrary, if the court's jurisprudence is stable, then citizens can predict that the court will rule in the same way in future cases, and will therefore act as if the court had issued a general rule.

Finally, the plurality of courts plays an important role. Since the 19th century, courts have been organized in two different court systems, with two supreme courts: the Court of Cassation at the head of civil, criminal, labor and commercial courts, and the Conseil d'État at the head of administrative courts. In the last few decades, the Constitutional Council, the ECJ and the ECHR have also been established. The Court of Cassation and the *Conseil d'État* have always competed with each other for jurisdiction in certain matters. Success can only be achieved by invoking general, moderate and stable principles. The same occurs with the Constitutional Council and the European courts.

II.

A second concept of the judicial function emerged after the Second World War.

One reason was the feeling that the so-called "positivist" attitude of judges was partly responsible for the efficiency of authoritarian regimes in Italy, Germany or Vichy France, or at least for the lack of resistance to tyranny and totalitarianism. The term "positivism" was used at the time to characterize the idea described in the first part of this chapter, and the attitude of judges who applied law regardless of its content; those who considered that only positive law, especially in statutes, was law. The claim was that such an attitude made things extremely easy for anti-democratic governments.

Instead, judges should enforce not only statutes, but also fundamental principles, and in the presence of a conflict between statutes and these principles, should let the principles prevail. According to this doctrine, fundamental principles ought to be considered either part of the law alongside positive law or the "real" law. In the German constitution for example, a distinction is made between *Gesetz und Recht* (statutes and Law) and judges are submitted to both. In France "positivism" was also blamed for smoothing the path for the Vichy regime.

This new attitude took hold in most European countries, with the notable exceptions of Britain and the Netherlands, where the principle of parliamentary sovereignty still reigns. As a consequence, it led to the creation of constitutional courts in charge of judicial review of legislation. This movement now includes France, where, since 2010, courts must refer a statute applicable to a given case to the Constitutional Council when one of the parties has raised the question of its constitutionality.

However, this type of centralized judicial review is significantly different from the American system, where judges, including lower judges, may decide alone on the constitutionality of a statute. The European model is formed in part by the influence of the ideas from the French Revolution: that judges should stick to the application of statutes as the expression of the will of the people.

A second reason for the development of a new concept of the judicial function is the influence of the American idea of the Rule of Law and of American Legal Realism. European judges began to understand the prestige and power of American Judges. That power stems from a long tradition, but also from the acceptance of the fact that judges necessarily enjoy discretion and create law. Unlike French Judges of the 19th century, the American realists did not hide the power of judges and did not pretend that they were merely mechanically applying statutes or even precedents. This acceptance was easy to justify because the application of a precedent cannot be mechanical. What is applied is not the decision itself but the principle of the *ratio decidendi*. There is room for discussion, and therefore discretion as to the question of whether the principle applies to the present case. Moreover, among the laws that have to be applied the most important is the constitution, which is extremely vague and ambiguous.

If judges do not stick to the mere application of statutes but create rules and exercise discretion in that activity, they must justify this power. This may seem to be a formidable task, but the acknowledgement of judicial discretion combines fairly easily with the Rule of Law. One of the best justifications is that they still apply law, but it is law in a higher sense; a law made of formal and substantive principles directed at the preservation of fundamental rights (Troper 2008).

In the modern day, European Judges are increasingly in similar situations. In France, and elsewhere, particularly in Italy, there are, as I said before, administrative courts, which do not apply codified statutes and never have. There were no administrative codes and very few statutes to apply. Administrative courts therefore had to develop a whole body of rules and principles, which they created. To this day administrative law is for the most part judge-made law. The only possible justification for this creation is to present it as the "discovery" of and, exactly as in the US, as the application of unwritten principles directed at the preservation of fundamental rights.

A third reason is related to the increasing influence of international law on the French national legal system, as on the legal systems of other European countries. For example, the French constitution prescribes that international treaties and law derived from international treaties (such as European directives or regulations created by institutions of the European Union and the European Convention of Human Rights) prevail over statutes. After a 1975 decision of the Constitutional Council, judges – even lower judges – can refuse the application of a statute if it contradicts international law. This is obviously an enormous revolution, especially if we remember that there was – and there still is – no judicial review of the constitutionality of statutes. Today, the judge is no longer submitted to the will of the people.

At the same time, French judges have to examine the mode of reasoning of international courts, and that of the Constitutional Council who certainly do not view their function as the mechanical application of the constitution, but rather as a balancing of competing principles.

A fourth reason is related to a new conception of public prosecutors. From the traditional point of view, prosecutors were a party to the case. They were not judges, but civil servants under the Minister of Justice who appointed them and could issue directives governing their actions. During the 19th century, prosecutors played an important role in the courtroom, and as judges were appointed and promoted by the executive, prosecutors were an instrument in the hands of the minister of justice to control the judiciary. The situation has changed very little. For example, prosecutors still have their offices in the Palace of Justice where judges have theirs. This is also where the courtrooms are. Moreover, they are recruited and trained in the same way and in the same school as judges. In criminal cases, prosecutors and *juges d'instruction* tend to form a team to devise and implement criminal policy. Therefore, prosecutors have developed solidarity with the judiciary rather than with the Minister, and they tend to claim a status and an independence from the Minister similar to that of judges. This tendency has been reinforced by the existence of unions grouping judges and prosecutors together. They view themselves as a body of magistrates exercising the function not of applying the law, but of delivering justice. They wish to be recognized together as forming a "judicial power", which – as we have seen – the constitution does not accept, and which could balance the other two constitutional powers. In fact they view the other powers as "political" and themselves as "neutral".

Indeed, occasionally there have been clashes between "judges", *largissimo sensu*, i.e. including prosecutors, and politicians. In France these clashes never attained the proportions as those in Italy, and nor did it have the same consequences, as in Italy operation *mani pulite* was a decisive factor in the dramatic change in the political system during the 1990s.

According to the new idea of the judicial function, the role of judges was no longer the mechanical application of statutes, but the delivering of justice. This could be done in different ways. Some are traditional: often several statutes are applicable to a particular situation and it is possible to choose one or the other; then it is always possible to interpret the text of the statute. It is therefore possible for courts to pursue a particular policy by these means. For example, the Court of Cassation has recently initiated a movement to limit the effects of its own jurisprudence to future situations only. Indeed, although the Court of Cassation decides a particular case and its decision is in principle only binding on the parties, the decision is, as we have seen, equivalent to a new rule, since all citizens in a similar situation will adapt their behavior. However, as the decision is presented as an interpretation of a statute, it is binding on situations regulated by that statute since the day it was first enacted, i.e. long before the Court of Cassation was involved. The court's decision is therefore retroactive. This has of course been known for a very long time. Even so, what is new here and particularly striking is the quiet recognition by the Court of Cassation that its decisions are general rules, that they are retroactive and that this conflicts with some of the basic principles that make the rule of law. One must also note their unilateral efforts to change it.

Another way in which the judiciary could deliver justice was to exercise pressure on the lawmaker to produce better or different legislation, in particular, legislation that would give courts greater discretion. Recently judges and lawyers have organized a campaign against laws that tend to restrict their margin of discretion.

Still another way is to use international rules to refuse the application of statutes, but also to use the hierarchy of norms to resist international rules. The *Conseil d'État* was very successful in this exercise when it decided that while international rules prevail over statutes, they do not prevail over constitutional principles, even unwritten ones. In case of a conflict between an international rule and a statute, judges have sometimes declared that the latter has the rank of constitutional principle, thus allowing it to prevail over the international rule. This is not as simple today, at least in the context of European law, as the European Court of Justice (hereinafter ECJ) has repeatedly declared that European law prevails over national law, including constitutional law. This idea is embodied in the Lisbon treaty. However, the French Constitutional Council has created another level of argumentation, by declaring that the prevalence of European law is not based on the treaties or the jurisprudence of the ECJ but on the French constitution alone. Since the French constitution could not possibly have ordered that its most fundamental principles be violated, the European Union law cannot prevail over those fundamental principles that form the constitutional identity of France: the ability to change them is left up to the French constituent power alone.

Obviously a considerable problem of legitimacy arises if it is recognized that judges exercise a formidable power that is essentially political, because it consists in making decisive policy choices. The problem arises because judges are not elected, nor appointed or controlled by elective representatives of the people. Nevertheless, this problem has for the time being been carefully avoided by denying the political nature of judicial power and maintaining that it is neutral.

This may have important consequences on an institutional level. Let me mention two: the first is a claim to build a real judicial power by creating the *Conseil Supérieur de la Magistrature* with the purpose of making it completely independent from the executive, and giving it a complete monopoly over the appointment and promotion of judges. Another is to export the model of a neutral power to the realm of elected professionals and to many government agencies in charge of regulating a particular domain, such as communication, business competition or financial transactions.

Conclusion

These two ideas of the judiciary have appeared at different historical moments, but one has not been replaced by the other. In spite of an obvious contradiction (as one is based on the idea that judges should be obedient servants of positive law, and the other on the opposite idea that they should be active discoverers of law) they coexist. The civil code and the prohibitions upon making law are still there. Courts are still prohibited from reviewing the constitutionality of statutes. Nonetheless, constitutional courts have been created, and the existence of judge made law is not only acknowledged but also justified.

Indeed, although they are very different and contradictory in many ways, they have the same effect: judges are not prevented from creating law, and their power is even reinforced by being concealed. In the revolutionary concept of judicial power, it is reinforced on the one hand by the denial that they interpret, so that they don't have to give reasons and bind themselves. On the other hand, it is reinforced by the distinction between *in abstracto* and *in concreto*, which allows them to make general rules, while pretending to decide only concrete cases. The second and more recent idea helps judges to keep the façade of neutrality by pretending either that they confine themselves to the mere application of the law, be it superior law, or to exercise precise balancing between objective principles.

This story may help us qualify some classical theories on interpretation. First, the distinction between interpretation *in abstracto* and interpretation *in concreto* is only relative because *in concreto* interpretation can be used as a precedent in similar cases and therefore produce the same effects as an abstract interpretation. Secondly, the two opposing conceptions on the nature of interpretation have similar practical consequences. The cognitivist view is that interpretation is directed at discovering the true or the best possible meaning of a text. The realist view is that there is no true meaning and that interpretation is just a means to create the meaning by the will of the interpreter.

Chaim Perelman frequently told a story drawn from the Talmud. There was a dispute between several rabbis about the meaning of one passage from the Torah. Rabbi Eliezer was alone in proposing one interpretation and the others urged him to bow to the majority. However, he argued that truth had nothing to do with the views of the majority and appealed to God for a sign that he was right. At that moment a loud sound of thunder was heard, but the majority refused to accept this as a sign. Then, Eliezer called to God to make Himself clearer, and the walls of the house started to shake. Yet, this again was not sufficient to convince the majority. Once more, Eliezer called to God and a voice came down from the sky saying that Eliezer was right. But the majority did not accept this as a valid argument, saying only that God had given the text of the Torah to men, and it was now theirs alone to interpret. At this point, God laughed and said "my children have defeated me". This story may help us to understand the problem of legal interpretation. On one hand it indicates that the meaning depends not on the lawmaker's intention but on the interpreter. Moreover the interpreter determines the meaning not because of superior skills, but merely because a group always contains a majority within, i.e. its power. Thus, the realist view appears to be vindicated. On the other hand, if God accepts the majority's view although he has Himself given a different interpretation, this is only because he gave the Torah to men, and empowered them to interpret it. Thus the majority, by going against God's recent interpretation is faithful to God's original intention. This supports the cognitivist view, as the meaning of the Torah – that interpretation should be determined by a majority – was already there, and has been discovered by an act of knowledge.

Theories of legal interpretation are certainly capable of being true or false when they are considered at the level of legal theory, but they are incorporated into positive law and serve as the basis for distribution of power. In that context, we can see that the theories can have similar practical consequences.

The French Revolution held to the realist view, and prohibited judges from interpretation with the hope of preventing them from making law. In this respect, not only did it fail, but this very prohibition increased the courts' power, as they could not avoid interpreting statutes, but did not have to give reasons for their interpretations and thus did not bind themselves. However, the rule making power of the judges can also be based on the cognitivist theory, as judges can pretend to find a meaning that is hidden in the text, while creating that meaning: thus the practical impact of these theories is entirely independent of their truth value.

Bibliography

Beccaria, C. 1764. *Of Crimes and Punishments.*, translation, annotations, and introduction by G. R. Newman and P. Marongiu. 5th ed. New Brunswick, NJ: Transaction Publishers, 2009.

Eisenmann, Ch. 1933. L'Esprit des Lois et la séparation des pouvoirs, ds. *Mélanges Carré de Malberg*, p. 190, reprinted in Eisenmann, Ch. 2002. *Essais de théorie du droit, de droit constitutionnel et d'idées politiques*. Paris: LGDJ.

Halpérin, J.-L. 1987. *Le tribunal de cassation et les pouvoirs sous la Révolution (1790–1799)*. Paris: LGDJ.

Hanley, S. 1983. *The 'Lit de Justice' of the Kings of France: Constitutional Ideology in Legend, Ritual, and Discourse*. Princeton, NJ: Princeton University Press.

Montesquieu charles-Louis de Secondat. 1748. *Spirit of the Laws*, edited by Anne M. Cohler, Basia Carolyn Miller, and Harold Samuel Stone. Cambridge Texts in the History of Political Thought. Cambridge: Cambridge University Press, 1989.

Troper, M., and C. Grzegorczyk. 1997. "Precedent in France", In *Interpreting Precedents. A Comparative Study*, edited by N. ds. Maccormick and R. S. Summers, 103 ff. Aldershot: Dartmouth.

Troper, M. 2008. "Constitutional Law", In *Introduction to French Law*, edited by G. ds. Berman and E. Picard, 1–34. Alphen aan den Rijn: Kluwer Law International.

Troper, M. new edit. 2010. *La séparation des pouvoirs et l'histoire constitutionnelle française*. Paris: LGDJ.

Chapter 9
The Craft of Legal Interpretation

W. Bradley WENDEL

Introduction

The lawyer's fundamental ethical obligation, as established by agency, contract, and tort law, is to represent her client effectively within the bounds of the law. In carrying out this obligation, the lawyer must ascertain and protect her client's legal entitlements. This duty does not mean doing whatever one may get away with, as long as it is in the client's interests. Rather, it requires the lawyer to represent a client with reference to what the law actually permits or requires. This can be called the lawyer's obligation of fidelity to law.[1] This obligation is grounded in the capacity of the law to solve what might be called social coordination problems, although in a thicker sense than the term "coordination" is used in game theory. What is meant is that citizens have a shared interest in stability and peaceful cooperation, but it is difficult to realize this interest given moral pluralism.[2] Citizens disagree over what rights and obligations they ought to have, how resources should be allocated, and so on, and they find themselves unable to resolve these disagreements

---

[1] I have argued at length for this conception of legal ethics in W. Bradley Wendel, *Lawyers and Fidelity to Law* (Princeton, NJ: Princeton University Press 2010). A version of this paper originally appeared as Chapter 6 in that book. I am grateful to Princeton University Press for permission to reprint it here.

[2] Compare Rawls' notion of the burdens of judgment. (Rawls 1993, pp. 55–58)

W.B. WENDEL (✉)
Law School, Cornell University, Ithaca, New York, US
e-mail: bradley-wendel@lawschool.cornell.edu

MORIGIWA, Y. et al. (eds.), *Interpretation of Law in the Age of Enlightenment*, Law and Philosophy Library 95,
DOI 10.1007/978-94-007-1506-6_9, © Springer Science+Business Media B.V. 2011

using reasoning alone.[3] The law responds to citizens in this predicament by establishing a provisions, but relatively stable and determinate, framework for action. Instead of being mired in uncertainty and disagreement, citizens can determine what is required and justify their actions to each other with reference to the rights and duties established by the law.

It follows from this conception of the function of law that a lawyer has an ethical obligation to ascertain what the law requires or permits, and give advice and assistance to citizens based on the content of this socially established framework for cooperation. To this notion of duty an objection is often raised, however, which notes the existence of ambiguity in the law. The content of legal entitlements cannot simply be read directly from legal texts. Rather, the content of many legal entitlements can be discerned only with some effort and with the use of judgment. Moreover, ambiguity creates the possibility of abuse, so that a clever lawyer may be able to manipulate the law into appearing to convey an entitlement that does not actually exist. If there is sufficient determinacy in the law that the set of inadequately supported legal positions is not empty, however, legal ethics could in principle require lawyers to refrain from relying on insufficiently supported legal positions when counseling clients and structuring transactions. The position defended here is that the law is not fully determinate, in the sense that in any given situation there is only one view that a reasonable lawyer could reach about the content of a citizens legal entitlements, but it possesses sufficient determinacy to ground ethical evaluation of lawyers' advising on the basis of whether their advice is adequately supported by legal reasons.

The idea of legal reasons is essential to this conception of ethics, and it is related to the function of the law in settling societal disagreement. Reasons given in support of an interpretation of a legal norm (a statute, regulation, or judicial decision) have a particular structure. They make reference to the underlying reasons that were contested among citizens who disagreed about some matter *ex ante*, but they replace or outweigh those reasons in the

---

[3]In Jeremy Waldron's terms, citizens are in the circumstances of politics. Jeremy Waldron, *Law and Disagreement* (New York: Oxford University Press 1999), pp. 86, 101. The circumstances of politics are the initial conditions of (1) a shared interest among members of a society or group in establishing a common framework for cooperative action, (2) despite disagreement over what that framework should be, yet (3) with a recognition that any procedures that are used for resolving disagreement must permit the competing positions to be heard and treat participants with as much equality of respect as is compatible with the need to reach at least a moderately stable provisional settlement.

practical deliberations of citizens subject to the law.[4] As a result, the law is always aimed at some end – that is, it is a purposive activity. A basic constraint on a permissible interpretation of law is therefore that it be aimed at recovering the substantive meaning of some legal norm. Another important constraint is that lawyers regard the law from the internal point of view – in other words, as creating genuine obligations and not merely inconvenient obstacles to be evaded or planned around. As this chapter shows, jurisprudential concepts of exclusionary reasons and the internal point of view can help clarify some practical problems in legal interpretation.

The Case of the Torture Memos

To make this argument somewhat less abstract, it will be useful to begin with a case study. The case study is from the United States, but it involves a controversy that received a great deal of international attention. The American invasion of Afghanistan soon after the September 11th attacks resulted in the capture of numerous detainees with possible al-Qaeda affiliation, who might have possessed information on the structure of the organization, personnel, or even future terrorist attacks. In particular, the capture of high-ranking al-Qaeda members such as Abu Zubaydah, Mohamed al-Kahtani, and Khalid Shëikh Mohammed raised the possibility that American officials may have custody over people with extremely valuable "actionable intelligence". The Bush administration was therefore faced with an urgent question regarding the limits it should impose on the interrogation techniques used by military, FBI, CIA, and other government agents and civilian contractors. Recently disclosed internal memos revealed, for example, that high-level government officials had been asked if it was permissible to subject Zubaydah to numerous "enhanced interrogation techniques", alone or in some combination, including waterboarding, "walling" (slamming the prisoner headfirst into a wall, albeit while wearing a collar to prevent his neck from being broken), stress positions, sleep deprivation, cramped confinement, and "insects placed in confinement box" to exploit Zubaydah's fear of insects.[5] In other

---

[4]Compare Joseph Raz's argument that the law provides exclusionary reasons for action. Joseph Raz, "Authority, Law, and Morality", in *Ethics in the Public Domain* (Oxford: Oxford University Press 1994).

[5]See Memo from Assistant Attorney General Jay S. Bybee to John Rizzo, Acting General Counsel of the Central Intelligence Agency (Aug. 1, 2002). Subsequent revelations show that Khalid Sheikh Mohammed (often referred to as "KSM") was subjected to waterboarding an astonishing total of 183 times in March 2003. See Scott Shane, *Waterboarding Used 266 Times on 2 Suspects*, New York Times (April 20, 2009).

words, Zubaydah and other detainees were systematically tortured in an effort to obtain information.[6]

Subsequent revelations showed that torture was not an isolated occurrence, and not the work of a few bad apples, as government officials had suggested in the wake of the Abu Ghraib prisoner-abuse scandal. Instead, the United States government had constructed a torture program,[7] complete with procedures, protocols, lists of approved techniques, and safeguards to ensure that the interrogations did not go too far, resulting in the deaths of detainees.[8] These techniques "had been vetted in the highest circles of government".[9] Naturally, where anything becomes regularized, even bureaucratic in this way, one expects that lawyers will have been involved. Indeed, lawyers were involved from the beginning, providing legal advice to the Defense Department, the CIA, the State Department, and the uniformed military services. Throughout the development of interrogation policy, military lawyers resisted the use of coercive techniques, citing the obligations of the Geneva Conventions, the War Crimes Act, and the Uniform Code of Military Justice. Some civilian lawyers objected, too, including William H. Taft IV, the legal advisor to the State Department. However, Secretary of Defense Donald Rumsfeld rejected the advice of lawyers who expressed concerns about aggressive techniques, turning instead to a small group of lawyers at the Office of Legal Counsel (OLC) within the US Department of Justice.[10]

---

[6]For a review of several books on the torture of detainees, and further thoughts on the legal ethics issues involved, see W. Bradley Wendel, "The Torture Memos and the Demands of Legality", *Legal Ethics* (2009) 12: 107–23.

[7]See Executive Summary, *Senate Armed Services Committee Inquiry Into the Treatment of Detainees in U.S. Custody*, available at http://levin.senate.gov/newsroom/supporting/2008/Detainees.121108.pdf. The first page of the summary concludes, "[t]he abuse of detainees in US custody cannot simply be attributed to the actions of 'a few bad apples' acting on their own. The fact is that senior officials in the United States government solicited information on how to use aggressive techniques, redefined the law to create the appearance of their legality, and authorized their use against detainees".

[8]A quote was widely reported, and is also referenced in the Senate Armed Services Committee Report (see Executive Summary, *supra*, p. xvii), from the chief counsel to the CIA's Counterterrorism Center. This lawyer noted that the definition of torture is "basically subject to perception. If the detainee dies you're doing it wrong".

[9]Jack Goldsmith, *The Terror Presidency: Law and Judgment Inside the Bush Administration* (New York: W.W. Norton 2007).

[10]See Executive Summary, *supra*, p. xxi, for this history. The Office of Legal Counsel exercises power delegated from the Attorney General of the United States to advise the President (in his capacity as the head of the executive branch), and to issue legal opinions that are binding on the entire executive branch unless overruled by the Attorney General. See Jane Mayer, *The Dark Side: The Inside Story of How the War on Terror Turned into a War on American Ideals* (New York: Doubleday 2008), p. 65.

These lawyers provided advice in a series of memos that the coercive techniques described in the recently released reports were consistent with the requirements of applicable domestic and international law.

These memos, which were dubbed the "torture memos" when they were leaked to the press following the revelation of prisoner abuse at Abu Ghraib, consider a wide range of legal issues, from whether the Geneva Convention protections afforded to prisoners of war extend to suspected *Taliban* or *al-Qaeda* detainees, to whether the President's power as commander in chief could be limited by an act of Congress criminalizing mistreatment of prisoners. One memo excluded detainees believed to be associated with the Taliban or al-Qaeda from the protection of the international norms regarding the treatment of prisoners of war.[11] Despite forceful objections from Secretary of State Colin Powell, White House Counsel Alberto Gonzales concluded that non-state terrorism is a "new paradigm" that "renders quaint" some provisions of the Geneva Conventions imposing limitations on the questioning of captured prisoners.[12] One of the most notorious memos concluded that certain methods of interrogation might be cruel, inhuman, or degrading, yet fall outside the definition of prohibited acts of torture.[13] Even if an act were deemed torture, the memo concluded that it might be justified by self-defense or necessity. And even if an interrogation technique would otherwise be deemed wrongful, the President as Commander-in-Chief had the unilateral authority to exempt government actors from application of domestic and international legal restrictions on torture.

---

[11] See Memorandum from Jay S. Bybee, Assistant Attorney General, to Alberto R. Gonzales, Counsel to the President, and William J. Haynes II, General Counsel of the Department of Defense (Jan. 22, 2002), in Karen J. Greenberg and Joshua L. Dratel, eds., *The Torture Papers: The Road to Abu Ghraib* (New York: Cambridge University Press 2005). The relevant international treaties are the Geneva Convention [III] Relative to the Treatment of Prisoners of War (Aug. 12, 1949), 75 U.N.T.S. 135, 6 U.S.T. 3517, as well as the protections contained in so-called Common Article III, which apply in all contexts covered by any of the four Geneva Conventions for the Protection of Victims of War.

[12] Memorandum for the President, from Albert R. Gonzales (Jan. 25, 2002), in Greenberg and Dratel, *supra*. According to sources at the State Department, Powell "hit the roof" when he read the analysis prepared by Justice Department lawyers. See John Barry, et al., "The Roots of Torture", *Newsweek* (May 24, 2004). For additional reporting on Secretary Powell's reaction, see R. Jeffrey Smith and Dan Eggen, "Gonzales Helped Set the Course for Detainees", *The Washington Post* (Jan. 5, 2005), at A1. Powell's objections are succinctly presented in a memo to Alberto Gonzales. *See* Memorandum from Colin L. Powell, Secretary of State, to Counsel to the President (Jan. 26, 2002), in Greenberg and Dratel, *supra*.

[13] See Memorandum from Jay S. Bybee, Assistant Attorney General, to Alberto R. Gonzales, Counsel to the President (Aug. 1, 2002), in Greenberg and Dratel, *supra*.

The ethics of fidelity to law maintains that the most relevant critical stand-point for evaluating the conduct of the OLC lawyers is not the horribleness of torture from the point of view of ordinary morality. The moral wrongful-ness of torture is not a "legal reason" as that term is used here. The objection to the advice given by lawyers for the Bush administration is not that it is bad moral advice; rather, it is that it is bad legal advice. The law simply does not permit what interrogators at Guantánamo Bay, Bagram Air Base, and other sites have done to detainees. When one criticizes the OLC lawyers *qua lawyers*, the terms of this criticism must make reference to the rea-sons embodied in the positive law governing the treatment of detainees. The role of the lawyer is to interpret and apply this law in good faith. To be a lawyer is to participate in a craft with its own internal standards of success or failure. Just as the evaluation that someone is a good chess player or a boring, derivative composer is an internal one, situated within the practices of chess or musicianship, the evaluation of lawyers as good or bad is internal to the practice of reasoning with reference to the law. Respect for the value of legality when advising others is what makes lawyers distinct from other occupational groups who deal with matters of public significance, and from ordinary citizens acting in that capacity. Ordinary citizens have views about the morality of torture, and members of other professions may have fur-ther expertise. Military and civilian interrogators, for example, might know something about how best to obtain reliable information from prisoners.[14] What makes lawyers distinct, however, is that their advice must always be given with respect to what the law permits or requires. The requirement that their actions always be grounded in the law creates the possibility of an inter-nal critique of the advice and assistance of lawyers in the establishment of a torture regime.

Even if this critical stance is valid in theory, however, it may not be help-ful in practice the law can be interpreted to permit whatever the client wants

---

[14]Jane Mayer reports that an FBI agent named Ali Soufan, who grew up in Lebanon and spoke fluent Arabic, was having "phenomenal" success and making progress in the interrogations of suspected terrorists. His method was to "argue religion and politics with terror suspects, drawing them out in the process. He would sit on the floor and drink tea with them, and learn about their families and their concerns". The progress he was making was not deemed fast enough, however, and interrogators began sub-jecting the detainee to "late-night interrogations using pounding music, bright strobe lights, extremely painful temperatures, dogs, and other oddities". Mayer, *supra*, p. 191. Soufan testified at a Senate Judiciary Committee hearing that he and other interrogators were able to obtain useful information from detainees before coercive techniques were used, but the nature of this information remains classified. See Testimony of Ali Soufan, http://judiciary.senate.gov/hearings/testimony.cfm?id=3842&wit_id=7906.

to do. Legal indeterminacy is not a problem only for theoretically inclined legal scholars. It is very much part of the popular understanding of the legal system, as revealed by public comments made by high-ranking government officials in the course of the debate over the Bush Administration's legal response in the war on terror. For example, after the US Supreme Court ruled that American personnel overseas had to comply with Common Article 3 of the Geneva Conventions, which prohibit outrages upon human dignity, President Bush noted, "[t]hat's like – it's very vague. What does that mean 'outrages upon human dignity'? That's a statement that is wide open to interpretation".[15] Similarly, former Attorney General Michael Mukasey equivocated on the question of whether waterboarding is illegal. In a letter he released in advance of a hearing on interrogation policy, he stated:

> If this were an easy question, I would not be reluctant to offer my views on this subject. But, with respect, I believe it is not an easy question. There are some circumstances where current law would appear clearly to prohibit the use of waterboarding. Other circumstances would present a far closer question.[16]

Although Bush and Mukasey did not say so explicitly, their comments suggest they would be willing to acquiesce in advice from their lawyers if the law was clear. In their view, however, the indeterminacy of the law gave them a legal permission to withhold the protections of the Geneva Conventions from detainees, and even in some cases to subject them to waterboarding.

The problem with this appeal to indeterminacy is that the law governing torture is one of those areas in which there really is not any disagreement, in good faith, about the meaning and application of core terms.[17] With respect to international law, the Third Geneva Convention, applicable to prisoners of war, prohibits the inflicting of physical or mental torture, or any form of coercion, on prisoners of war. The Fourth Geneva Convention, applicable to civilian detainees, requires the protection of civilians from all acts

---

[15]Press Conference of the President (Sept. 15, 2006), available at http://www.whitehouse.gov/news/releases/2006/09/20060915-2.html. The unedited comment is reported in Richard Leiby, "Down a Dark Road: Movie Uses Afghan's Death to Ask Tough Questions About U.S. and Torture", *The Washington Post* (April 27, 2007), at C01.

[16]Quoted in Scott Horton, "'Reasonable Minds Can Differ'", *Harpers* (Jan. 31, 2008), available at <http://www.harpers.org/archive/2008/01/hbc-90002285>. The letter is available online at <http://i.a.cnn.net/cnn/2008/images/01/29/letter.to.senator.leahy.pdf>.

[17]See the discussion in David Luban, *Legal Ethics and Human Dignity* (New York: Cambridge University Press 2007), Ch. 5 ("The Torture Lawyers of Washington"); and Harold H. Bruff, *Bad Advice: Bush's Lawyers in the War on Terror* (Lawrence, KS: University Press of Kansas 2009). pp. 237–39.

of violence or threats thereof. Common Article 3, which is part of all of the separate Geneva Conventions, outlaws cruel treatment and torture, as well as outrages upon personal dignity, and humiliating and degrading treatment. The Convention Against Torture prohibits not only torture, but also cruel, inhuman, and degrading treatment that does not amount to torture. The Convention contains an express non-derogation provision blocking the appeal to a national emergency as a justification of torture.[18] Moreover, the prohibition on torture is a *jus cogens* norm in international law – a peremptory standard that may not be deviated from under any circumstances. There are similar prohibitions in US domestic law. These include a general federal assault statute, prohibiting assaults by striking or beating within the special maritime and territorial jurisdiction of the United States,[19] and a federal criminal statute specifically addressing torture, which prohibits anyone outside the United States to commit torture, which is defined as an act specifically intended to inflict severe mental or physical pain or suffering.[20]

As one might expect, the administration's lawyers had an explanation for why these prohibitions do not apply to prohibit the treatment inflicted upon detainees. They argued that the POW convention does not apply because *al-Qaeda* was not a contracting party to the Geneva Conventions, ignoring the past American practice of treating all armed combatants, not just soldiers of signatory states, as POWs under the Third Geneva Convention. With respect to the Fourth Geneva Convention on civilian detainees, the lawyers contended that the President has deemed *al-Qaeda* and *Taliban* fighters "unlawful combatants".[21] The deficiency in this argument is that it

---

[18]Convention Against Torture and Other Cruel, Inhuman or Degrading Treatment or Punishment, G.A. Res. 39/46, 39 U.N. GAOR, Supp. (No. 51), U.N. Doc. A/39/51 (1984), Art. 2(2) ("No exceptional circumstances whatsoever, whether a state of war ... or any other public emergency, may be invoked as a justification of torture".).

[19]18 U.S.C. § 113.

[20]18 U.S.C. §§ 2340–2340A. The "severe pain" language of this statute became notorious when the OLC analysis leaked showing that government lawyers used a federal health-benefits statute as an analogy to support the definition of severe pain as only that pain equivalent to pain accompanying organ failure or death. The benefits statute actually defined "emergency", not "severe pain". See 42 U.S.C. § 1395w-22(d)(3)(B). Emergency is, in turn, defined in the alternative as a situation involving severe pain or one associated with organ failure or death. Former OLC head Jack Goldsmith, among many others, criticized this reasoning. Goldsmith, *supra*, pp. 144–50. The OLC subsequently expressly repudiated its reliance on this statute. See Memorandum from Daniel Levin, Acting Assistant Attorney General, to James B. Comey, Deputy Attorney General (Dec. 30, 2004), available at http://www.usdoj.gov/olc/18usc23402340a2.htm.

[21]See Executive Order of George W. Bush (Feb. 7, 2002); Executive Order of George W. Bush (July 20, 2007), http://www.whitehouse.gov/news/releases/2007/07/20070720-4.html (reaffirming "unlawful combatant" determination).

may be possible for a detainee to lose POW status by being a nonprivileged or unlawful combatant, but that simply throws that detainee into civilian status, protected by the Fourth Geneva Convention. One is either a POW or a civilian detainee; it is not possible to be a kind of legal non-person, totally outside the coverage of the Geneva scheme. As the International Committee of the Red Cross has stated, "nobody in enemy hands can fall outside the law".

Regarding Common Article 3, which applies to all detainees no matter how they are categorized, the administration lawyers reasoned that the conflict with *al-Qaeda* is "international in scope". Common Article 3 applies to conflicts "not of an international character" and the Global War on Terrorism is, obviously enough, global. But this reasoning is simply wrong as well, because the point of Common Article 3 is to fill in the gaps in coverage created by the application of the rest of the Geneva Conventions to conflicts between nation-states. A conflict is one or the other – a war between nation states, or a conflict not of an international character – there is no such thing as an inherently non-law-governed conflict. In order to avoid the force of these arguments, the OLC lawyers backstopped them with a highly implausible "commander-in-chief override" position, claiming that the President had the authority to suspend the Geneva Conventions unilaterally.[22] This argument is untenable, however, because the President's constitutional power as commander-in-chief of the armed forces is meant to ensure only that civilian government officials play a supervisory role with respect to the military. It certainly does not mean that Congress has no coordinate role in setting legal limitations on what executive branch officials may do in the conduct of war, and it also does not mean that international legal norms are ousted by the President's authority to supervise the uniformed services.[23]

Interpretive Judgment

Considering the legal issues in the torture memos suggests that the evaluation of the ethical permissibility of a lawyer's advice can turn, in practice, on how well supported a legal position is. A lawyer who knew enough about international humanitarian law and the law of warfare would respond to the administration lawyers' arguments with incredulity. This incredulity is

---

[22]See Memorandum from Jay S. Bybee, Assistant Attorney General, to Alberto R. Gonzales, Counsel to the President (Aug. 1, 2002), in Greenberg and Dratel, *supra*.

[23]For a magisterial analysis, see the book-length two-part article on the commander-in-chief power, written by two former OLC lawyers who have since rejoined the OLC in the Obama Administration, see David J. Barron and Martin S. Lederman, "The Commander in Chief at the Lowest Ebb" Parts I and II, *Harvard Law Review* (2008) 121: 689–804.

a product of participating in an activity, a *craft*, which carries with it certain internal standards of good practice – excellences, or virtues, one might say.[24] A craft grounds the possibility of normative criticism for violation of craft standards. Recognizing what it means to be a practice aimed at some end means also recognizing what it is to do well or poorly at realizing that end. This is a long tradition in ethics, with its roots in Aristotle, but it has a contemporary application to complex institutional activities such as serving as an advisor to clients within the legal system. In the case of legal ethics, being a good lawyer means exhibiting fidelity to law, not distorting its meaning to enable the client to do something unlawful. The torture memos are deficient lawyering, as one can tell by participating in the craft of making and analyzing legal arguments.

References to craft should not be taken as appeals to some mysterious faculty of intuitive judgment, or "I know it when I see it" reasoning. An experienced lawyer may have an intuitive negative reaction to an argument, buy that intuition is only a symptom of something that has gone awry in the argument. How do we know what has gone awry? It is not easy to give a simple answer to this question, but that is not because professional craft is mysterious. Rather, it is something that takes some practice to familiarize oneself with, but with experience one can recognize good and bad legal arguments. Certain argumentative "moves" are ruled out by the existing body of law. Lawyers may not be conscious of the tacit norms regulating the exercise of interpretive judgment, but if called upon, they can generally give reasons why one interpretation is persuasive and another strikes them as implausible.[25] Going back to the torture memos example, it is well understood that the structure of the law of war is intended to create gapless coverage: There is no such thing as a person who is neither a POW nor a civilian detainee, or a war that is neither "of an international character" or "not of an international character". Someone familiar with this structure would recognize that many of the categories of non-persons and non-wars were invented by Bush administration lawyers out of whole cloth. Thus, they do not represent good-faith attempts to determine what the law means; rather, they are evasions of the law, using legal-looking arguments that do not actually hold up under scrutiny.

---

[24]David Luban, "Natural Law as Professional Ethics: A Reading of Fuller", in Luban (2007), *supra*, pp. 107–8.

[25]Owen M. Fiss, "Objectivity and Interpretation". *Stanford Law Review* (1982) 34: 739–63; Donald Schön, *The Reflective Practitioner: How Professionals Think in Action* (New York: Basic Books 1983).

Lawyers frequently assess legal positions using informal judgments of plausibility. They may say an argument is solid, sensible, plausible, within the range of reasonableness, a stretch, adventurous, barely colorable, frivolous, and so on. Scholars and regulators have occasionally experimented with defining these confidence judgments in mathematical terms, for instance asking whether a position has a 10 percent chance, a 30 percent chance, and so on, of success on the merits. The American Bar Association (ABA), for example, has advised tax lawyers that they may counsel a client to take a position on a tax return as long as there is a reasonable basis in law for the position.[26] Although the ABA's ethics committee warned that a reasonable basis is more than a "colorable" claim, it also said that a lawyer may advise the taxpayer that a position is permissible even if the lawyer believes the client's position will not prevail. All that is necessary is a good-faith belief that the position is warranted by existing law. Subsequent regulations issued by the Internal Revenue Service have defined reasonable basis as approximately a one in three chance of success.[27] However, expressing judgments of plausibility in mathematical terms creates an illusion of precision that can never be obtained in legal reasoning. A lawyer may believe an argument is "pretty strong" or "not as strong, but not a complete loser", but if asked to translate those evaluations into numerical terms, will just be pulling numbers out of the air. Even worse, a lawyer may be misled into thinking that her inability to express a judgment regarding confidence in numerical terms means that the judgment is purely subjective. But one can feel confident in some prediction or evaluation in certain domains without being able to quantify that judgment precisely.

Although mathematical definitions of plausibility are unlikely to be forthcoming, it may be possible to articulate an informal but nevertheless robust standard of plausibility in terms of attitudes of conviction. For example, if the lawyer could stand behind an interpretation, take pride in it, and offer it to a third party the lawyer respects for her sound judgment, then the interpretation is one that satisfies a fairly high standard of plausibility. This attitude or conviction on the part of a lawyer who offers an interpretation may be fleshed out with reference to a kind of hypothetical ideal observer. One possible heuristic using an ideal observer is that if a lawyer would be comfortable making the argument to the judge for whom she clerked, a professor she respects, or a colleague who is known for her good sense and judgment, the argument is plausible. This standard is more stringent than

---

[26]ABA Standing Comm. on Prof'l Ethics, Formal Op. 85–352 (July 7, 1985).

[27]Treasury Dept. Circular 230, 31 C.F.R., Subtitle A, Part 10, § 10.34(a), (d)(1). This regulation uses the language of "a realistic possibility of being sustained on the merits".

the "laugh test" commonly employed by lawyers (i.e., whether it would be possible to make an argument in court without laughing at the ridiculousness of it). It is closer to the test proposed by Charles Fried for determining when an account of the law as given by a judge is twisted: If the lawyer offered an interpretation of law in an oral argument, or a law student offered it on an exam, would the lawyer or student be accused of being disingenuous?[28] Lawyers are comfortable making these kinds of judgments and, as we have seen, these are the sorts of arguments that have been leveled against the OLC lawyers who prepared the torture memos.

It is important not to expect the law to provide too much determinacy. In fact, in many cases, reasonable lawyers may differ on what the law permits or requires. Even if there is some indeterminacy in the law, however, it still may be possible to pick out instances in which lawyers are creating the appearance of indeterminacy where there is actually considerable certainty. To illustrate, consider this colorful quote from a former manager at Enron, describing his company's attitude toward compliance with accounting rules:

> Say you have a dog, but you need to create a duck on the financial statements. Fortunately, there are specific accounting rules for what constitutes a duck: yellow feet, white covering, orange beak. So you take the dog and paint its feet yellow and its fur white and you paste an orange plastic beak on its nose, and then you say to your accountants, "This is a duck! Don't you agree that it's a duck?" And the accountants say, "Yes, according to the rules, this is a duck".[29]

One's intuition here is that the accountants at Enron are abusing or manipulating the applicable law. There are criteria of duck-ness and dog-ness that may not be coextensive with formal legal norms ("according to the rules", as the accountants say in the example), but there are nevertheless standards of plausibility that regulate the permissibility of asserting that something is a dog or a duck. The manipulation engaged in by the Enron lawyers depends on a spurious identification of law with formal legal norms. There may be apparent ambiguity in the governing rules, but the ambiguity is only apparent. Lawyers acquainted with the craft of making and evaluating legal arguments would recognize the duck-creation of the Enron lawyers as what it is, namely a charade.

The problem of legal interpretation is of course one that has received considerable attention from legal scholars. The problem is different in important ways, however, when considered from the point of view of lawyers, not

---

[28]Charles Fried, "A Meditation on the First Principles of Judicial Ethics", *Hofstra Law Review* (2008) 32: 1227–44, at 1232.

[29]Quoted in Bethany McLean and Peter Elkind, *The Smartest Guys in the Room: The Amazing Rise and Scandalous Fall of Enron* (New York: Portfolio 2003), pp. 142–43.

judges. The permissibility of taking a legal position – in litigation, as the basis for a transaction, or as a ground for legal advice to a client – depends on the institutional features of the situation. Some of these features include whether there is meaningful constraint as a result of an adversarial process of briefing and argument, whether the lawyer's reasoning is public or secret, and whether the law itself contemplates flexibility in application. The most important aspect of the distinction between judges and lawyers is that, for lawyers, the obligation of fidelity to law must be understood in context. The question is, if the client "needs a duck", *when* may a lawyer say on behalf of the client, "This is a duck"? The answer is, "It depends".

To stick with the illustration (at the cost of making it a bit silly), suppose the client has been accused of the crime of possessing a dog, but wants to claim that what looks like a dog is actually a duck, which one may legally possess. It is helpful to start with this variation, because in legal ethics discourse, the criminal defense paradigm always hovers in the background, subtly informing our tacit assumptions about what a lawyer's duties ought to be.[30] It is well accepted that the criminal defense lawyer's job is to resist the application of state power to her client's case, and argue for virtually any interpretation of the law that will enable the client to avoid punishment.[31] The usual rule prohibiting lawyers from asserting claims or defenses without a good-faith basis in existing law is expressly subordinated to the constitutional entitlements of a criminal defendant, which permit (and arguably even require) the assertion of weak legal positions right up to the boundary of frivolousness.[32] Criminal-defense lawyers rightly believe that

---

[30]See, e.g., David Luban, *Lawyers and Justice* (Princeton, NJ: Princeton University Press 1988), pp. 58–66.

[31]For a strong defense of the idea that criminal defense lawyers have no obligation at all to respect the law, see Abbe Smith "The Difference in Criminal Defense and the Difference it Makes", *Washington University Journal of Law and Policy* (2003) 11: 83–140. Smith argues that criminal defense lawyers are only prudentially (she says "pragmatically") required to respect the bounds of the law, which is an untenable position. However, a lawyer's belief that she does not have a genuine nonprudential obligation to respect the law would entail the belief that other actors within the legal system, including the prosecutor and judge, also do not have an obligation to respect the law. There would be a practical contradiction if the criminal defense lawyer held that belief while simultaneously demanding compliance by prosecutors and judges. Nevertheless, Smith's conclusion, that a criminal defense lawyer should "engage in advocacy that is as close to the line as possible, and, indeed, should test the line", ibid., p. 90, is supportable on the basis of a reasonable division of labor among prosecutors, defense lawyers, and judges, who collectively aim at a plurality of competing ends.

[32]Model Rules of Professional Conduct, Rule 3.1, cmt. [3] ("The lawyer's obligations under this Rule are subordinate to federal or state constitutional law that entitles a defendant in a criminal matter to the assistance of counsel in presenting a claim or contention

they are permitted to "put the state to its proof", requiring the prosecution to establish every element of its case beyond a reasonable doubt, even if the defense lawyer knows there is no question of the state's ability to prove its case.[33] Thus, if there is any argument, even if it is barely possible to make it with a straight face, that a dog is a duck, then the lawyer may, and arguably must, make it.

The criminal defense lawyer has virtually no obligation to ascertain that a legal argument is plausible. Lawyers may have tactical reasons not to make such laughable arguments that they lose credibility with the court and thereby diminish their effectiveness as advocates, but these are prudential reasons only, not legal or ethical obligations. Underlying this broad permission to advance practically any interpretation of the law consistent with a criminal defendant's interests is the American political tradition, emphasizing as it does the rights of the individual against the bogey of the all-powerful state.[34] The Orwellian vision of the omnipotent state may be more caricature than reality,[35] but the power differential between individuals and the state is not the whole story behind criminal defense advocacy. The real basis for the practically unlimited license of criminal defense lawyers to make creative and aggressive legal arguments is threefold. First, criminal prosecution and defense involves a substantial threat to important interests of the client, and for this reason it is situated within an institutional context that provides for fairly robust adversarial checking by partisan advocates, whose duties are oriented solely (or at least substantially) toward protecting the rights of

---

that otherwise would be prohibited by this Rule".) (hereinafter "Model Rules"). The American Bar Association, which is formally nothing more than a voluntary trade association, promulgates models for the lawyer disciplinary rules adopted by the highest court in each US jurisdiction. The actual rules in effect in each state vary somewhat in content but are close enough to the promulgated models that it is possible to generalize about the obligations of lawyers across the US with reference to the ABA Model Rules.
[33]Restatement (Third) of the Law Governing Lawyers (2000) § 110(2) ("a lawyer for the defendant in a criminal proceeding ... may so defend the proceeding as to require that the prosecutor establish every necessary element".) (Herein after "Restatement"). The criminal defense lawyer's right, and even duty, to put the state to its proof is derived from several constitutional rights enjoyed by the defendant, including the presumption of innocence and the evidentiary requirement that the state prove its case beyond a reasonable doubt, *In re Winship*, 397 U.S. 358 (1972), *Mullaney v. Wilbur*, 421 U.S. 684 (1975), and the due process requirement that the jury find all elements of the state's case beyond a reasonable doubt, *Apprendi v. New Jersey*, 530 U.S. 466 (2000).
[34]Monroe H. Freedman and Abbe Smith, *Understanding Lawyers' Ethics* (Newark, NJ: Matthew Bender & Co., 2d ed., 2002) §§ 2.03, 2.04.
[35]William H. Simon, *The Practice of Justice: A Theory of Lawyers' Ethics* (Cambridge, MA: Harvard University Press 1998), pp. 173–79.

clients. Second, permitting lawyers to argue for less well-supported conclusions of law builds some capacity for change into the legal system. For this reason, lawyers for the parties in civil litigation also have some latitude to press weaker legal arguments, subject to legal prohibitions on relying on totally unsupported positions. Finally, and most importantly, in criminal or civil litigation, one can be a zealous advocate and assume, for the most part, that the procedures and personnel of the tribunal will take care of the "bounds of the law". Adversary briefing and argument, rules of procedure and evidence, the presence of a judge and law clerks, and the possibility of appeal all serve to mitigate excesses of interpretive creativity. In other words, there is an *institutional* solution to the problem of the indeterminacy and manipulability of the law.

Where institutional checks and balances are not present, in counseling and transactional planning matters, a lawyer cannot rely on some other actor to ensure that the law is correctly interpreted and applied. In non-litigation representation, there may be no institutional mechanism to safeguard against one-sided interpretations of law. Little can be said in the abstract about all transactional practice. Some aspects, such as filing disclosures with the Securities and Exchange Commission, are quite extensively subject to procedural oversight. Lawyers in transactions also sometimes provide opinion letters on behalf of clients to third parties (lenders, guarantors, etc.) – since lawyers are exposed to civil liability for providing misleading opinion letters, there is significant constraint on lawyers' creativity in evaluating the applicable law.[36] In the absence of some effective procedural checking of the lawyer's interpretation, however, the lawyer in effect acts as a private lawgiver to the client, in that whatever interpretive judgment the lawyer renders is unlikely to be challenged by another party and tested for adequacy by a court. The law can essentially be manipulated out of existence under the guise of "zealous advocacy" if the lawyer's advice is uncoupled from the possibility that the legality of the client's actions might actually be subject to evaluation by an impartial decision-maker.

The law governing lawyers accordingly places more responsibility for getting the law right on a lawyer counseling clients, creating private ordering within the law (e.g., by contracts or incorporation procedures), or advising a government agency on its conduct. The state bar disciplinary rules provide that an attorney serving as an adviser must use independent professional judgment and render candid advice, while a lawyer representing a client in

---

[36]See the analysis in Geoffrey C. Hazard, Jr., et al., *The Law and Ethics of Lawyering* (New York: Foundation Press, 4th ed., 2005), chs. 2 & 3.

a litigated matter may assert any non-frivolous legal argument.[37] Lawyers have an obligation to use reasonable care in representing clients, and this duty may include making a reasonable evaluation of the legal basis for the client's actions, and advising the client not to do something that is legally impermissible.[38] Similarly, the Securities and Exchange Commission's regulations implementing the Sarbanes-Oxley Act require lawyers in some cases to report information "up the ladder" within a corporation where they reasonably believe their client is committing certain wrongful acts, but do not require reporting up where the lawyer is representing the client in litigation over the wrongful act.[39] Lawyers may not make materially misleading statements to third parties in the course of representing clients, and this includes statements made in documents drafted by lawyers on which third parties might reasonably rely.[40] Finally, generally applicable tort and agency law principles, as well as the rules of professional conduct, require lawyers to refuse to assist a client in an action that is not permitted by the law.[41] This requires lawyers to make an assessment of whether their clients are legally entitled to assert some right with respect to others, and to either advise the client against a course of conduct not supported by legal entitlements, or to withdraw from representing a client who wishes to do something not permitted by the law.

---

[37]Compare Model Rules, *supra*, Rule 2.1 (advisor) and Rule 3.1 (advocate).

[38]See, e.g., *FDIC v. O'Melveny & Myers*, 969 F.2d 744 (9th Cir. 1992), *rev'd*, 512 U.S. 79 (1994), *aff'd in relevant respects on remand*, 61 F.3d 17 (9th Cir. 1995).

[39]Compare 17 C.F.R. § 205.3(b)(2)–(3) (duty to report where representing issuer in non-litigation context) with 17 C.F.R. § 205.3(b)(7)(ii) (no duty to report up where lawyer retained "[t]o assert, consistent with his or her professional obligations, a colorable defense on behalf of the issuer ... in any investigation or judicial or administrative proceeding relating to such evidence of a material violation").

[40]See, e.g., *Klein v. Boyd*, Fed. Sec. Rep. ¶ 90,136 (3d Cir. 1998), *vacated on grant of rehearing en banc* (reprinted in Hazard, *supra*, p. 191).

[41]The Model Rules provide that "[a] lawyer shall not counsel a client to engage, or assist a client, in conduct that the lawyer *knows* is criminal or fraudulent". Model Rules, *supra*, Rule 1.2(d) (emphasis added). The knowledge requirement here may cause lawyers to believe they are permitted to advise clients on the basis of weakly supported interpretive judgments. However, this argument reflects a misunderstanding of the relationship between the disciplinary rules and other law such as tort and agency principles. The Restatement, which was designed to take generally applicable law into account, would not permit lawyers to engage in the evasion of advising the client on the basis of weakly supported interpretive judgments. Referring to agency and contract law, it states that "a lawyer retains authority that may not be overridden by a contract with or an instruction from the client to refuse to perform, counsel, or assist future or ongoing acts in the representation that the lawyer *reasonably believes* to be *unlawful*". Restatement § 23(1) (emphasis added).

In transactional practice, these legal rules may mean that the lawyer is required to refuse to certify compliance with legal or accounting standards, usually in an opinion letter, where this certification would be required as a condition for the deal closing. This is the sense in which lawyers are sometimes called upon to be "gatekeepers".[42] Lawyers have a tendency to strongly overreact to the characterization of their role as gatekeepers, but this idea is far from novel or radical. Lawyers have always been potentially exposed to criminal and administrative penalties, as well as civil liability to third parties, for actively participating in their clients' fraudulent transactions. Gatekeeping liability goes beyond penalizing lawyers for knowing, active participation in client fraud, and reaches instances of what might be called, with an awkward double negative, "failure to not-participate". Contrary to popular usage of the term, gatekeeping does not require lawyers to "blow the whistle" on client misdeeds, by disclosing confidential information to the authorities. The predicate for liability as a gatekeeper is not failure to disclose, but failure to timely disassociate oneself from unlawful conduct. Opinion letters given by counsel certify compliance with regulatory requirements, and legal liability for giving misleading opinion letters ensures that the responsibility for ensuring compliance with the law rests on the party with the best access to the facts needed to evaluate the legality of the transaction. As a result, business lawyers reduce transaction costs, reduce information asymmetries, and enable the parties to cooperate. Given that a lawyer's professional obligation is to obtain and protect legal entitlements on behalf of clients, it is hard to see how imposing liability for failure to assist a client in unlawful conduct changes the normative landscape of legal ethics in any way.

Lawyers tend to react negatively to the suggestion that they should interpret the law from a quasi-judicial point of view, when acting as advisors or transactional planners. Superficially, at least, this resistance is understandable. Lawyers and judges occupy discrete roles in the legal system, and should be expected to have different responsibilities. The adversary system enacts a normative division of labor among various institutional actors, responding to political needs such as limiting government power and enhancing accountability. Lawyers in litigation need not assert only the legal positions they believe to be the best view of the law, or even those reasonably well founded. As long as a legal argument is adequately grounded, which means it has some chance of success on the merits, it is permissible to urge it to a court. While that is an accurate description of lawyers'

---

[42] John C. Coffee, Jr., *Gatekeepers: The Professions and Corporate Governance* (New York: Oxford University Press 2006).

responsibilities in litigation, it is mystifying that this argument from the adversary system is thought to prove anything about legal advising outside the litigation context. The argument that lawyers should have the same interpretive freedom in counseling as in litigation proceeds by taking the lawyer's litigation-advocacy role as the baseline, and then demanding a justification for any deviation from that baseline. But why should we take the lawyer's litigation-related duties and permissions as the baseline, and not as a special case? The normative baseline is the principal<n->agent relationship between clients and their lawyers. What "good lawyering" means varies by context, but it is always oriented toward the client's legal entitlements. There may be room to contest the content of those entitlements in litigation, and there may be areas of transactional practice in which it is permissible to rely on somewhat doubtful interpretations of the law, but in all cases the law sets a boundary on what lawyers justifiably may do on behalf of clients.

The Jurisprudence of Lawyering

Even if one grants that the obligation of fidelity to law should vary by context, one might nevertheless ask whether the law is the sort of thing that is capable of possessing determinacy at all, and how it would have this quality. The argument defended here is that the nature of legal interpretation and the nature of law are related, and that law should be fundamentally understood as a practice of reason-giving, subject to certain kinds of constraints. The most basic constraint on what counts as an interpretation of law is that law must be viewed as a purposive activity, as having some point or end.[43]

---

[43]The argument here is influenced by the Hart and Sacks legal process tradition in American law. (The Hart in question is no relation to the English legal philosopher H.L.A. Hart, whose views figure prominently in the argument below.) See Henry M. Hart, Jr. and Albert M. Sacks, *The Legal Process: Basic Problems in the Making and Application of Law* (William N. Eskridge, Jr. and Philip P. Frickey eds., Westbury, NY: Foundation Press 1994), pp. 143–50. Hart and Sacks are talking about attributing a single purpose to a piece of legislation, but their legal process materials have come to be understood as embodying the more general point that the law should be understood as a purposive activity. As David Luban shows in an insightful discussion, Lon Fuller is another legal theorist who emphasizes the purposive nature of law. Luban, *Legal Ethics and Human Dignity*, supra, pp. 108–9. Outside the specific context of law, Alasdair MacIntyre relies on the concept of a *practice*, as "any coherent and complex form of socially established cooperative human activity through which goods internal to that form of activity are realized in the course of trying to achieve those standards of excellence which are appropriate to, and partially definitive of, that form of activity". Alasdair MacIntyre, *After Virtue* (Notre Dame, IN: University of Notre Dame Press, 2d ed., 1984),

That is true of the law in general, and of specific areas within the law. Legal reasoning can be said to exhibit "immanent rationality", in the sense that a competent lawyer or judge working within some domain of law (such as tax, commercial, or national security law) knows how to deploy and respond to arguments using a distinctive form of reasoning, which can be differentiated from ordinary moral or political argument.[44] The rationality of each domain is, in turn, subject to the immanent rationality of law in general. The structure of legal reasoning at this level is constrained by familiar rule-of-law values, such as the necessity that legal reasons be general, public, consistent with other legal reasons, and so on.[45]

Returning to the Enron example, the law governing structured-finance transactions involving special-purpose entities may appear on its face to be subject to almost infinite manipulation. But the range of plausible interpretations of these accounting and securities-law rules narrows quite a bit if they are understood against the background of structured finance, with attention to the purpose for having and regulating this activity. Structured finance is designed to have certain economic benefits, most notably enhancing access to capital markets for institutions that are not investment banks, reducing transaction costs by eliminating certain intermediaries from the financing process, while all the while remaining relatively transparent from the point of view of managers and investors.[46] A proposed interpretation of law that

---

p. 187. The theory of interpretation set forth here is indebted substantially to the idea that the purposiveness or goal-directedness of any practice – what it is all about, so to speak – is a non-circular source of obligations internal to the practice, because it would be incoherent to claim to be engaging in any activity without caring about the goods that are internal to that form of activity. Ibid., pp. 190–91.

[44] Ernest J. Weinrib, "Legal Formalism: On the Immanent Rationality of Law", *Yale Law Journal* (1988) 97: 949–1016, at 953–54. On the idea of internal or immanent rationality, Rawls says something important and general about how objectivity is a property of a discipline of reasoning, not something "outside" that can be used as a yardstick:

> [W]e assert a judgment and think it correct because we suppose we have correctly applied the relevant principles and criteria of practical reasoning. This parallels the reply of mathematicians who, when asked why they believe there are an infinity of primes, say: any mathematician knows the proof. The proof lays out the reasoning on which their belief is based .... [B]eing able to give the proof, or to state sufficient reasons for the judgment, is already the best possible explanation of the beliefs of those who are reasonable and rational.

Rawls, *Political Liberalism, supra*, p. 120.
[45] Joseph Raz, "The Politics of the Rule of Law", in Raz, *Ethics in the Public Domain, supra*.
[46] See Steven L. Schwarcz, "Enron and the Use and Abuse of Special Purpose Entities in Corporate Structures", *University of Cincinnati Law Review* (2002) 70: 1309–18.

would permit a transaction that does not reduce transaction costs, does not enhance access to capital markets, and that requires transparency-reducing complexity, should be viewed with suspicion, as being more likely within the zone of colorable, but not plausible interpretations. This conclusion is justified not by the text of the relevant statutes and regulations, because in many cases the language is ambiguous or susceptible to manipulation. Rather, a lawyer would regard some interpretations as implausibly aggressive because they go against the whole point of the law of structured finance.

When interpreting any legal norm (a case, statute, regulation, etc.), lawyers and judges must consider the background of reasons against which the rule was established, locating it within a context and fleshing out its meaning with reference to the understandings of the players in the legal system who had a role in creating the norm in the first place and sustaining it over time. The dynamic and evolving nature of many legal norms – particularly common law rules, but also statutes and regulations as interpreted by courts and administrative agencies – links these norms with a multitude of internal legal reasons that may be relied upon as guides to interpretation. Taken together, these internal reasons structure the arguments that may be given in support of an interpretive judgment.

> [J]udges confronting an "indeterminate" norm do not simply put on their policy-making hats, even if their view is that they must make new law. They attempt to understand the meaning of the relevant norm in light of what the situation demands; they argue, by analogy, for the salience of certain facts, and they try to find principles which have some toe-hold in the existing law.[47]

The demand for a reasoned justification requires that an interpretation of legal norms be grounded in materials (texts, principles that are fairly deemed to underlie and justify legal rules, interpretive practices, hermeneutic methods, and so on) that are properly regarded in the relevant community as appropriate reasons.

Of course, even if legal argumentation is structured by the immanent rationality of some domain of law, if there is a multitude of legal reasons that bear on any interesting interpretive question, it is unlikely that there will be only one obviously right answer. In the structured-finance example, the goals of reducing transaction costs and increasing the transparency of financing arrangements may conflict in many cases. (Requiring additional disclosures for the sake of transparency will almost inevitably increase transaction costs.) More generally, one might argue that every area of law is

---

[47]Martin J. Stone, "Formalism", in Jules Coleman and Scott Shapiro, eds., *The Oxford Handbook of Jurisprudence and Legal Philosophy* (New York: Oxford University Press 2002), p. 192.

structured around oppositions between conflicting values, such as individualism and altruism.[48] For this reason, legal interpretation almost always involves the exercise of judgment, or what some scholars of statutory interpretation refer to as practical reasoning.[49] One may question whether this is enough for coordination and settlement, particularly if internal legal reasons can be plural and conflicting. There still seems to be a subjective element in interpretation if it is thrown back on judgment, which is a virtue or characteristic of a judge or lawyer, not a property of the law itself. But judgment, in turn, is not a subjective process. Judgment is not a faculty of individual interpreters, and is certainly not a matter of punting the weighing or balancing of plural factors to the subjective discretion of the decision-maker. Rather, the exercise of judgment is fundamentally a community-bound process, in that it makes reference to inter-subjective criteria for the exercise and regulation of judgment.[50] "Objectivity in the law connotes standards. It implies that an interpretation can be measured against a set of norms that transcend the particular vantage point of the person offering the interpretation".[51]

This must be true in order for a judgment of the form, "The client may do such-and-such", to be a conclusion of *law*, and not something else, like politics or morality. Law is the enactment of a political community, and a legal judgment must therefore make reference to standards that transcend the individual making the judgment. The law is purposive; it is *about* something, and legal interpretation is aimed at recovering that meaning. As I have been arguing, the whole point of the law is to differentiate between something you can get away with, and something that is authorized, as a matter of right, and regulated by rules of general application. The legal system enforces that distinction by rhetorical practices that take certain considerations into account, as part of the justification of legal judgments, and exclude other considerations as irrelevant. Only considerations that are part of the law count in favor of an interpretation of law. That sounds tautological, but it is actually a significant implication of the theory of authority defended here. If citizens disagree about matters of importance to their communal life, and cannot resolve these disagreements using ordinary practical reasoning (including

---

[48]Duncan Kennedy, "Form and Substance in Private Law Adjudication", *Harvard Law Review* (1976) 89: 1685–778.

[49]See, e.g., Daniel A. Farber, "The Inevitability of Practical Reason: Statutes, Formalism, and the Rule of Law", *Vanderbilt Law Review* (1992) 45: 533–48; William N. Eskridge and Philip P. Frickey, "Statutory Interpretation as Practical Reasoning", *Stanford Law Review* (1990) 42: 321–84.

[50]Gerald J. Postema, "'Protestant' Interpretation and Social Practices", *Law and Philosophy* (1987) 6: 283–319; Fiss, *supra*.

[51]Fiss, *supra*, p. 744.

moral reasoning), they can fall back on the procedures made available by
the legal system for establishing a communal position with respect to the
matter. Determining what considerations are part of law is a task for the
interpretive community, comprised of judges, lawyers, scholars, and interested citizens who have learned to differentiate between legal and non-legal
reasons. In other words, the authority of law is founded in social practices,
much as H.L.A. Hart explained in *The Concept of Law*.[52]

In order for any official, institution, or practice to have authority, it
must be conferred somehow – say, by a rule authorizing the subject of the
rule to promulgate authoritative rules. Consider the authority of a federal
statute, passed pursuant to Congressional authorization under Article I of
the Constitution. Saying that the Constitution confers authority on Congress
only raises the further question of where the Constitution gets its authority. In response one might point to Article VII which provides that the
Constitution would be established by ratification by the conventions of nine
states. However, the appeal to state ratification is either circular (because it
is specified by the very document whose authority is in question) or leads
to an infinite regress, as we then ask on what basis state conventions have
the authority to ratify some document which can then confer authority on
Congress. Without authority, one cannot confer authority, but there has to
be some original source of authority – a first cause, unmoved mover, or
Grundnorm. The nature of this original source is deeply paradoxical, however, because in order for it to claim authority it must have the power to
change the normative situation of others, but it must derive this power from
something other than a grant of authority, which would just get the regress
rolling again. As Hart observed, law creates reasons for action that are
acknowledged by citizens using the language of obligation, such as "ought",
"duty", "right", and "wrong".[53] The solution to the circularity or regress of
legal authority must be something that accounts for the obligatory nature of
law, at a fundamental level.

The startling thing about Hart's solution to the problem of the foundation
of legal authority is that he grounds the normativity of law in something
empirical. Social practices validate the existence of a law and fix its content.
"[A] statement about what the law is is made true by certain social facts –

---

[52]The discussion in this paragraph is drawn from two careful and helpful articles
on Hart's practice conception of rules. See Scott J. Shapiro, "On Hart's Way Out",
and Benjamin C. Zipursky, "The Model of Social Facts", both in Jules Coleman, ed.,
Hart's Postscript: Essays on the Postscript to The Concept of Law (New York: Oxford
University Press 2001).
[53]H.L.A. Hart, *The Concept of Law* (Oxford: Oxford University Press, 2nd ed., 1994),
p. 57.

facts regarding the conduct and attitude of certain persons in the community".[54] This is a philosophically adventurous position – every student in an introductory ethics course learns that you cannot derive an "ought" from an "is". In order for anything to be normative – that is, to provide a justification for doing something – it is not enough for that thing simply to be practiced. Instead, it must have "ought-ness" about it somehow, in the sense that one has a duty to do what is practiced.[55] Hart seeks to locate the ought-ness of the rule of recognition in the community's practices, which seems to beg the question of how the rule of recognition creates a duty.[56] The way out of this apparent circle is to appeal to the notion of a practice as having normativity built in.[57]

For Hart, what stops the regress is the critical reflective attitude displayed by judges, who believe that certain considerations ought to be regarded as standards to be followed by other judges.[58] This is not a mere preference or hope on the part of judges, but part of a *practice* that regards deviation from these standards as an occasion for justified criticism.[59] Hart says that

---

[54]Zipursky, *supra*, p. 225.

[55]Ronald Dworkin, *Taking Rights Seriously* (Cambridge, MA: Harvard University Press 1977), p. 51.

[56]Scott J. Shapiro, "What Is the Internal Point of View?" *Fordham Law Review* (2006) 75: 1157–70, p. 1166.

[57]Jules Coleman, "Incorporationism, Conventionality, and the Practical Difference Thesis", in Coleman, *supra*, pp. 110–11.

[58]Hart, *supra*, p. 56 ("[I]f a social rule is to exist some at least must look upon the behavior in question as a general standard to be followed by the group as a whole".).

[59]Hart writes: "What is necessary is that there should be a critical reflective attitude to certain patterns of behavior as a common standard, and that this should display itself in criticism (including self-criticism), demands for conformity, and in acknowledgments that such criticism and demands are justified, all of which find their characteristic expression in the normative terminology of 'ought,' 'must,' and 'should,' 'right' and 'wrong'". Ibid., p. 57. He returns later to the idea that the legitimacy of a norm is bound up with the acceptance by others of the norm as a standard for justified criticism: "[W]here rules exist, deviations from them are not merely grounds for a prediction that hostile reactions will follow or that a court will apply sanctions to those who break them, but are also a reason or justification for such reaction and for applying the sanctions". Ibid., p. 84.

In his plenary lecture at the IVR World Congress in Krakow, Fred Schauer cited Brian Simpson's insight that Hart really should have talked about a "practice of recognition", with "practice" being understood in the Wittgensteinian sense, rather than a *rule* of recognition. A.W.B. Simpson, "The Common Law and Legal Theory", in William Twining, ed., *Legal Theory and Common Law* (Oxford: Blackwell 1986). I believe Schauer and Simpson are absolutely right that the notion of a practice, as developed by Wittgenstein and Alasdair MacIntyre, is crucial to understanding what legal reasoning and argumentation is all about, beyond solving the theoretical problem of how social facts can create obligations.

judges who adopt this critical reflective attitude are regarding the law from
the internal point of view, not looking at it merely as observers interested
in predicting behavior, but as participants in a meaningful social practice.[60]
When judges regard something as a standard for deciding cases, criticize
other judges for not following that standard, and accept the criticism of others as justified to the extent they do not adhere to the applicable standard,
a "rule of recognition" comes into existence.[61] The rule of recognition is a
standard that establishes criteria of validity or legality.[62] Primary rules governing the conduct of citizens are then validated by the rule of recognition;
these rules create obligations that are backed by the authority of the legal
system's master norm, the rule of recognition. "Jaywalking . . . is prohibited
by law in New York City even though nearly everyone ignores the rule. It is a
law because it is valid, not because it is practiced".[63] The rule of recognition,
on the other hand, is law only because it is practiced.

Judges' acceptance of the rule of recognition from the internal point of
view is conceptually necessary in order for there to be a legal system. If
judges did not acknowledge legal norms as legitimate reasons for action
(indicating this by the use of words like "ought", "right", and so on), then
there would be no way to differentiate an authoritative legal command,
issued as part of a legitimate legal *system*, from the demand of a mugger,
and the state from the gunman writ large.[64] To see Hart's point about the
systematicity of official decisions, imagine some kind of strange hypothetical society in which disputes are resolved by the whim of decision-makers,
but as it happens the class of decision-makers is remarkably homogeneous,
in terms of socioeconomic background, ideology, education and training,
and other determinants of beliefs and preferences. If these decision-makers
consistently favored certain litigants – say, prosecutors or big corporations –
there would be an observable regularity in their decisions, but we would not
call those decisions *lawful* unless they were justified by reasons that made
reference to the sorts of values that should make a difference in how legal
disputes are resolved. The system would deserve the label "legal" only if

---

[60]Hart, *supra*, p. 89.

[61]Ibid., p. 116 ("if [the rule of recognition] is to exist at all, [it] must be regarded from
the internal point of view as a public, common standard of correct judicial decision, and
not as something which each judge merely obeys for his part only".).

[62]Ibid., pp. 100–101.

[63]Shapiro, "On Hart's Way Out", *supra*, p. 155.

[64]Hart draws the distinction in terms of acting out of obligation from acting because one
feels obliged. Hart, *supra*, pp. 82–83, 88–89. Giving up one's wallet at gunpoint reveals
a sense of being obliged to act, for fear of experiencing the consequences of inaction.
When someone acts out of obligation, by contrast, the explanation of the person's action
makes reference to normative standards, not merely the desire to avoid harm.

the officials regarded themselves as duty-bound to make decisions on the basis of certain reasons and not others. We may disagree in some particulars over what criteria differentiate a lawful decision from one based on whim or partiality. But if we are to speak intelligibly of legality and legitimacy, there must be some criteria for distinguishing between actions that respect a regime of law and those that are responsive to other sorts of concerns.

It is important to point out that this account of the normativity of practices does not depend on the motivations of judges. Hart protests that "[t]he internal aspect of rules is often misrepresented as a mere matter of 'feelings' in contrast to externally observable physical behavior".[65] But as he emphasizes, facts about beliefs and motives "are *not necessary* for the truth of a statement that a person had an obligation to do something".[66] Judges have an *obligation* to follow the rule of recognition, which identifies the society's laws and differentiates them from other norms.[67] Nevertheless, a judge may be *motivated* by the desire to be promoted to a higher court, to win glory, or simply to continue in employment in a cushy job. Whatever specific motivations a judge may have, however, there must be something distinctive about law that provides a different sort of reason for action – otherwise there would be no such thing as a legal system as opposed to a fortuitous convergence of behavior by a bunch of people sitting on high benches wearing black robes.[68] As long as the law makes a practical difference to how a judge decides cases, in the sense that the judge accepts the legitimacy of measuring her own conduct against the standard of lawfulness articulated by the relevant community, the specific motivation a person has for being a judge is immaterial. Similarly, a citizen may not believe herself morally obligated to perform some action required by law, or may be morally indifferent yet think the law is silly. Despite having no particular motivational state toward the law, to the extent the citizen wishes to describe her conduct as lawful, she is necessarily committed to viewing the law from the internal perspective, as creating obligations.

Several points in this discussion are relevant to the jurisprudence of lawyering. The first is the difference between an obligation accepted from the internal point of view and something else. In order for a government to be

---

[65] Ibid., p. 57.

[66] Ibid., p. 83.

[67] Ibid., p. 116. Hart insists that "if [the rule of recognition] is to exist at all, [it] must be regarded from the internal point of view as a public, common standard of correct judicial decision, and not as something which each judge merely obeys for his part only". And since he further argues that the rule of recognition is necessary for there to be a legal system at all, *see* ibid., p. 100, it is clear that the recognition by judges that the law is a reason as such for making decisions is the conceptual heart of legality.

[68] Ibid., p. 116.

characterized by the virtue of legality, legal officials must regard themselves as duty-bound to consider some reasons, and not others, as the grounds for a judgment of law. This obligation applies to lawyers as well as judges, to the extent a lawyer intends to give *legal* advice, as opposed to merely counseling on what would be moral or prudent. This is the way legal entitlements are differentiated from mere client interests. The second point is that the rule of recognition in an actual legal system may be complex and contestable. For example, judges often make reference to tacit criteria of legality.[69] There is no requirement that the rule of recognition refer only to official acts of political actors such as legislators and judges – what Dworkin refers to as pedigree criteria.[70] Moreover, the rule of recognition may have a hierarchical structure, may consist of a series of disjunctive tests, or may have a number of exceptions that are triggered by certain facts.[71] What matters from the internal point of view is whether a consideration has "been consistently invoked by courts in ranges of different cases" in support of a decision.[72]

Conclusion

Hart's theory of law, which emphasizes its foundation in social practices, shows the relationship between reason-giving and the value of legality. The larger project, from which this chapter is taken, seeks to build the ethics of lawyers on a similar practical foundation of reason-giving. The fundamental ethical obligation of lawyers is to engage in the craft of legal argumentation. Doing so poorly is an occasion for criticism. The way in which the internal, practice-based normative critique is connected with morality more generally is beyond the scope of this chapter. What is established here is only that if lawyers can reason from the internal point of view, then critics of lawyers' ethics may ground an ethical evaluation in the practice of giving legal reasons.

Bibliography

Rawls, John. 1993. *Political Liberalism.* New York, NY: Columbia University Press.

---

[69]Zipursky, *supra*, p. 228.
[70]Scott J. Shapiro, "The 'Hart-Dworkin' Debate: A Short Guide for the Perplexed", in Arthur Ripstein, ed., *Ronald Dworkin* (New York: Cambridge University Press 2007).
[71]Zipursky, *supra*, p. 235.
[72]H.L.A. Hart, "Postscript", in Hart, *supra*, p. 265.

Part V
Concluding Remarks

Chapter 10
Legal Interpretation in 18th Century Europe: Doctrinal Debates Versus Political Change

Jean-Louis HALPÉRIN

As the different studies contained in this book have shown, it is not so easy to characterize the legacy of the Age of Enlightenment as a "new paradigm" of legal interpretation. Debates about legal interpretation have a long history. In particular, for the European tradition based on Roman culture, the debate began with Cicero's *De inventione* and the works of Quintilian, and blossomed with mediaeval canon literature and Roman law commentators. At the same time, as Jan Schröder has explained with numerous examples, many of the "rules of interpretation", which we still use today (by quoting Latin formulas supposedly from Roman origins), are not so aged, but rather were produced by the writings of Humanists during the 15th and the 16th centuries. For instance, Schröder argues that the maxim *In claris cessat interpretatio* was "invented" by Italian and French lawyers of the Renaissance such as Guy Pape (who died in 1477), Philippus Decius (1454–1535) and Petrus Paulus Parisius (1473–1545).[1]

Saverio Masuelli's study of the same maxim concluded that its origins are found in the works of Cicero and Quintilian – specifically in a passage of Paulus (D. 32, 25, 1) which concerned the unambiguous terms of a will. Masuelli also notes the more recent construction of the sentence, which appears in the works of Cardinal Del Luca and in the writing of an anonymous commentator on his *Theatrum veritatis* in 1726 – both of which

---

[1] Jan Schröder, *Theorie des Interpretation von Humanistik bis zur Romantik. Rechtswissenschaft, Philosophie, Theologie*, Stuttgart, Steiner, 2001, pp. 166–167.

J.-L. HALPÉRIN (✉)
École Normale Supérieure, UMR 7074 "Centre de Théorie et Analyse du droit", Paris, France
e-mail: jean-louis.halperin@ens.fr; jean-louis.halperin@wanadoo.fr

MORIGIWA, Y. et al. (eds.), *Interpretation of Law in the Age of Enlightenment*, Law and Philosophy Library 95, DOI 10.1007/978-94-007-1506-6_10, © Springer Science+Business Media B.V. 2011

appear before the well-known passage of Vattel's *Droit des gens* (1758), which denounces the use of interpretation when faced with a clear text.[2]

This sole example indicates how complex and interconnected the *longue durée* is with the history of legal interpretation. However, I would like to propose a few guides to understanding the innovative tendencies that appeared in Europe (and not only in Germany or France) between the middle of the 17th century and the beginning of the 19th century. As Paul Hazard argues in his ground-breaking book (1935), if the period chosen for this European panorama appears too large, and exceeds the so-called Enlightenment period itself, it must be noted that the crisis of European conscience began in the second half of the 17th century. Paul Hazard found support for this turning point in the works of the Biblical exegesis, which questioned the traditional interpretations of sacred texts.[3] In relation to legal questions, there is no doubt that Hobbes's *Leviathan* (1651), with its important passage about the interpretation of civil laws, can be chosen as a point of departure for a kind of new era.

Based on his fundamental "nominalism", with major implications about logics and the theory of language,[4] Hobbes's concept of legal interpretation is particularly developed in chapter 26 of the Leviathan: according to Hobbes, "all laws, written and unwritten, are in need of interpretation" (*Leviathan*, ch. XXVI, 8). Even for written laws, the task of interpreting legal texts is not an easy one. Interpreters must use the "black letter" (or the "bare words") and the "sentence" (the relationship between words created by the discourse) of the law. However, "the significations of almost all [words] are either in themselves, or in the metaphorical use of them, ambiguous; and may be drawn in argument to make many senses; but there is only one sense of the law". This passage illustrates that Hobbes is not, in fact, the founding father of the hermeneutic turn of the 20th century, as rather he considered that laws had only one meaning. However, his conception of the arbitrary choice and interpretation of words (contrary to the Aristotelian tradition of the existence of essences represented within words) led him toward new questions about the risks of legal interpretation. In line

---

[2]Saverio Masuelli, "In claris non fit interpretatio. Alle origine del brocardo", *Rivista di Diritto Romano*, 2002, II, pp. 401–424.

[3]Paul Hazard, *La Crise de la conscience européenne 1680–1715*, Paris, Boivin et Cie, 1935, pp. 186–197.

[4]Foucault has used Hobbes's *Logics* (1655) as a first step for a new critical analysis of language: Michel Foucault, *Les mots et les choses*, Paris, Gallimard, "Bibliothèque des sciences humaines", 1966, pp. 95, 108 and 133.

with the interests of his intellectual master, Francis Bacon (1560–1626),[5] (but with less confidence in judges and common law institutions), Hobbes focused in particular on the variety of private opinions about the interpretation of legal texts. Hobbes had no confidence in the reasons of lawyers, which were as various as the number of Schools and sources of "erroneous sentences", to quote Lord Coke. Hobbes further argued that the will of the sovereign had to prevail against the *juris prudentia,* or the purported wisdom of subordinate judges.

From a European perspective, it seems that one of the new trends in legal writing since the second half of the 17th century consists in the growing doubts over the variety of interpretations proposed by advocates and recognized by *judges* (even if the criticism of lawyers' differing opinions is older). In a passage of *Il Dottor volgare* (1673), often quoted by Italian lawyers during the 18th century, Cardinal Giovanni Battista De Luca (1614–1683) argued (as did his contemporaries) that laws needed to be interpreted or explained, and that a variety of interpretations was an unavoidable consequence of two facts. First, legal texts cannot foresee all possible cases (a principle coming from Roman law, especially from D. 1, 3, 12); and second, human intellects are so different that the outcome will necessarily be a variety of opinions about the same text.[6] It is the same anxiety about the weakness and the diversity of human reasons which led Jean Domat (1625–1696) to write *Les Lois civiles dans leur naturel* (1689) in order to guide judges and to give them good principles for interpreting legal texts. Domat was a close friend of the French philosopher Pascal, who complained about what was considered as truth or error on both sides of the Pyrénées Mountains. If we return to England, 60 years after Hobbes's *Leviathan,* we find the famous speech of Bishop Benjamin Hoadly (1676–1761). It is part of a sermon delivered before the King in 1717, which was quoted by American jurists from John Chipman Gray[7] onwards. The sermon discusses the enormous powers of the interpreter: "whoever hath an absolute authority to interpret any written or spoken laws, it is he who is truly the lawgiver, to all intents and purposes, and not the person who first spoke or wrote them".[8]

---

[5]Donal R. Coquillette, *Francis Bacon*, Edinburgh, Edinburgh University Press, 1992, pp. 277–280.

[6]Giovanni Battista De Luca, *Il Dottore Volgare*, Rome, G. Corvo, 1673, Proemio, p. 38; the same writer has rejected the interpretation of clear laws, but noted that this case was rare: *Lo stilo legale*, Bologna, Il Mulino, 2010, pp. 82–83.

[7]John Chipman Gray, *The Nature and the Sources of the Law*, New York, Columbia University Press, 1916, pp. 162–166.

[8]William Gibson, *Enlightenment Prelate: Benjamin Hoadly 1676–1761*, Cambridge, James Clarke, p. 36.

The debates about legal interpretation thus moved from medieval questions about *interpretatio* of Roman texts by Christian lawyers,[9] to the modern discussion about the powers of the judiciary in relation to the legislative sovereign. During the 18th century, one can note three kinds of doctrinal answers to these questions. The first, as a central point and an ambiguous proposition (open itself to various interpretations) is Montesquieu's well known formula about the judge as the *bouche qui prononce les paroles de la loi* ("mouth of the law", *Esprit des Lois,* XI, VI 1748). This formula is supported by other passages of the *Esprit des Lois,* in which Montesquieu distinguishes between republican regimes where judges are subject to the black letter of statutory laws, and monarchies where judges are authorized to interpret according to the spirit of the law. Not only this, but it is also further supplemented by the *Pensées* (Montesquieu's personal diary, written before and after the publishing of the *Esprit des Lois*) which discusses the French Parliaments as a "depository of laws": for this reason the legislative history into which new laws are integrated, is known.[10] Thus, the "mouth of the law" formula can be interpreted either as a strict subjection of judges towards the legislative power, or as the recognition of a creative power of judges (who make the law to speak through their own speech).

It can be observed that Montesquieu's formula was interpreted in both ways throughout the 18th century, according to two different "national" trends in Italy and in England. In Italy, the debate launched by De Luca was developed, before the publishing of the *Esprit des Lois*, through the work of Ludovica Antonio Muratori, *Dei difetti della giurisprudenza* (1742).[11] Muratori lived from 1672 to 1750, and was librarian of the Duke of Modena. His works examined historical and religious questions, and among the different flaws of legal science described by Muratori, the problems linked with the obscurity of laws (of which every word is "distilled" and refined by the advocates) were numerous. He focused upon the silences in the legislation, and the difficulties in interpreting the will of the legislator and the variety of human opinions (with quotes from De Luca) as the main source of the failure to discover a scientific way in which the "right" law could be applied to a particular case. It must be noted that Muratori does not use the word "syllogism" even if his developments allude to this logical form. Muratori

---

[9]Paolo Grossi, *L'ordine giuridico medievale*, Roma-Bari, Laterza, 1996, pp. 162–168 about this conception of legal science as *interpretatio*.

[10]Montesquieu, *Pensées. Le Spicilège*, ed. Louis Desgraves, Paris, Robert Laffont, coll. "Bouquins", 1991, especially *pensée* n° 1226 (p. 411) and n° 2266 (p. 658).

[11]Ludovica Antonio Muratori, *Dei difetti della girusprudenza*, reedited by Elio Tavilla, Bologna, Forna, 2001, especially pp. 10–18.

defended a solution, and a rather modest one, in the writing of a small code of laws and of authentic interpretations.

Twenty two years later, Beccaria published his famous book *Dei delitti e delle pene*. In the fourth chapter, devoted to the interpretation of laws, Beccaria affirms the ideas of De Luca, Muratori and Montesquieu, without quoting them expressly. The power of interpretation cannot belong to the judges, who are neither legislators nor depositary (as some family heirs) of the laws. Interpretation according to the spirit of the law is a dangerous path, open to variable opinions depending on the passions and characters of the judges (almost a declaration of "legal realism"!). Thanks to a precise penal code, judges will be able to form a perfect syllogism with the law as the major proposition, the facts as the minor proposition and the penalty (or acquittal) as the conclusion. Here is the "legalist" (favourable to the control of judges through an authentic process of interpretation depending upon the legislator) interpretation of Beccaria's interpretation, shared by his friend in Milan, Pietro Verri,[12] and defended by some French deputies (such as Duport[13]) during the French Revolution.

At the same time, Blackstone's *Commentaries on the Laws of England* (1765–1769) proposed another interpretation of Montesquieu (who was much admired by Blackstone as by Beccaria). In this no less famous Introduction (§ 3[14]) of the *Commentaries*, Blackstone defended the English judges as "oracles of the laws" or as a "depository of the laws" (the second formula is the nearest to Montesquieu's words), with his theory of the common law as a customary (pre-existing) law declared by the courts. As Blackstone had not recognized the judiciary as a third power and rejected the idea of judicial review, his cautious theory can appear as a way of "cloaking" the real power of judges, through the defence (not so different from Hobbes's point of view) of precedents.[15] It is noteworthy that one of the arguments

---

[12]In his work *Sulla interpretazione delle leggi* (1765): Paolo Alvazzi del Frate, *L'interpretazione autentica nel XVIII secolo. Divieto di interpretatio e riferimento al legislatore nell'illuminismo giuridico*, Torino, Giappichelli, 2000, pp. 123–125.

[13]Discourse of the 29th March of 1790 (using the notion of judicial syllogism), *Archives parlementaires*, vol. XII, pp. 411–429.

[14]William Blackstone, *Commentaries on the Laws of England, A Facsimile of the First Edition of 1765–1769*, Chicago, University of Chicago Press, 1979, vol. I, pp. 69–71 and 86–91 about the rules of interpretation of statutory laws.

[15]Paul O. Carrese, *The Cloaking of Power. Montesquieu, Blackstone and the Rise of Judicial Activism,* Chicago-London, The University of Chicago Press, 2003, pp. 138–154 for this convincing interpretation of an hidden plan in Montesquieu's and Blackstone's formulas.

used by Blackstone to support this influence of precedents is the development of (private) law reports, that have furnished "numerous volumes" in the "lawyer's library".

At the end of our period, the first works of Bentham (most notably his unpublished essay *On Laws in general* (1789)) were critical of Blackstone, but influenced by him as by Beccaria. They extended the discussion on the difficulties of interpreting laws (as assemblage of signs), the great power of the interpreters ("to interpret a law is to alter it") and the balance between a strict or liberal interpretation of legal texts.[16] One also knows how the Chief Justice Marshall could have interpreted Blackstone's ideas to support the revolutionary thesis of constitutional review in *Marbury v. Madison* (1803).

From this doctrinal "bifurcation" between an Italian-French "strict legalism" and the common law defence of "judge-made law", one does not come to conclusions on the decisive authority of legal writing inside national traditions. As Michael Stolleis has shown, these debates about legal interpretation from the second half of the 17th century are dominated by the progress of modern States to control the process of creating binding norms through statute law. This trend is the main cause of numerous texts imposing authentic interpretation as stemming only from the sovereign (with a procedure of referee or *référé* to the Prince), such as: the 1667 Ordinance about civil procedure in France, the 1723, 1729 and 1779 *Leggi e Constitutioni del Regno di Sardegna* in Piedmont, the 1771 *Codice di Leggi e Costituzioni del Ducato di Modena* in this Italian principality, the 1774 *Dispaccio del re di Napoli Ferdinando IV* in Naples, the French revolutionary law of 16th–24th of August 1790 and finally, the 1795 *Allgemeines Landrecht* in Prussia.[17]

Even if many of these texts did not succeed in preventing the judges from interpreting legal texts, there is no doubt that this pressure from legislators was more important than legal writings in imposing a stricter subjugation of judges to a growing statutory legislation. The lack of unification and the survival of Roman law as a source of positive law in parts of Germany can also explain why the German writers of the 19th century, beginning with Zachariae[18] and Thibaut[19] before Savigny's famous works, could continue to develop a more independent (and more intellectual) thought about legal

---

[16]Jeremy Bentham, *Of Laws in General,* ed. by H. L. A. Hart, London, The Athlone Press, 1970, pp. 152–163.

[17]Paolo Alvazzi del Frate, op. cit., pp. 72–81; Giovanni Tarello, *Storia della cultura giuridica moderna*, Bologna, Il Mulino, 1976, p. 492.

[18]Karl Salomo Zachariae, *Versuch einer allgemeiner Hermeneutik des Rechts*, Heidelberg, 1805.

[19]Anton Friedrich Justus Thibaut, *Theorie der logischen Auslegung des römischen Rechts*, Heidelberg, 1806.

interpretation. The German specific way about legal interpretation has also political origins: the debate was launched again, at the end of the 19th century (with the works of von Bülow and Zitelmann) with the preparation of the German Civil Code (BGB).

A last remark about the changes begun in the Age of Enlightenment concerns the case-law books. Here, we can likely see a point of contact between the French tradition and that of the common law (Germany again is a special situation with the development of these case law books later in the 19th century). One could perhaps even say that the progress accomplished during the 18th century in publishing more "rational" case-law books prepared the mixture of statutory law and judge-made law in European countries that we see in the modern day.

Name Index

A
Accursius, 4, 52
Albrecht, W. E., 12
Austin, J. L., 130

B
Bähr, O., 120
Beccaria, C., 29, 140, 185–186
Bodin, J., 4–5, 69, 73, 75, 102

C
Caepolla, B., 93, 97–99
Connanus, F., 101–102

D
de Ghewiet, G., 50–54
de Montaigne, M., 102
de Montesquieu, C., 6–7, 28, 34, 36,
    38–39, 64, 80, 140, 184–185
de Phedericis, S., 93, 98–99
de Saxoferrato, B., 4–5, 52, 98
Donellus, H., 97–98, 102

E
Everardus a Middelburg, N., 93–94, 97

F
Frederik II. (Friedrich), 9–10

G
Gadamer, H.-G., 131
Gandinus, A., 98
Gans, E., 108, 110, 117–118

H
Haferkamp, H.-P., 14, 85, 107–121
Heise, G. A., 12
Hobbes, T., 3–6, 8, 71, 102, 182–183, 185
Holderrieder, J. L., 96, 99–101
Husserl, E., 14, 128

K
Kant, I., 102–103, 127
Klüber, J. L., 11
Kreittmayr, W. A. X., 101
Kuntze, J. E., 114

M
MacIntyre, A., 170, 175
Maurenbrecher, R., 11–12
Mugellanus, D., 98
Mukasey, M.(U.S. Attorney General), 159

N
Napoleon, B., 10, 24, 125, 134, 144

O
Ogorek, R., 7, 9, 12, 14, 109
Ogris, W., 9–10

P
Perelman, C., 150
Pinault des Jaunaux, M., 47–49
Placcius, V., 92, 100
Pollet, J., 48–52, 54
Puchta, G. F., 108, 109–110, 112–113,
    118–119, 121
Pufendorf, S., 39, 71–72, 95, 99, 101–103

MORIGIWA, Y. et al. (eds.), *Interpretation of Law in the Age
of Enlightenment*, Law and Philosophy Library 95,
DOI 10.1007/978-94-007-1506-6, © Springer Science+Business Media B.V. 2011

Subject Index